The Sufi Message of Hazrat Inayat Khan

Centennial Edition

Volume VI
The Alchemy of Happiness

Hazrat Pir-o-Murshid Inayat Khan

The Sufi Message of Hazrat Inayat Khan

Centennial Edition

Volume VI
The Alchemy of Happiness

Sulūk Press
Richmond, Virginia

Published by Sulūk Press
112 East Cary Street
Richmond, Virginia 23219
sulukpress.com

©2024 Omega Publications, Inc.
All rights reserved. No part of this publication may be reproduced, stored in a retrieval system, or transmitted by any means, electronic, mechanical, photocopying, recording, or otherwise without prior written permission of the publisher.

Cover ornament from Shutterstock.com
Cover design by Sandra Lillydahl

This edition is printed on acid-free paper.

ISBN 978-1-941810-50-7 paper
ISBN 978-1-941810-49-1 hardcase
ISBN 978-1-941810-51-4 e-book

Names: Inayat Khan, 1882–1927, author. | Inayat Khan, Zia, 1971–, author of introduction.
Title: The Sufi Message of Hazrat Inayat Khan, Centennial Edition, Volume VI: The Alchemy of Happiness
Description: First Edition, Richmond, VA: Sulūk Press, 2024. | Includes introduction, biographical note, glossary, index.
Identifiers: LCCN 2016940929 | ISBN 9781941810491 (hardcase) | ISBN 9781941810507 (paper) | ISBN 9781941810514 (e-book)
Subjects: LCSH: Sufism BISAC: Religion/Sufi | Religion/Mysticism

Printed and bound in the United States of America

CONTENTS

Introduction by Pir Zia Inayat Khan	vii
Acknowledgments	ix
1. The Alchemy of Happiness	1
2. The Aim of Life	7
3. The Purpose of Life (1)	14
4. The Purpose of Life (2)	23
5. The Art of Personality	35
6. Reconciliation	46
7. Attitude	49
8. The Secret of Life	56
9. What Is Wanted in Life	64
10. Life, a Continual Battle (1)	71
11. Life, a Continual Battle (2)	76
12. The Struggle of Life (1)	83
13. The Struggle of Life (2)	88
14. Reaction	93
15. The Deeper Side of Life	102
16. Life, an Opportunity	112
17. Our Life	123
18. Communicating with Life	127
19. The Intoxication of Life (1)	135
20. The Intoxication of Life (2)	143
21. The Meaning of Life	150
22. The Inner Life	157
23. The Inner Life and Self-Realization	168

Contents

24. The Interdependence of Life Within and Without	181
25. Interest and Indifference	186
26. From Limitation to Perfection (1)	193
27. From Limitation to Perfection (2)	205
28. The Path of Attainment (1)	211
29. The Path of Attainment (2)	220
30. Stages on the Path of Self-Realization	223
31. Human Beings, Masters of Their Destiny (1)	234
32. Human Beings, Masters of Their Destiny (2)	241
33. The Law of Action	250
34. Purity of Life	258
35. The Ideal	266
36. The Journey to the Goal (1)	274
37. The Journey to the Goal (2)	281
38. Acknowledgment	288
39. Responsibility	294
40. The Continuity of Life	298
Glossary	305
Sources	307
Biographical Note	309
Index	311

INTRODUCTION

What makes human happiness possible? Hedonists hold that happiness consists of a favorable ratio of pleasant to unpleasant experiences. According to this view, the aim of life is to successfully obtain the world's choicest gratifications. Aristotle saw matters differently and located happiness in virtuous action. Such is the view of Imam Muhammad al-Ghazali, the author of the original *Alchemy of Happiness* (*Kimiya as-sa'ada*), but with a difference. Al-Ghazali maintained that virtue was defined by the prescriptions of Divine revelation, and that the happiness that comes with fulfilling these prescriptions will be realized in the hereafter. The present volume echoes the title of al-Ghazali's influential work. What does Hazrat Inayat Khan tell us about happiness?

In this sixth volume of the Centennial Edition of the *Sufi Message* series, Hazrat Inayat Khan approaches the question of happiness from various angles. Sometimes the context is a discussion of desire, other times an analysis of ethics. What links these investigations is that, in every case, Hazrat identifies happiness with the soul. "Happiness is your own being, your own self, that self that is the most precious thing in life." From this perspective, happiness is something to be discovered rather than acquired.

It bears emphasizing that for Hazrat Inayat Khan the soul's self-realization is not confined to the trackless territory beyond time and space. Human life is a domain abounding in possibilities for the expression of the soul's nature. The ability to touch the depths of life through meditative silence, however, is indispensable as a foundation for soulful action. A person undergoing the discovery of the soul's intrinsic happiness is therefore moved to live simultaneously in inner and outer worlds. Such a person is learning how to be "in tune with the infinite and in rhythm with the finite."

The chapters that make up this volume comprise discourses given by Hazrat Inayat Khan in various places during the last five years of his earthly life. Many of the lectures were delivered in France, where Hazrat settled with his family in 1920; others took place in Belgium, England, Italy, the Netherlands, Switzerland, and the United States. In France, the venue was often the home of Baroness d'Eichthal (d. 1929), whom Hazrat described as the "backbone" of the French branch of his Sufi Order. Outside of the baroness's salon, settings were as varied as the Sorbonne, the Sufi meeting hall in Suresnes, the Waldorf Astoria in New York, a high school in Wichita, L'Hotel Splendide in Bern, and a cruise liner ferrying passengers across the Atlantic.

The volume before you is a book to study. But to study in which way? "In order to find truth, there is something greater than the study of books," says Hazrat Inayat Khan. Hazrat is alluding here to the process of illuminative unlearning that lays bare the mind behind the mind, which to say, the soul. While the disclosure of the soul's consciousness involves, in the first instance, the dissolution of mental constructs, what is revealed is not so much an absence as a presence. The nature of that presence is pure and unalloyed happiness.

"It is not that happiness belongs to the soul; it is that the soul itself is happiness." Here are words to live by.

Pir Zia Inayat Khan

ACKNOWLEDGMENTS

Many thanks to Anne Louise Wirgman at the Nekbakht Foundation for locating the source texts in the Complete Works and finding the previously unpublished material in the Nekbakht Archives in Suresnes. Thanks as well go to Sandra Lillydahl for her design, to Beatrice Upenieks for preparing the texts for editing and for laying out the pages, and to Dorothy Craig for proofreading.

This volume of the Centennial Edition is dedicated to the memory of Sharif Munawwir Donald Graham (1942–2024), editor in chief of the Complete Works from 1992 to 2012, and a dedicated and tireless worker for the Message of Love, Harmony, and Beauty.

—Cannon Labrie, editor

1

THE ALCHEMY OF HAPPINESS

Beloved Ones of God, my subject tonight is the alchemy of happiness.[1] The soul in Sanskrit and in the terms of Vedanta is called *atman,* which means happiness or bliss itself—not that happiness belongs to the soul, but that the soul itself is happiness. Today we often confuse happiness with pleasure. Pleasure is only an illusion of happiness, a shadow of happiness, and in this delusion one perhaps passes one's whole life, seeking after pleasure, and never finding satisfaction. There is a Hindu saying that a person looks for pleasure and gets pain. Every pleasure that seems to be happiness in outward appearance promises happiness, for it is the shadow of happiness, but just as the shadow of a person is not the person and yet represents the form of the person, so pleasure represents happiness but is not so in reality. According to this idea one finds that there are rarely souls in this world who know what happiness is; they are constantly disappointed in one thing after another; but such is the nature of life in the world—it is so deluding that if one were disappointed a thousand times, one would still take the same path, for one knows no other. The more we study life, the more we realize how rarely there is a soul who can honestly say,

---

1. A report of a lecture that appeared in *Sufism* magazine of December 1922.

"I am happy." Almost every soul, whatever their position in life, will say that they are unhappy in some way or another, and if you ask for a reason, perhaps they will say, "I cannot attain to the position, power, property, possessions, or rank for which I have worked for years." Perhaps they are craving for money, and do not realize that possessions give no satisfaction; or perhaps they say they have enemies, or that those whom they love do not love them; there are a thousand excuses for unhappiness that the reasoning mind will make. But is even one of these excuses ever entirely correct? Do you think even if they gained their desires they would be happy? If they possessed all, would these things suffice? No, for still they would find some excuse for unhappiness, and all these excuses are as coverings before their eyes, for deep within is the yearning for the true happiness that none of these things can give. Those who are really happy are happy everywhere: in a palace or a cottage, in riches or poverty, for they have discovered the fountain of happiness that is situated in their own heart; so long as one has not found that fountain, nothing will give one real happiness. Those who do not know the secret of happiness often develop avarice. They want thousands; and when they get those they do not satisfy, and they want millions; and still they are not satisfied—they want more and more. If you give them your sympathy and service, they are still unhappy; all you possess is not enough—even your love does not help them, for they are seeking in a wrong direction, and life itself becomes a tragedy.

Happiness cannot be bought or sold, nor can you give it to a person who has not got it. Happiness is in your own being, your own self, that self that is the most precious thing in life. All religions, all philosophical systems, have in different forms taught how to find it by the religious path, or the mystical way, and all the wise ones have in some form or another given a method by which the individual can find that happiness for which the soul is seeking. Sages and mystics have called this process alchemy. The stories of the *Arabian Nights* that symbolize these mystical ideas are full of the belief that there is a philosopher's stone that will turn metals into gold by a chemical process. No doubt this symbolic idea has deluded people in both the East and West; many have thought that a process exists by which gold can be produced. But this is not the idea of the wise; the pursuit after gold is for those who are as yet children. For those who have the consciousness of reality gold stands for light or spiritual inspiration. Gold represents the color of light, and therefore an unconscious pursuit after light has made people seek for gold. But there is a great difference between real gold and false. It is the longing for true gold that makes people collect the imitation gold, ignorant that the real gold is within. They satisfy the craving of their soul in this way, as a child satisfies itself by playing with dolls. But this realization does not depend upon a person's age. A person may have reached an advanced age and still be playing with dolls, may still be involved in the search for this imitation gold, while another may begin in youth to see life in its real aspect. If one studied the transitory nature of life in the world, how changeable it is, and the constant craving of everyone for happiness, one would certainly endeavor, whatever happened, to find something one could depend upon. Placed in the midst of this ever-changing world one yet appreciates and seeks for constancy somewhere—one does not know that one must develop the nature of constancy in oneself; it is the nature of the soul to value that which is dependable. But think: Is there anything in the world on which one can depend, which is above change and destruction? All that is born, all that is made, must one day face destruction; all that has a beginning also has an end; and if there is anything one can depend upon it is hidden in the human heart, it is the divine spark, the true philosopher's stone, the real gold that is the innermost being of a person.

Those who follow a religion, and have not come to the realization of truth, of what use is their religion to them if they are not happy? Religion does not mean depression and sadness.

The spirit of religion must give happiness. God is happy. God is the perfection of love, harmony, and beauty. A religious person must be happier than the one who is not religious. If a person who professes religion is always melancholy, in this way religion is disgraced; the form has been kept, but the spirit is lost. If the study of religion and mysticism does not lead to real joy and happiness, it may just as well not exist, for it does not help to fulfill the purpose of life. The world today is sad and suffering as the result of the terrible war;[2] the religion that answers the demand of life today is that method of morals that invigorates and gives life to souls, that illuminates the human heart with the divine light that is already there, not necessarily by the outer form, although for some a form is helpful, but by the showing forth of that happiness that is the desire of every soul.

Now, as for the question of how this method of alchemy is practiced, the whole process was explained by the alchemists in a symbolical way. They say gold is made out of mercury; the nature of mercury is to be ever moving, but by a certain process the mercury is first stilled, and once stilled it becomes silver; the silver then has to be melted, and the juice of an herb is poured onto the melted silver, and then the melted silver turns into gold. Of course this method is given in outline, but there is a detailed explanation of the whole process. Many childlike souls have tried to make gold by stilling mercury and melting silver; they have tried to find the herb, but they were deluded, and it would have been better had they worked and earned money.

The real interpretation of this process is that mercury represents the nature of the ever-restless mind, something realized especially when a person tries to concentrate; the mind is like a restive horse: when it is ridden it is more restive than when it is in the stable. Such is the nature of mind: it becomes more restless when you desire to control it; it is like mercury, constantly moving. When by a method of concentration one has

2. World War I.

mastered the mind, one has taken the first step in the accomplishment of a sacred task. Prayer is concentration, reading is concentration, sitting and relaxing and thinking on one subject are all concentration. All artists, thinkers, and inventors have practiced concentration in some form; they have given their minds to one thing, and by focusing on one object have developed the faculty of concentration; but for stilling the mind a special method is necessary, and is taught by the mystics, just as singing is taught by the teacher of voice production. The secret is to be learned in the science of breath.

Breath is the essence of life—the center of life—and mind, which is more difficult to control than a restive horse, may be controlled by a knowledge of the proper method of breathing. For this, instruction from a teacher is a necessity, for since the mystical cult of the East has become known in the West, books have been published, and teaching that had been kept as sacred as religion has been discussed in words that cannot truly explain the mystery of that which is the center of a person's very being; people read the books and begin to play with breath, and often instead of receiving benefit they injure both mind and body; there are also those who make a business of teaching breathing exercises for money, so degrading a sacred thing. The science of breath is the greatest mystery there is, and for thousands of years has been kept as a sacred trust in the schools of the mystics.

When the mind is under complete control, and no longer restless, one can hold a thought at will as long as one wishes. This is the beginning of phenomena.[3] Some abuse these privileges, and by dissipating the power, before turning the silver into gold, they destroy the silver. The silver must be heated before it can melt, and with what? With that warmth that is the divine essence in the human heart, which comes forth as love, tolerance, sympathy, service, humility, unselfishness, in

---

3. Inayat Khan customarily used this word to refer to paranormal phenomena.

a stream that rises and falls in a thousand drops, each drop of which could be called a virtue, all coming from that one stream hidden in the heart—the love element—which, when it glows in the heart, the actions, the movements, the tone of the voice, the expression, all show that the heart is warm. The moment this happens a person really lives; that person has unsealed the spring of happiness that overcomes all that is jarring and inharmonious. The spring has established itself as a divine stream.

After the heart is warmed by the divine element, which is love, the next stage is the herb, which is the love of God. But the love of God alone is not sufficient; knowledge of God is also necessary. It is the absence of the knowledge of God that makes one leave one's religion, because there is a limit to a person's patience. Knowledge of God strengthens a person's belief in God, throws light on the individual and on life. Things become clear; every leaf on a tree becomes as a page of a holy book to one whose eyes are open to the knowledge of God. When the juice of the herb of divine love is poured onto the heart, warmed by the love of one's fellow humans, then that heart becomes the heart of gold, the heart that expresses what God would express. The human being has not seen God, but has then seen God in the human being, and when this is so, then verily everything that comes from such a person comes from God.

2

THE AIM OF LIFE

Beloved Ones of God, I ask your indulgence on my subject for this evening which is the aim of life.[1] As to the main object of life there cannot be but one object, though there may be as many external objects as there are things and beings. There is one object of life for the reason that there is one life, and this in spite of the fact that outwardly it appears to be many lives. It is in this thought that we can unite, and it is from this thought that true wisdom is learned. No doubt that main object of life cannot be understood all at once, and therefore the best thing for one is to pursue one's object in life first, and in the accomplishment of one's personal object one will arrive some day at accomplishing that inner object. When one does not understand this one goes on thinking there is something else to accomplish, and thinks of all that is before one that is not yet accomplished, and therefore one remains a failure. One who is not definite about one's object has not yet begun one's journey in the path of life. One should therefore determine one's object for oneself. However small that object is, once it has been determined one has begun one's life.

We find in the lives of many people sometimes that all through their life they do not happen to find their vocation in

---

1. A talk given in rue de Loxum, Brussels, on May 22, 1924.

life, and what happens? In the end they consider their life a failure. All through their life they go from one thing to another; yet not knowing their life's object they can accomplish so little.

When people ask: Why do I not succeed? In answer to that I always say: because you have not yet found your object. As soon as one has found one's life's object one begins to feel at home in this world. Before that one feels in a strange world. No sooner one has one found one's way, one proves to be fortunate, because all things one wants to accomplish will come of themselves. Even if the whole world was against one, one gets such a power that one can stand on one's object against the whole world. One gets such patience when one is on the way to one's object that whatever misfortune happens, it will not discourage one. No doubt as long as one has not found it, one goes in one thing and then in another, and one thinks that life is against one. Then one begins to find fault with individuals, conditions, planets, climate—with all things. Therefore what is called being fortunate or successful is having the right object. When one is wearing clothes that were not made for one, then one says they are too loose or too short. When wearing one's own clothes one feels comfortable in them. The real thing therefore is to give every soul the freedom to choose its object in life, and if one finds one's object one knows that one is on the right path.

When a person is on the path, there are certain things to be considered. When one has a knot to unravel, to loosen, and one is given a knife to cut it, one has lost a great deal in one's life. It is a small thing, but by not accomplishing it a person has gone backward. It is like taking a backstep. This is a little example I have given, but in everything one does, if one does not have that patience and confidence to go forward, then one loses a great deal. However small a work one has undertaken, if one accomplishes it, one has accomplished something great. It is not what work one has accomplished, it is the very fact of accomplishing that gives one the power.

And now coming to the question of the object that is the object of every soul: that object may be called spiritual attainment. One may go all one's life without it, but there will come a time in one's life when, although one may not admit it, one will begin to look for it. Because spiritual attainment is not only an acquired knowledge, it is the soul's appetite. And there will come a day in life when a person will feel the soul's appetite more than any other appetite. No doubt every soul has an unconscious yearning to satisfy this soul's appetite, but at the same time one's absorption in everyday life keeps one so occupied that one has no time to pay attention to the soul's appetite.

Now, the definition of spiritual attainment can be found in studying human nature, for human nature is one and the same, whether one be spiritual or material. There are five things that a person yearns for: life, power, happiness, knowledge, and peace, and the continual appetite that is felt in the deepest self yearns for one or the other of these five things. In order to answer one's appetite what does one do?

In order to fulfill the desire to live, one eats and drinks and protects one's self from all dangers of life. And yet the appetite is not fully satisfied because all danger one may escape, but the last danger, which is called death, one cannot escape.

In order to obtain the next thing, which is called power, a person does everything in order to gain physical strength, influence, or rank; a person seeks every kind of power in order to be powerful. And one always knocks against disappointments, because one always sees that if there is a power of ten degrees, there is always another power of twenty degrees to knock against it. Just think of the great nations whose military power was once so great that one could not have thought that in a single moment they would collapse. One would have thought that it would take thousands of years for them to fall, so great was their power. We need not look for it in history, we have just seen it in these past few years; we have but to look at the map.

Then the third kind of appetite is happiness. A person tries to satisfy it by pleasure, not knowing that the pleasures of this world do not answer for that happiness that the soul really seeks after. One's attempts are in vain: one finds in the end that every effort one made for pleasure one made with a greater loss than gain. Besides, that which is not enduring, that which is not real in its nature, is never satisfactory.

Then comes the desire for knowledge. This desire gives a tendency to study. And one might study and study all through one's life, but even if one read all the great libraries, all the books, there will still remain that question, "why?" That "why" will not be answered by the books one might study, by exploring the facts that are on the outside of life. In the first place the depth of nature is so profound that one's limited life is not long enough to probe its depths. Yes, comparatively or relatively you might say one is more learned than another, but no one arrives at satisfaction by the outer study of life.

And then there is the appetite for peace. In order to find peace one leaves one's environments that trouble one. One wants to get away from people. One wants to sit quietly and rest. But one not ready for that peace, even if one went to the caves of the Himalayas, away from the whole world, even there would not find it.

When considering these five appetites, which are the deepest the human has, one finds that all the efforts made to satisfy these appetites seem to be in vain. And how can these five desires be satisfied? They can be satisfied by spiritual attainment, for that is the only thing that answers these five different appetites.

And now to explain how these five appetites are answered by spiritual attainment: The desire to live can only be satisfied when the soul realizes its eternal life. For mortality exists in conception rather than in reality. From a spiritual point of view mortality is the lack of the soul's understanding of its own self. For instance, it's like one who always thought that one's coat was oneself and lived all one's life in that conception, and when that coat was torn thought that he or she died. One experiences the same in life. It is a kind of illusion that the soul gets from this physical body and identifies itself with this mortal being. It is just like identifying oneself with one's overcoat. And by the loss of the coat one thinks: I am lost.

Nevertheless an intellectual knowledge of this is but of little use. Because when the inner self has identified itself with the body and when in imagination the person thinks: No, no, the body is but my overcoat. It is therefore that meditations are done by the wise people of all times in order to give a chance to the soul to find itself independent of the physical body. Once the soul has begun to feel itself, its own life, independently of its outer garb, it is beginning to have confidence in life and is no longer afraid of what is called death. As soon as this phenomenon is vouchsafed one, one no longer calls death "death"; one calls it a change.

And now on the idea of power. The true power is not in trying to gain power. The true power is in becoming power. But how is one to become power? It requires an attempt to make a definite change in oneself, and that change is a kind of struggle with one's false self, and when that false self is crucified, then the true self is resurrected. Before the world this crucifixion appears to be the lack of power; in truth, all power is attained by this resurrection.

As to knowledge, there are two aspects. One knowledge is that which one learns by knowing the names and forms of this life, what we call learning. That cannot be the answer of this appetite. It cannot satisfy this appetite, it is only a stepping stone to that appetite. This outer learning helps one to get to the inner learning, but the inner learning is quite different from the outer learning, and how is it learned? It is learned by studying the self. One finds that all the knowledge that one strives to learn and all that exists to study—it is all in oneself. Therefore one finds a kind of universe in one's self, and by the study of the self one comes to that spiritual knowledge that satisfies the soul's appetite.

And then comes the question of happiness. One thinks that if my friend is kind to me then I will be happy; when people respond to me, or when I will get money, then I will be happy. But that is not the way to become happy. It is a mistake, because the lack of happiness makes one blame others, because they are in the way of that person being happy. But in reality, it is not so. True happiness is not gained; it is discovered. One's soul itself is happiness. That is why one longs for happiness. What keeps happiness out of one's life is the closing of the doors of the heart. When the heart is not living, then happiness is not living there. Sometimes the heart is not fully living, but a little living, and it expects life from the other heart. But the real life of the heart is to live independently in its own happiness. And that is gained by spiritual attainment.

For those who have found peace within themselves, they may be in a cave of the mountain or amidst the crowd, but in every place they will experience their peace.

Now the question is how these five things can be gained. As I have said, the first thing necessary is for one to accomplish the object that is immediately standing before one. However small, it does not matter. It is by accomplishing it that one gains power. As one goes further in this way through one's life, always seeking for the real, one will in the end come to reality. Truth is attained by the love of truth.

When a person runs away from truth, truth runs away from that person. If not, truth is more near to the person than what is without truth. There is nothing more precious in life than truth itself, and in loving truth and in attaining to the truth, one attains to that religion that is the religion of all people and of all churches. It does not matter then to what church one belongs, what religion one professes, to what race or nation one belongs; when once one realizes the truth, one is all because one is with all. There is disagreement and misunderstanding before a person has attained to the truth. When once a person has attained to the truth there is no more misunderstanding. It is among those who have only learned the outer knowledge that disputes arise. But those who have attained to the truth, whether they come from the North Pole or the South Pole, from whatever country, it does not matter. For when they have understood the truth, they are at-one-ment. And it is this object that we should keep before us in order to unite the divided sections of humanity. For the real happiness of humanity is in that unity that can be gained by rising above the barriers that divide people.

3

THE PURPOSE OF LIFE (1)

Beloved Ones of God, every living being has a purpose in life, and it is the knowing of that purpose that makes every soul able to fulfill his or her life's purpose.[1] As it says in the *Gayan*, "Blessed is the one who knoweth his or her life's purpose." Be not surprised if you find many groping in darkness all through life, doing one thing or another, going from one thing to another, always dissatisfied, always discontented; and everything they undertake has no result. The reason is the absence of knowledge, the knowledge of the purpose of life.

Individuals apart, every object has its purpose. The mission of science is to discover the purpose in objects. It is from that discovery that science has come: be it medical science or philosophy, all different aspects of science are the result of discovering the purpose of things. But the aim of mysticism is to find the purpose in the lives of human beings—the purpose in one's own life and the purpose in the life of others. As long as one has not found this purpose, one may have success or failure, one may be seemingly happy or unhappy, but in reality one does not live; for life begins from the moment that one has found the purpose of one's life.

---

1. A talk given at the Waldorf Astoria Hotel in New York City, December 27, 1925.

The Purpose of Life (1)

You will find people with all riches, with position, with comfort, and conveniences through life, and yet they are missing something, missing the main thing that can alone make them happy, and that is knowing the purpose of their life. This is the very thing they miss, and at the same time humankind is ignorant of this. One will have interest in a thousand things, one will have an interest in one thing and then go on to another thing, and so on. But one will never come to that point where one finds the purpose of one's life. Why? Because one does not look for it.

And now coming to children's education, to the education of youth: very often the parents never think about it. Whatever seems to them beneficial for the child to do, they recommended that the child do. They do not pay attention to the fact that it is in one's childhood that one has to find the purpose of one's life. How many lives have been ruined for this reason! The child may have been brought up with every facility, and yet he or she is always kept away from the purpose of this life. Sa'di, the writer of the *Gulistan*, says that every infant is born for a certain purpose, and the light of that purpose is kindled in its soul. This is a psychological and mystical secret that people, however unhappy they may be, the moment they know the purpose of their life, a switch is turned and the light is on. They may not yet be able to accomplish it, but the very fact of knowing the purpose gives them all the hope and vigor and inspiration and strength to wait for that day. If they had to strive after that purpose for their whole life, they would not mind so long as they know what that purpose is. Ten such persons have a much greater power than a thousand people working from morning till evening not knowing the purpose of their life.

Besides, what we call wrong or right, good or bad, that is also according to the purpose of life. There is one person whose vocation through life is to write plays, and there is another person who is studying medicine. Both have their examination before them. They see an advertisement for a play, and they both feel that, "I must go and see it." The medical student thinks that, "My examination is near, I must stay home and study, but this is an attractive play, and I must see it." The student who is the playwright thinks, "Going to see this play would perhaps be beneficial." Both act the same act, both see the same play, but one loses the sense and purpose of studying. It is not the action but the purpose. For one, the purpose is to see it. For the medical student, it's the passing of the examination that will bring success, not attending the play. The more one studies life, the more one will realize that it is not the action but the purpose that makes things right or wrong, good or bad.

And now coming to the purpose of all, and that is the ultimate purpose. We begin our lives with an individual purpose, but we come to a stage where the purpose of every soul is one and the same. And that purpose can be studied by studying the inclinations of people. Every soul has five inclinations in the depth of its heart. Being absorbed in the life of the world a person may forget that ultimate purpose. But at the same time there is a continual inclination toward it. That shows that the ultimate purpose in the life of all is one and the same.

One of the five points is the love of knowledge. It is not only intellectual and intelligent beings who seek after knowledge. Even an infant wishes to know what every little noise is. Every child in seeing a beautiful color and line in a picture inquires about it. And therefore, in greater or less degree, every individual is striving after knowledge. No doubt, in life as it is today, many are put into a situation where they never have a moment to gain that knowledge after which they seek. From morning till evening they have their duty to perform; they are so absorbed in it that after some time that hunger for knowledge is gone and their mind becomes blunted. It is not just one person, it is thousands and thousands of people whom life has put in a certain situation where they cannot help but have their mind on some particular work and never have time to think about things that they would like to think about, that they would like to know.

We have made this life. And what do you call it? Progress? We call it freedom. What freedom? It is not freedom of mind. The mind is thrown into a limited horizon and we call it a sphere. Besides that, every day in education one finds that the examinations for different things are becoming more and more difficult. Why? In order to make them difficult, not for the sake of knowledge, but in order to make them more difficult for people. I happened to ask the captain of the ship if he had to pass an examination, Yes, he said, and every year it is more difficult. I asked him for what reason. He said, "We have to read so much; it is not all useful for our work, it is only to make it difficult. There are so many candidates for this examination that it is made more difficult for them to learn." If all thought in life is to study something only in order to earn one's bread and butter, then when can one give thought and mind to what one's soul is seeking after?

Among those who have a little freedom in life, who have time for thinking about gaining some knowledge, there are many who seek only after novelty. They think that to learn means to know something they did not know before. You will find very few seekers who will see that in every idea, however simple, a revelation arises when they put their mind to it, and then it begins to teach more and more things that they had never known. I can tell you of my own experience regarding a couplet of a Persian verse I had known for twelve years. I liked it. It was a simple everyday expression. But after twelve years, one day a glimpse of inspiration came, and that very couplet became a revelation. It seemed as if there was once a seed and then a seedling came from it and turned into a plant from which sprung fruits and flowers.

The difficulty that so-called truth-seeking people have is that when they have a little time to look after it, they are restless. One thing does not satisfy them and so they go from one thing to another thing, and so on. And instead of coming to the real idea, they get into confusion because every new idea becomes confusing too. Someone asked an artist, "Can you make a new picture?" "Yes," the artist said, "I can." The artist put two horns and two wings on the body of a fish. And they said, "How wonderful, this is something no one has seen. Everyone has seen wings on birds and horns on beasts." And so there are many souls who need that novelty. And there are many souls who admire it, and few think as Solomon has said that "there is nothing new under the sun,"[2] especially when we come to the domain of wisdom, of knowledge. For one does not arrive at concentration, contemplation, and meditation by studying many, many things, nor by going from one idea to another.

And the next inclination is the love for life. Human beings apart, even little insects, if you want to touch them, they escape. Their life is dear to them. What does it show? It shows that every being wishes to live, however unhappy a person may be, however difficult one's life may be. Perhaps in the sadness of a moment a person would wish to commit suicide. But if the person was in their normal condition, they would never think of leaving this world. Not because the world is so dear, but because it is the soul's inclination to live. As it says in the *Gayan*, "Life lives, death dies." Since life lives, life longs to live, and nobody for one moment wishes that death should ever take them. The great prophets, masters, saints, sages, philosophers, mystics—what was their striving? Their striving was to find some remedy to cure people from mortality. But was their mortality their conception or their condition? It is a condition when seen outwardly; in reality it is a conception. The soul has the physical body as its garb, and when it cannot carry its garb any longer, then its purpose is fulfilled, and it wishes to leave this garb. For no one wishes always to carry his heavy coat. Even the king feels more comfortable when the crown is put in the cupboard. It is the soul's happiness when it is free from its

2. Ecclesiastes 1:9.

physical burden. But it only can be happy when it can be itself. As long as one thinks one is one's body, so long is one mortal, being only conscious of one's mortal existence. What is it? It is a garb. But this, intellectually understood, will not help. The soul must see itself. The soul must realize itself. And how to do it? In the scriptures it is said, "Die before death."[3] What is this dying? This dying is playing at death. The mystics have all through their life on earth practiced playing at death. By playing at it, they were able to see what death is. Then it was not only intellectual knowledge. They actually saw that their soul stands independently of this physical garb. Buddha has called it *jnana*, which means realization. The absence of it is called *ajnana*, the lack of realization.

All thoughtful people, when they think of that day when they will have to depart from this earth where they have their friends whom they once loved and their treasures, feel very sad that there should come a day that they should leave. Not only that, but it makes them sadder still to feel that, "Once I am gone, I will be nothing," for life does not wish to become death; life wants to live. But this shows ignorance; this means the false conception of life that is gained by the senses, by experiences through the senses. The one who has lived through the senses, realized life through the senses, thinks through the senses, does not know life. Life can be very different from this.

And the third inclination a person shows is to gain power in any way whatsoever. Every person strives through life to gain power. The reason is that the soul strives to exist against the invasion of life because the life's conditions seem to sweep away everything that has no strength. When the leaf has lost its strength, it falls from the tree; when the flower has lost its strength it is thrown away. Naturally the soul wishes to keep its strength. Therefore, every individual seeks for power. But the mistake lies in the fact that however much power a person may have, it is limited. And therefore with the increase of

---

3. A hadith of the Prophet Muhammad.

power, there comes a time when one sees there can be another power greater than what one possesses. This limitation makes one suffer; one becomes disappointed. Besides, when we look at the power that one possesses, the power of the world, what is it? Powerful nations that were built over thousands of years can be crushed in a very short time. Then what is their power? If there is any power, it is the hidden power, the almighty power. And by getting into touch with that power, one begins to draw from it all the power that is necessary. The secret of all miracles and phenomena of sages and masters is to be seen in that power they are able to draw from within. Perhaps you have heard of fakirs and dervishes practicing jumping into the fire or cutting the body and healing it instantly. But there exists a power even greater than that. And those who can do great things, they do not show them. If they can do small things, they show them. But at the same time there is this power that gives proof that spirit has power over matter. Spirit may be buried under matter for some time. And that makes one powerless.

And the fourth inclination a person shows is to be happy. One seeks happiness in pleasure, in joy, but these are only shadows of happiness. The real happiness is in the human heart. But one does not look for it. In order to look for happiness, one seeks pleasure. Anything that is passing, and anything that results in unhappiness is not happiness. Happiness is the very being of a person. Vedantists have called the human soul *ananda*, happiness, because the soul itself is happiness. That is why it seeks happiness. And because the soul cannot find itself, therefore it is looking for something that will make it happy; but what it finds can never make it happy, perfectly happy. Besides that, sin and virtue, good and bad, right and wrong, can be distinguished and determined on this principle. What brings real happiness is virtue. What is called right is that which leads to happiness. That which is called good is good because it gives happiness. And if it does not do so, it cannot be good, cannot be virtue, cannot be right. Whenever one has found virtue in unhappiness, one has been mistaken; whenever one was wrong, one has been unhappy. Happiness is the being of a person; that is why one craves for it.

And the fifth inclination a person shows is for peace. It is not rest or comfort or solitude that can give peace. It is an art that must be learned, the art of the mystics, by which one comes to experience peace. But one may ask why, if it is natural for the soul to experience peace, must one strive for peace by practice, by meditation, by contemplation? The answer is, yes, it is natural to experience peace, but life in the world is not natural. Animals and birds all experience peace, but not humankind, for human beings are the robbers of their own peace. They have made their life so artificial that they can never imagine how far they are removed from what may be called a normal, natural life for them to live. It is for this reason that we need the art of discovering peace within us.

We shall not experience peace by making outside conditions better. People have always longed for peace, and have always caused wars. It was not only in the ancient times that people sought for wars. And at the same time every individual says, "I am seeking for peace." Then where does war come from? Because the meaning of peace has not been fully understood. Therefore, people live in a continual turmoil, in a restless condition, and in order to seek for peace, they seek war. If this goes on for many years more, we shall have the same condition as before; we will not have peace unless every individual will begin to seek first for peace within.

And now coming to the question, what is peace? Peace is the natural condition of the soul. The soul that has lost its natural condition that practically belongs to it becomes restless. The normal condition of mind is tranquility, yet at the same time, the mind is anything but tranquil. The soul experiences anything but peace.

Now, the question that arises in the mind of every thoughtful person is, what was the reason, what was the purpose for the creation of this world? The answer is, to break the monotony. Call it God, call it the only Being, call it the source and goal of all; being alone, God wished that "There should be something that I should know." The Hindus say that the creation is the dream of Brahma. Call it dream, but that is the main purpose. The Sufis explain it that God, the lover, wanted to know his own nature. And therefore, through manifestation the beloved was created, in order that the love may manifest. And when we look at it in this light, then all that we see is the beloved. As Rumi, the great writer of Persia says, "The Beloved is all in all, the lover only veils the Beloved; the Beloved is all that lives, the lover a dead thing."

Sufis have therefore called God the Beloved. And they have seen the Beloved in all beings. They have not thought that God is in heaven, apart, away from all beings, but in everything, in all forms, they have seen the beauty of God, and in this realization the main purpose and the ultimate purpose of life is fulfilled. As it is said in the ancient scriptures that when God asked Adam, "Who is thy Lord?" he said, "Thou art my Lord." When briefly explained, this means that creation was purposed so that every soul may recognize its source and goal and surrender to it and attribute to that source and goal all the beauty and wisdom and power, and by doing so may become perfect. As the Bible says, "Be ye perfect as your Father in heaven."[4]

---

4. Matthew 5:48.

4

THE PURPOSE OF LIFE (2)

Beloved Ones of God, my subject this afternoon is the purpose of life.[1] Every intelligent person comes to a stage in life, sooner or later, when he or she begins to question what purpose there is in life, in being on earth, asking: "Why am I here?" "What am I to accomplish in life?" No doubt, the moment this question has arisen in a person, that person has taken the first step in the path of wisdom. Before this, whatever one did without being conscious of one's life's purpose, one remained discontented. Whatever one's occupation in life, whatever one's condition in life, whether one is wise or foolish, learned or illiterate, there is always discontent. One may have success or failure in one's life, but that desire that "My life's purpose should be accomplished" remains there, and unless it is accomplished, a person cannot be satisfied. That is why many people who are successful in business, doing very well in their profession, comfortable in their domestic life, and well-off in the life of society yet remain dissatisfied because they do not know the purpose of their life. And after knowing the purpose of life you may be handicapped by many things, you may lack means, but the conditions will be favorable to go forward in spite of all that. There is a strength in

---

1. A talk given at the Twentieth Century Club, Detroit, May 9, 1926.

that conviction, that the knowledge itself gives, when a person knows that, "I am here for this particular purpose."

There is a story told of the Prophet Muhammad. At the time when the Prophet, who was born for that particular purpose in life, felt a kind of restlessness, a dissatisfaction with all things in life, he thought he'd better go into the forest, into the wilderness, into the mountains and sit there alone to get in touch with himself and to find why there was some yearning after something that he did not know. He asked his wife if she would allow him that solitude that his soul longed for, and she agreed. Then he went into the wilderness and sat there for days together. And when the vibrations of the physical body and mind, which are always upset and in turmoil in the midst of the world, when these vibrations calmed down, and when his mind became quiet and his spirit was tranquil, when the heart of the Prophet became restful, he began to feel in touch with all the nature there, the space, the sky, the earth; and then it seemed as if everything was talking to the Prophet, as if the water and the clouds were talking to him. He was in communication with the whole world, with the whole of life. And then the word came to the Prophet, "Cry out the name of thy Lord." This is the lesson of idealism, not only to be in touch with nature but to idealize the Lord.

In these days there is the great drawback that when people become very intellectual, they lose idealism. If they want to find God, they want to find him in figures. There are many who would rather meditate than worship, than pray. In this way there has always been conflict between the intellectual person and the idealistic person. The Prophet was taught as the first thing to idealize the Lord, and when his ideal became his conception of God, then in that conception God awakened, and he began to hear the voice saying, "Now you must serve your people, you must awaken in your people the sense of religion, the ideal of God, the desire for spiritual attainment, and the wish to live a better life." And then he knew that all the prophets that came before were always intended to accomplish the same thing that it was now his turn to accomplish. We all are born in this world to accomplish a certain purpose, and as long as one does not know this purpose, one remains ignorant of life, one cannot call oneself a living being. A machine has no choice, it cannot find its life's purpose, but an individual is responsible to a great extent. Very often out of weakness one gives in to something that otherwise one would have refused to accept. This weakness comes through the lack of patience and endurance, lack of self-confidence, and lack of trust. A person who does not trust in Providence, who cannot have patience, who cannot endure, will take what comes in the moment, will not wait till tomorrow. Perhaps the purpose of life would open before one if one had more power of endurance, more self-confidence, more trust in Providence. But when one possesses none of these things, one is just like a machine. One is not pleased with what comes in life, one is grudging every day, and confused, and yet one goes on like a horse that is not willing to go on, but at the same time is yoked to the cart, and has to go on. The first knowledge that we must gain is the knowledge of the purpose of our life.

It is a great pity that education as it is today gives very little attention to this question. Children, youths, and grown-ups all go through life toiling morning till evening, studying or working, and at the same time not knowing what purpose in life they have to accomplish. Among a thousand persons there may be one exception, but nine hundred ninety-nine are placed in a situation whether they desire it or not, where they are working just like a mechanism, a machine put in a certain place that is made for it and where it must work. Out of a hundred perhaps ninety-nine are discontented with the work they are doing. Either it is their life's condition that has put them there or it is because they must work to make a living, or because they have an idea that they should first gather what they need. By time they have gathered the means to make themselves able to do something in life, the desire of accomplishing something is gone.

It is a great drawback that, in spite of progress, individuals have no opportunity to accomplish something they desire to. Therefore, many youths never think about it. They think, "We must do that work and that is all," and they have no time to think of the purpose of their particular life. Thus, lives are wasted—hundreds and thousands of lives are wasted. In spite of all the money they make, their hearts are not satisfied because it is not the wealth one gains that can give that satisfaction.

When we look at life with a philosopher's view we see that every person is like one note in this symphony of life, that we all make this symphony of life, each contributing the music that is needed in that symphony. But if we do not know our own part in the symphony of life, naturally it is as if one of the four strings on the violin is not tuned. If it is not tuned, it cannot give the music that it should produce. So we must each produce that part for which we are born. If we do not contribute what we are meant to, what we should contribute, we are not in tune with our destiny. It is only by playing that particular part that belongs to us that we shall get satisfaction.

Maybe many people will not think as I do; for instance, those who believe strongly in pacifism, or those who believe in the peace ideal, will say, "Is it not madness that anybody should make a war?" To that I say that everything one does, though it may look better or worse, yet belongs somewhere in the scheme of life, and we have no right to condemn it. The principal thing is for every individual to become conscious of the duty for which they are born.

And now coming to the question of the purpose of life. There are two purposes. One is the minor, the other is the major purpose of life. One is the preliminary, the other is the final purpose of life. The preliminary purpose of life is just like a stepping stone to the final purpose of life. Therefore, one should first think about the preliminary purpose of life. For instance, if one wishes to collect wealth, one's whole thought is absorbed in it. And if one were told, "No, no, that is not a good thing. What is wealth after all? Is it not material, useless? You ought to be devotional, spiritual." But that one's mind will not be there. One cannot be spiritual when one is concentrated on that particular thing, and because one cannot collect the money one wants to have, one is unhappy. If you force upon one spirituality, religion, devotion, prayer, they will not help one. Very often people in the place of food give water, in place of water they give food. That is not good. Spirituality comes in its time. But the preliminary purpose is what a person will contribute to the world as the first step before awakening to spiritual perfection.

All great teachers of humanity have taught that preliminary purpose of life in their religions. Whatever teachings they have given to their followers, their motive was that they help them to accomplish that first purpose in life. For instance, when Christ called the fishermen, he said, "Come hither, I will make you fishers of men." He did not say, "I will make you more spiritual." That was the first step. He wanted them to accomplish the first purpose of life. And the next lesson was, "You will become more spiritual." To the teachers of spiritual knowledge who look at it in this way, their first duty is to show the person or help the person to accomplish the first purpose in life. When they have done this, then they show the second purpose.

And now coming to the preliminary purpose of a person's life. There are four different ways people take in their lives. One way is the way of material benefit. By profession, by occupation, business, or industry, a person wants to make money. Something can be said both for and against this ideal. Against this ideal it may be said that while working for money, very often one loses the right track, thought, and consideration. One overlooks the rights of others. And what is to be said for it is this: that it is after all those who possess wealth who can use wealth for better purposes. All charitable institutions, hospitals, schools, colleges, they are all raised by charitable people who have given generously to such organizations. Therefore, there is nothing wrong in earning money, and in devoting one's time to it as long as the motive was right and good.

Another aspect is duty. One thinks that one has a duty to one's community, to one's town, one's city, or one's country. One does some social work, one tries to do good to others, and considers it one's duty. It may be that one has a duty toward one's parents; one may be looking after one's mother and sacrifices one's life for her, or for one's wife and children. There is a great merit in this also. No doubt, what speaks against it is that very often such lives are spoiled and they have no chance to do anything worthwhile in the world. But if it was not for the sense of duty, the world would be void of love and affection. If the wife had no sense of duty toward her husband, nor the husband to his wife, nor the neighbor to a friend, then we would be living like creatures of the lower creation. It is the sense of duty that makes a person greater than ordinary beings; that is why we admire it. Heroes who give their lives for their country are not doing a small thing. It is something great when a person gives his or her life for the sake of duty. Besides, duty is a great virtue.

There is a story from the last war about a young woman who was always displeased with her husband and always wished for a separation. When the call to arms came, this young man went to the battlefield, and he hoped that in his absence she would marry someone else. And as the war was going on, she thought that while her husband was in battle she could go as a nurse. It so happened that in the same ward where she was working, her wounded husband—he had lost his eyes—arrived. She happened to be his nurse. And when she saw him in that condition she was astonished that it so happened that she was to be his nurse. And she had just received a letter with a marriage proposal. She tore it up and changed her mind in an instant and said, "Now that he has lost his eyes and he is helpless, I shall remain his wife, I shall take care of him all through life." Duty, the sense of duty, is a great virtue, and when it is perfected and deepened in the heart of a person, it wakens a person to greater and higher consciousness. In that way, people have accomplished great things. The great heroes have lived a life of duty. The sense of duty comes from the love of the ideal. The greater one's ideal of duty, the greater one will be. According to the Hindus the observers of duty are considered religious, because *dharma*, the Sanskrit word that means religion, also means duty.

The third aspect one chooses in life is to make the best of the present. It is the point of view of Omar Khayyam in the *Rubaiyat*, where he says,

> O my Beloved, fill the cup that clears
> Today of past regrets and future fears.
> Tomorrow, why tomorrow, I may be
> Myself with yesterday's twenty thousand years.

This is this point of view of the person who says, "If I was great in the past, what does it matter? The past is forgotten, and the future, who knows what will come out of it? No one knows his future. Let us make the best of this moment, let us make life as happy as we can." It is not a bad point of view; it is a philosophical point of view. Those who adhere to this point of view are happy and give happiness to others. No doubt, all these different points of view have a wrong side just the same. But when we look at their right side, there is something in it to appreciate.

People nowadays use a phrase: "He's a jolly good fellow." In songs and at different occasions this phrase is used to appreciate that tendency of mind that tries to make this moment happy. It is difficult, and not everyone can manage to do it, for life has so many conflicts and troubles. One has to face so many difficulties in life that to be able to keep on smiling is not everyone's work. In order to keep smiling a person must either be very foolish and not feel or think about anything, but just close both eyes and heart to the world, or a person must be as high as the souls meant by the story of the miracle of Christ walking upon the water. There are some who sink and some who swim and others who walk over the water. Those who are drowned in life's misery are those who cannot get out of it; they are tied down in the depths of life; they cannot get out, and they are miserable there. They are the ones who sink. Then there are others who are swimming; they are those who want to strive through the conflicting conditions of life in order some day to reach the shore. And then there are others who walk upon life. Theirs is the life that is symbolically expressed in the miracle of Christ walking upon the water. It is like living in the world and not being of the world, touching the world and not being touched by it. It needs a clear perception of life, keen intelligence, and thorough understanding of life, together with great courage and strength and bravery. By this I do not mean to say that the one who makes the best of this moment is the same as the one whom we call happy-go-lucky, the one who is a simple person. That one is someone who lives in another world, is not aware of life's conditions, is not awake to the conflicting influences of life. If that one is happy, it is not surprising; for that one is happiness itself. I mean those who are wakened to life's conditions, those who are tender and sensitive to the thoughts and feelings of others. For them is very difficult to go on living and at the same time to keep smiling. And if one can do it, it is no doubt a great thing.

The fourth aspect is the thought of those who think that, "What is life on earth after all; is it not only a few days to pass somehow or other? The day ends, the months and years pass, and so time slips by, and one comes to the end of life before one has expected it, and the whole past becomes like a dream of one night." Ask one who has lived a hundred years, "What do you think about life on earth?" That one will say, "One night's dream, my child, it is no longer than that." If that is all there is to life, then those who think about it that way say, "We should think of the hereafter." Just as some say, "If we are able to work, we must strive in order to make a provision for our old age to be more comfortable," so those who think of the hereafter say, "Life is a short stay; it is nothing but an opportunity. We must prepare something so that later we shall have the benefit of it." Maybe there will be some who have the right understanding, but there are others who make too much of it and have the wrong conception of the hereafter. But at the same time, the wise ones who think "We must use the time and opportunity which is given to us in this life to prepare for the next one" have accomplished a great deal. It is something to admire.

I have now explained the four different ways people take in order to accomplish the purpose of their lives: making wealth, being conscientious of their duty, making the best of every moment of life, and preparing for the future. All four of these have their good points. And once you realize this there is no need to blame anyone for having taken a different path from the one we have taken in order to accomplish our life's purpose. By understanding this we become tolerant.

And now we come to the ultimate purpose of life, which is always one and the same; for every person has in the end to accomplish the same purpose in whatever way that person will, coming to it consciously or unconsciously, easily or with difficulty. But one has to accomplish it. That is spiritual attainment. You may ask, "People who never think about it, who are so material that they never think about it, who refuse to consider this question, do you think they attain to spiritual realization?" Yes, everyone consciously or unconsciously is striving after spiritual attainment. Sometimes they do not take the same way as we do, sometimes their point of view and their method differ, and sometimes one person attains to spiritual realization much sooner than another. For one person it may be reached in a day, and for another person a whole life may not be enough to have attained it. And then one may ask, "What determines it?" It is the evolution of a particular soul.

There are stories told in India of how a person was awakened to spiritual consciousness after having heard one word from their guru. That one word inspired the person instantly to touch the higher consciousness. And then again we hear the stories in the East of people who went to the forest, to the mountains, who fasted for months or for days and days, who were hanging by their feet, their head downward, or who stood erect for years and years. This explains how difficult it is for one person and how easy for it might be for another. We make a very great mistake today when we consider every person's evolution in the same way. We say, "Every person is a human being just the same." It is not so. There are great differences between people. One is creeping, one is walking, one is running, and another is flying. And yet they all live under the same sun.

It is the custom in the East for those who begin to seek for a spiritual purpose to look for a spiritual teacher. They do not set forth on the spiritual journey by themselves, because after thousands of years of experience have taught that to tread the spiritual path it is necessary to have some leader to whom we can give our confidence and trust in order to follow that one to the end. The difficulty in America is that there is a general wakening, no doubt, and everyone wishes to know something about it, but at the same time they do not stick to one and the same thing. There are many who will go first to one school and then another, and then to another esoteric school, and so on. In the end they have learned so much but do not know what is true and what is false, which is right and which is wrong. It is just like visiting a restaurant and eating so much that one is not able to digest it. Besides, when a person takes in all that is false and true, there remains no discrimination between false and true. In addition, the greatest merit seekers after truth can show is the confidence and trust that they give their teacher. It

The Purpose of Life (2)

is according to the confidence one gives that the heart is able to receive the knowledge that leads one to the higher
 . . . [*text blank*].

And now one might ask: How are we to realize the preliminary purpose of our life? By coming to our natural rhythm. Today people adopt wrong methods. They go to a clairvoyant and ask about the purpose of their life. They do not know it themselves. Anybody else must tell them except their own spirit, their own soul. They ask others because they do not tune themselves to that pitch where they can feel intuitively what they live for. If another person says, "You are here to become a carpenter, or lawyer, or a barrister," that does not satisfy your need. It is our own spirit that must speak to us. We must be able to quiet our condition, to attune our spirit to the universal consciousness, in order to know the purpose of our life. And once you know the purpose of your life, the best thing is to pursue it in spite of all difficulties. Nothing should discourage you, nothing should keep you back once you know, "This is the purpose of my life." Then go after it at the sacrifice of everything. For when the sacrifice is great, the gain in the end gives a greater power, a greater inspiration. Rise or fall, success or failure does not matter as long as you know the purpose of your life. If ninety-nine times you fail, the hundredth time you will succeed. And the ultimate purpose for which our soul is seeking every moment of our life—that is our spiritual purpose.

And you may ask how to attain to that purpose. My answer is that what you are seeking for is within yourself. Instead of looking outside, you must look within. The way to proceed to this accomplishment is for some moments to suspend all your senses, such as sight, hearing, smell, touch, in order to put a screen before the outside life; and by concentration and by developing that meditative quality, sooner or later you will get in touch with the inner self that is more communicative, that speaks more loudly than all the noises of the world; and this gives joy and creates peace, and produces in you a self-sufficient spirit, a spirit of independence, of true liberty. The moment you get in touch within yourself, you are in communion with God. It is in this way, if God communication is sought rightly, that spirituality is attained.

5

THE ART OF PERSONALITY

Beloved Ones of God, my subject this evening is the art of personality.[1] First of all, let me explain why I call it art, because what one thinks of art is that it is something inferior to nature. But I do not think art is inferior to nature. I think art finishes nature, that in art there is something divine, that it is God who through the human finishes this beauty that is called art. In other words, art is not only an imitation of nature, art is the improvement upon nature, be it painting, drawing, poetry, or music. But the best of all arts is the art of personality, which must be learned in order to use it in every walk of life. It is not necessary for every person to become a painter, nor is it necessary to become a musician, a drawer, or an architect. But it is necessary for every person to learn the art of personality. Once a person came to me and said with great contentment and satisfaction that, "I was brought up by my parents just like a plant in the forest, naturally growing." And I answered, "It is a pity. If your parents wanted you to grow naturally they ought to have kept you in the forest. It is a pity that you are in the midst of the world. The world is made by art. In order to be in the world you ought to know the art of personality."

---

1. A talk given at the Twentieth Century Club, Detroit, May 14, 1926.

Very few of us distinguish between individuality and personality. Individuality is that which we have brought with us at our birth, we are born as a separate entity. That itself makes us individual. But personality is something that is acquired. It has not come with us; it is something we gain. Therefore, in ancient times, education meant to learn and practice the art of personality. That was the culture of ancient times. Today a person has to pass examinations. As long as one has a degree, one thinks one is safe, one thinks, "Now I can go into the world and will get on." But that is not enough. Besides, the examinations are becoming all the more difficult. The other day I met a man who has passed the examination in Europe to become a sea captain. And he told me that, "Within these ten years the examination has become so difficult. And yet, when we think of what we have to study, there are unnecessary books and things we never use in the work we do. And why? In order to make as few captains as possible." I saw a man working to become doctor of philosophy. And when I asked him what he has to study, he said he has taken the mystical line and that he is reading some German philosophers. But at the same time, there are so many books on language and books of grammar—every year there are added more and more—that it is difficult to pass the examination. By the time they have passed the examination their nerves are wrecked and they have lost the best time of life. And when they have their degree, then it is even difficult for them to obtain a job. And if you ask, "What have you learned?" they say, "I have read so many books." That central theme of culture, that thing that alone can be called education, seems to be totally forgotten—and that is the art of personality. That is why, in general, in the midst of the crowd there is a lack of manner, a lack of ideal. An external qualification is different. It is the inner qualification, the inner culture that matters, and it can only be obtained by the development of personality.

And now I come to the idea of the use of personality. In a business, salespeople have success according to the power of their magnetism; their influence solely depends on their personality. It is their personality that attracts, whether they go to other offices or to a shop. It is their personality that stands out, that gives you the thought of buying or selling or dealing with them, and the lack of this makes one go away and never come back. A statesman or stateswoman, a politician, a teacher, a solicitor, barrister, or lawyer—all require personality. A physician may be a great physician, a most qualified one, and yet if their personality is not agreeable, if they are rude, crude, unsympathetic, however many patients they may have their medicines will make them feel bad, their personality will make them feel worse. And very often a doctor with a sympathetic personality, good manner, and wisdom can cure a person by a word of consolation before the medicine reaches that person. It is the same with barristers and lawyers. They can dishearten a person in one visit. And when a person has lost courage and hope, then naturally there is little hope of being successful. Because power of mind is needed. If the power of mind is strong, then a lawyer can succeed. Therefore, in all walks of life what counts is the personality. Those whose personality is against them, the world is against them.

There are four categories of personality. The first personality is likened to a date, the next is like a walnut, the third is like a pomegranate, and the fourth is like a grape. The date-like personality is soft outside and hard inside. As soon as one puts a date in one's mouth and feels the seed between the teeth one has a horror of it. And then there is the next personality that is walnut-like. There is a hard shell, hard to penetrate, but when you know the person more, it is like breaking the walnut, and out comes a nut that is soft. And then there is a pomegranate personality. It is hard outside and hard inside. The pomegranate is hard, the skin is hard, and the seed inside is hard too. And then there is the grape-like personality that is soft outside and soft inside. You will always find these four classes of persons. The personalities of those who are hard outside are repellent at first, but in the end you will become their friend. You understand them only when you come to their inner being. Therefore, they do not always make many friends. And those whose personality is soft outside and hard inside will at once attract people, but those people will not stay with them. They will stay for some time, but then they leave. People know them and turn away from them. And the personalities who are hard outside and hard inside are isolated in the world. This is not the place for them. Everyone will want to keep away from them, and after some time they will find themselves in difficulties. And those whose personality is soft outside and soft inside naturally will be most magnetic. The grape is the most attractive fruit.

There are also stages in the evolution of the human being, and at every stage there is a different kind of magnetism. There are four different aspects of magnetism: physical magnetism, intellectual magnetism, sympathetic magnetism—which is sometimes called personal magnetism—and spiritual magnetism. Freshness, newness, good health, cleanliness, harmonious movements, regular form, all these things help physical magnetism. But it endures for a short time. The next magnetism is the intellectual magnetism: keen perception, ready conception, clear vision, wit, and the art of expression, all these things create intellectual magnetism in a person, which lasts longer. And then we come to sympathetic or personal magnetism. People who are sympathetic, loving, affectionate, kindly, gentle, and who have developed a sympathetic nature will always attract without them knowing it, because sympathy has the greatest power, and this magnetism is lasting. Whatever relation you may be to a person, if there is no link of sympathy, there is no attraction. Very often a person may be very qualified, very intellectual, imposing in appearance, and yet being without feeling will lack magnetism, and in many cases fails to succeed because of the lack of sympathy. And the fourth kind of magnetism is spiritual magnetism. It can be recognized in the innocence of a person, in the purity of a person, in the simplicity of a being. One might think a spiritual person is most evolved. But in appearance the spiritual person is the most simple one, the innocent one, not ignorant, but less complicated, broader in outlook, keen in perception, with lofty ideals, with raised consciousness, and yet humble and democratic in the true sense of the word.

The idea of democracy is wrongly understood by many today. The principle that, "I am as good as you" is a wrong principle of democracy. It takes away humbleness, gentleness, and the high ideal. Besides, to think that camphor and bone, chalk and sugar are all equal! It is a very sweet idea that everybody is equal. But when you tune the piano with each note the same you have no more music. When one has a wrong conception of democracy, one tunes the piano to the same note. Therefore, the music of one's soul becomes dull. It is more an obsession with democracy than democracy itself. Real democracy is raising oneself higher by appreciating the ideal one meets. In this way one rises to a higher ideal. The high ideal is not appreciated by many. It is being equal on a higher plane instead of being ignorant. Pulling a high person down to the earth and then speaking of democracy is wrong democracy; it is the spirit of the revolutionary, of people who make revolutions by being mad about one particular idea and regardless of anything else, as has been seen in many places. For instance, when there came a revolt against the Catholic Church, what happened? It was not only against the church, but against the ideals of the church. Every good thing about it was disregarded. It was not only a revolt against what was not desirable, but everything about it. It is from that time that the sense and depth of religion that existed in the Western world seem to have been diminishing, and they are diminishing further every day. In spite of the many churches, there is less idealism. The ideal that is necessary in some form or other for every soul has been drowned. It is drowned because people revolt against something regardless of what is good about it. The tendency is, when a person disregards the God-ideal, that person disregards everything that belongs to it—not only something that is undesirable, but everything. And so it is with the world today, that the art of personality has been lost in the obsession with democracy instead of it being realized as a higher spiritual evolution. For instance, it is spirituality alone, a spiritual outlook alone, that gives a person real democratic feeling. That is to say, that for every person any other person is their parent, their brother, their enemy, or their great friend. According to the spiritual outlook, spiritual people see every person as themself. They see their own spirit, their own soul reflected in the other one. That is the real democracy, when one sees oneself in both a higher and a lower person. That is the highest ideal of spiritual attainment, and that is what makes one really democratic. No doubt, one rises to such an ideal by degrees. And the first degree of this highest ideal is gentleness. It is therefore that in English language word *gentleman* was used. Why gentle? Because he took the first step toward the accomplishment, toward the art of personality. It is not necessary that a person was rich, or in good position, or occupied a high rank. That does not necessarily make a person gentle. With all the position and high rank one may have, one may not be gentle. Once a person has become thoughtful, that person's first step is to become gentle. As soon as this one thing, thoughtfulness, is developed in one, one takes one's first step toward real evolution. But one might think, "Everyone tries to be thoughtful." And yet, when we consider two things in our daily life—the necessity for silence and for speech—we might find that we make a thousand mistakes every day. Often we speak more than we need to speak, or we give our confidence to someone to whom it might have been better not to have given it, Or we have spoken to someone and we should not have done it. But it is too late when we think of it afterward. Sometimes in a mood of haste, or opposition, or in a distressed condition, a person might say something hurtful without meaning it. One says it, and then one repents for it. By speaking one has not gained anything, but has lost more. There is no gain. And very often in speaking there is no gain except that it is a pastime, that one feels a desire to say something, that little pleasure of saying anything. And then afterward the result is the same. The human heart is so delicate; it is just like a fragile glass that once it is broken is very difficult to mend. It never really gets mended. Every hurt and harm once given is never mended. One can apologize and ask forgiveness. But what is done is done. What is said is said. The word is not lost. Every word we speak remains somewhere, in the heart of the one listening, in space, in the ground, it stays and results in something.

Then very often people make a habit of being talkative. They waste their own time, their own thought, and the thought and time of others. And very often it ends in confusion. One accomplishes nothing in useless argument. It is amusing to see that very often one argues because one does not know. One goes on arguing because one does not know something and wants to find out from the other what that one knows about it. Besides, how can one understand by discussing and arguing what one can only understand by one's own wisdom, by the intuition within? It is very often a loss of time.

Then there are others who have a passion for talking; it is a kind of amusement, a pastime. But in the end they exhaust themselves and become nervous, and nothing is gained. Silence sometimes seems to be very hard to keep but at the same time has its great benefit. Very often disagreement and inharmony can be avoided. Silence is good for both the wise and foolish. For the wise it is good because it avoids unnecessary talk; one can keep one's precious thought well cherished within oneself. And so one rears the good thought that is like a plant. And for the foolish, as long as one keeps silence, one covers one's stupidity, and so much the better. Silence raises the dignity of the wise, and covers the stupidity of the foolish. Besides, friends, the more you evolve, the more you will find the different grades of people just like the different keys on the piano. One is lower, another is higher. So every person has a different grade of evolution. And the higher you evolve the more you will necessarily find that you cannot drive everyone with the same whip. You have to talk to everyone differently. In other words, you have to speak to every person in his or her own language. If you speak to people in a language they do not understand, it will be gibberish. They will not understand it. If they are less evolved, they will abuse the word you have said. If they are highly evolved and you say something that does not reach their level of evolution, it will make you small in their eyes. What is the use? Besides, you will always find that inharmony is caused unnecessarily by words. There is no need of it. On the other hand, however inharmonious the atmosphere created by other persons may be, if you have the words of wisdom you can scatter the clouds of inharmony.

I will tell you an amusing story. It is from my own experience. In traveling I met a man of a very dense evolution, a soldier who always lived in the military and who had his own ideas. A modern educated man in the East understands differently and sometimes is criticized by uncultured men. And when we were talking together I happened to say, in order to harmonize, "Well, we are brothers!" He looked at me with great anger. He said, "Brothers! How dare you say such a thing!" I said, "I forgot. I am your servant, sir." He was very pleased. I could have argued. It would have created disharmony without reason. The foolishness of that man arose just like fire; I put water on it and extinguished it. It did not make me small. We are all servants of one another. It pleased him and satisfied him.

There is a story about a wise healer. A woman went to him and asked, "Can you tell me how to avoid this? I am having a difficult time with my husband. There is a quarrel at home every day." He said, "That is very easy." She said, "I would be so grateful." He said, "I will give you these lozenges, these sweets. You keep them in your mouth when your husband comes home, and it will all be well. They are magnetized sweets." And every day she experienced that there was no quarrel anymore. After ten days when the sweets were finished, she said, "Anything I would give if you can give me more sweets. They were wonderful." Then the teacher said, "My friend, you must understand after ten days of having the sweets that your husband after toiling all day was nervous and tired and weary when he came home. And naturally he was not in tune, and you made him worse by talking. By keeping silence he had nothing to quarrel about, and your home became more harmonious. This must teach you a lesson, that silence is the key to harmony."

Dear friends, the sages in the East, many of them either for some hours or perhaps all day long, keep silence. And one might think that it is very difficult to do. But once a person gets into this habit it is not so difficult. And the atmosphere they create, the healing power they show, and the harmony they spread all over is so wonderful that sometimes a single sage can spread an atmosphere of peace over the whole village. That sage is just like the peacemaker of the whole village. Silence has a silent power that spreads out and has wonderful phenomena associated with it.

In addition, anything that is odd, whether movement or words or action or thought, takes away the magnetism and hinders harmony. And therefore, the wise always avoid all that is odd. Besides that, to understand the law of harmony one must compare it with the harmony in music. Sometimes there are two notes of the same kind that harmonize. And so the wise will harmonize with the wise and foolish. The foolish could be in harmony with the wicked for the reason that they share the same note but with the difference of an octave. But it is the same. Then there is another law of harmony and that is the note that harmonizes with it. It is not the same note, but it harmonizes with it, it responds to it. In that there is the positive and negative. If one is positive, then the negative will harmonize. If one is negative, then the positive will harmonize. Two persons who are negative will not harmonize, and two persons who are positive will not harmonize.

And then there is a third law to be observed, that there may be two notes that will be quite different. But if you add a third note, they will make a chord. In that way, there may be two persons who do not harmonize, but there is a third who will create harmony between them. And at the same time there may be two persons who are most harmonious and a third will perhaps create inharmony.

And there is yet another law: that the wise will be in harmony with the foolish one, but will not be in harmony with the semi-wise. The law of attraction and repulsion depends upon the law of the harmonious blending of persons. If they do not blend harmoniously, then there is repulsion. If they blend harmoniously, then there is attraction. Just like different colors, the same colors used according to the law of harmony will harmonize. If they are not used according to that law, they do not harmonize. It is the blending. Every person does not harmonize with every other person. But whether they blend or not is all according to the law of notes in music. You will always find that it is always similar to the law of notes.

In India Brahmins believed that there were four kinds of persons: the angelic person, which they call *deva*; then *manusha*, a human person; then an animal person; and then *rakshasa*, a monstrous person. And very often whenever there was a marriage they went to consult with the Brahmin. And the Brahmin said he would make out the horoscope and according to the horoscope he would give advice. But he did not always advise according to the horoscope, but according to the psychological idea. That Brahmin was a person who had a more developed intuition and had insight into the law of harmony, the law of attraction and repulsion. He knew if the boy was *rakshasa* and the girl angelic, it would not go. And then he said it was against the horoscope. But most often it was his own conception. The same thing is with friendship and also in marriage. Neither friendship lasts nor marriage if there is a difference of kind.

In order to develop this law of personality there is no study or any particular practice that is required. If there is anything most necessary, it is first to acquire a right attitude of body and of mind: the body working regularly, rightly, and steadily, and mind working steadily and rightly. Perhaps you have known or read in books that in the East the adepts sat in certain posture for hours together in order to get even the attitude of the body right. And then we hear that they concentrated for hours together. That was to make the mind right. When the attitude of body and mind is right, then naturally the personality becomes right. It is right living and right thinking that develops personality. But the principal thing is development of the heart quality. There are many people who intellectually develop. But the greater the sympathy is developed in a person, the keener is the perception. One develops in oneself that outgoing nature that one's atmosphere embraces all those in one's presence. The spiritual magnetism that finishes the art of personality is gained by meditation, by the realization of the oneness of all, by getting in union with God, by having high ideals and high aspiration.

6

RECONCILIATION

Any efforts made in developing the personality or character building, must not be for the sake of proving oneself superior to others but in order to become more agreeable to those around one and to those with whom we come in contact.[1]

Reconciliation is not only the moral of the Sufi: it is the sign of the Sufi. This virtue is not learned or practiced easily, for it needs not only goodwill but also wisdom. The great talent of the diplomat is to bring about such results as are desirable with mutual agreement. Disagreement is easy. Among the lower creation one sees it so often. What is difficult is agreement, for it needs a wider outlook, which is the true sign of spirituality. Narrowness of outlook makes the horizon of one's vision small. The person with a narrow outlook cannot easily agree with another. There is always a meeting ground for two people, however much they differ in their thought. But the meeting ground may be far off and one may not always be willing to take the trouble to go so far in order to come to an agreement. Very often one's patience does not allow one to go far enough to where one can meet with the other. In an ordinary case what

1. A talk given at the Summer School in Suresnes, France, July 16, 1923. In the original *Sufi Message* volume this chapter was called "The Development of Personality" and included material from other talks. In the *Complete Works* this talk had two titles, "Saluk" and "Reconciliation."

happens is that one wants another to meet one in the same place where one is standing. There is no desire on one's part to move from the place where one stands. This does not mean that one, in order to become a real Sufi, should give up one's own ideas in order to agree with another. There is no benefit in always being lenient to every thought that comes from another, nor is there always benefit in erasing one's own idea from one's own heart. For that is not reconciliation. The one who is able to listen to another is the one who will make another listen to him or her. It is the one who will easily agree with another who will have the power of making another easily agree with him or her. Therefore in doing so one gains in spite of the apparent loss that might sometimes occur. When one is able to see from one's own point of view as well as from the point of view of another, one has a complete vision and a clear insight. One—so to speak—sees with both eyes. No doubt friction produces light, but light is the agreement of the atoms. If two people have their own ideas and argue about their different ideas as a stimulus for thought, it does not matter so much. But when a person argues for the sake of argument, the argument becomes that person's game. That one has no satisfaction in reconciliation. Words provide the means of disagreement. The reasons become the fuel for that fire. But wisdom is found where the intelligence is pliable, where it understands all things, seeing the wrong of the right and the right of the wrong.

The soul that arrives at perfect knowledge has risen above right and wrong. That one knows them and yet knows not. That one can say much and yet what can he or she say? Then it becomes easy for that one to reconcile with each and all.

There is a story of two Sufis who met after having traveled many years along their own lines. They were glad to meet each other after many years' separation, and for the reason that they were both murids of the same murshid. One said to the other: "Tell me please of your life's experiences." The other one said, "After all this time of study and practice of Sufism, I have learned one thing: how to reconcile with another, and I can do it very well now. Will you please tell me what have you learned?" The other one said, "After all this time's study and practice of Sufism, I have learned how to master life, and all that there is in this world is for me, and I am the master. All that happens, happens by my will." Then came the murshid whose murids both of them were. And both spoke of their experiences during this journey. The murshid said: "Both of you are right. In the case of the first, it was self-denial, in the right sense of the word, that enabled him to reconcile with others. In the case of the other there was no more of his will left; if there was any, it was the will of God."

7

ATTITUDE

Beloved Ones of God, I will speak this day on the subject of the attitude.[1] It is the attitude of mind that very often makes right and wrong; at the same time it is the attitude of mind that draws friends to you or gives you a repulsive influence. Also, it is the attitude of mind that brings happiness or unhappiness. It is true that there is the influence of time. There is a certain time in your life that has an influence for good or bad, for rise or fall, for happiness or unhappiness. But at the same time your attitude either controls it or is controlled by it. And if the attitude is controlled by it, then the situation, at that time conquers you. But if your attitude is in your hands, then there is a chance of you conquering the situation.

There is a phrase in Hindustani, known by every person, and the phrase is this: if your attitude is right, life becomes easy. Most often one's failure, one's unhappiness, and one's differences from one's friends come from a wrong attitude. When one takes up an enterprise and is not sure about it, and does not think about its success, and doubts whether one will have success or not, and doubts whether one's partners in business will help one or not, in that situation one's attitude will create

---

1. A Sunday public lecture given at the Suresnes Summer School, July 4, 1926.

all that one imagines. The partners in business will act wrongly toward one, unjustly toward one, and the situation will turn toward the attitude.

Because the attitude is the current that molds the situation; therefore however promising a business or a work may be, if one's attitude is not right, it must go wrong, it cannot come right. It is a hidden yet most powerful influence under all circumstances of life. It is the same way with your attitude toward friends. If one feels with friends whether this friend will prove to be kind and nice, faithful and constant, or whether this friend will change and we think "I doubt if I can hold this friend. I feel this friend will one day deceive me. I think this friend will disappoint me one day." Then one is creating that outcome, one is inspiring the friend, and the friend, without knowing it, will act in the same way as the person's attitude was. I repeat again the Hindustani saying: if your attitude is right, life becomes easy. In any enterprise, anything you wish to accomplish, what is most wanted is right attitude. Besides the attitude about right and wrong, if a person thinks that "Everything I touch, and everything I do, and everywhere I look, it is all wrong," certainly it is wrong. There is no doubt about it. It is one's attitude that is wrong, and therefore whatever one does is wrong. It is just like taking a red lantern and throwing the light upon everything; every object that appears in that light will appear red. One will become frightened and see danger wherever one looks, but the danger is in one's hand: it is the red lantern.

Sometimes, one gets into a wrong attitude out of humbleness. By correcting oneself, one grows to correct too much. And then one calls oneself wrong, and with every move one makes, thinks: "I have done something wrong, something dangerous." One has only made a turn, nothing else, and it results in a great danger, too.

Very often people do not progress in their lives because of their attitude toward life. They are very often enemies to themselves. And they themselves are the hindrance to their progress.

They might think this is the reason, or that is the reason: lack of money, unkindness of friend, a lack of acquaintances, the planets are against me—a thousand things. But what is most against them is themselves; they cannot progress. When one's attitude is analyzed and understood, and when one has controlled oneself so as to be able to take any attitude one wishes, then the latent influence in one naturally begins to manifest.

There are three gifts of God given to some in this world, and these gifts are greater than jewels and gems, wealth, and anything else in the world. And nothing can buy these three gifts of God; they are born with the person and very often the person does not know it. One gift is the influence to progress; another gift is the influence to attract; and the third gift is the influence to make difficult situations easy. I will tell you about the first gift. Nothing in the world can keep back a soul who has the gift of progress, in other words, the means to flourish, to prosper, to come out. There is a story, a well-known story, about a poor man who was selling empty bottles in Bombay who came to a merchant and asked for a salary to do this job for him. And from that time he began to sell empty bottles. From the day the merchant engaged him he gradually became more prosperous. So one day he thought, "I have worked for twenty years in this shop, and it is only since this young man has come that I have prospered." He did not tell this to the young man, but he thought, "Let us see what will happen next." He made this young man his partner in his business. And from that time he began to flourish a hundred times more. After six months he was flourishing and prospering in every way. This young man was the secret; he did not tell him. In the end, as this man had no son, no children, he gave his business to the young man who, in the end, in thirty years' time, became the wealthiest man in the whole country.

I do not mean to say that it is a spiritual influence, and yet it is the influence of spirit; there is no doubt about it. It is not a material influence, influence cannot be material. An influence that works from within and works toward perfection, in whatever form, is a wonderful influence. And there are some who are born with that influence. Whether they do it alone or with someone else, in whatever they do, there is a progress; it cannot be helped. Whatever they touch flourishes.

Then there is another influence, and that influence is that a person will never be without friends. If such a person left the whole of humanity and went to live among lions, tigers, bears, and rhinoceroses, these will be their friends. Let that person go among the educated and illiterate, among the wise and the foolish, wherever that person goes, they will attract friends. That person will never be alone, in riches, in poverty, in health, in sickness; at all times they will attract friends from all sides. That person is born with that gift. People may have relations or friends, perhaps three or four or five or six. But when someone possesses this influence, every person is their friend, and very often their friends will prove greater than relations. I think of this when some of my collaborators come and tell me that in that particular place where I am placed to work for the cause, they do not respond to it. That the place is such, the people are such that they do not respond to it, and this thing comes to my mind. Human beings apart, even go to the animals: cats, dogs, foxes, and wolves—they will all come to you. It is an influence.

Very often wandering dervishes, without one penny, wandering here and there, have that influence. And if they sat in a place somewhere in the desert, or in a forest, or somewhere in the country, people were attracted to them. It may be that six months or one year or two years had passed and that only the animals of the country knew them, only the birds recognized them. But then the time comes when human beings begin to come and then they are attracted. Very often people say that a place has an attraction because of its beautiful nature, nice mountains, beautiful riverbanks, seashores, deserts, forests; but a human being has a greater influence than all these places. Imagine, Prophet Muhammad was born in Mecca, a place in

Hejaz without anything interesting. For industry there were no gold mines, there were no coal mines, there was no oil. In nature there was nothing beautiful there, nothing to take from that country, nothing interesting—no art, no science, no literature—there was nothing there. There was only one soul who was interesting there. The soul who was a magnet and attracted the people of the whole world. And after the Prophet had passed, then the tomb of the Prophet attracted; it attracted millions. During his life thousands were attracted and after his death millions, to this same spot without any interest.

Then there is a third influence, and this influence is that however difficult a situation may be, when a certain person handles it, it becomes easy. For instance, there may be a strike of thousands of miners and workmen, and after everybody tries to make peace, and no one can, there comes a person with some influence given to that person by God. It is not intellect, knowledge, or psychology—it is influence. With that influence the person goes among them and makes everything right.

A person of that influence may go after the war, or during the war, or when there is a disagreement between nations. That person, by merely going there and touching the condition, will make it easier. If one wanted to develop this influence, one cannot develop it: it is God's gift. It is, therefore, that they call such a one: the "person of the day." That person may be in politics, or in industry or business; whatever form of work, it does not matter, the influence is there. But no doubt, any of these three great gifts may be in a person and yet, if the person's attitude is not right, it is just like a lantern that is dimly burning. It could burn much better if the attitude were right. There are many examples of those who are born with this in them. There is this gift; anyone who sees it can find out that they have it. And yet they never use it. They do not know it. The reason may be that their attitude is wrong. A person may have the greatest occasion and chance to progress in life and to flourish, to make things easy, and in spite of this, in spite of having all the power to make things easy for oneself, one may fail because of one's wrong attitude.

And now one might ask: What do you mean by the right attitude? And how can one have the right attitude? One can have right attitude by right thinking and by keeping one's mind focused on what is just and true. Wrong always attracts wrong, and right always attracts right. And one might ask: What is right and what is wrong? I say, what you think is right at this moment is right for you, and what you think is wrong at this moment is wrong for you. Wrong is wrong. I do not mean to say that what another person says is wrong is wrong for you, or what another person says is right is right for you.

The real basis of that is what you are thinking at this moment; and never for one moment think that those who do wrong think it to be right. It is not true. They do not believe it. They know it is wrong and yet they do it either out of weakness, or lack of power, or lack of discrimination, or something. They are not clear in their mind. It is not true that there are many who do wrong and that they think that it is right. They know that it is wrong. But the ones who think that this is right, that is right for them. Maybe tomorrow they will think that what they thought right is wrong. Well, then tomorrow it will be wrong, but today it is right.

Besides that, all one says, does, and thinks comes out of an impulse; one end of it is in one's own mind, and the other end is in the mind of God. And, therefore, every impulse, whatever people think about it, whether they think it right or whether they think it wrong—every impulse that comes, one end of that impulse is in the heart of God. It is the spark that first manifests in the heart of God, then it manifests outwardly.

Then one might say God cannot guide a person wrongly, because God is just and good and perfect. And the answer is that God's justice and goodness and perfection cannot be compared with what we consider just and good and right. It may be that God's justice and what is considered right and perfect by God is thought to be quite imperfect and unjust by human beings, because the horizon of their vision is very narrow; they cannot think and they cannot imagine what is meant by God in every action that takes place.

In the Qur'an it is said that there is not one atom that moves without the command of God. Yes, one might say, then how about perfect and imperfect things, all things wrong and right; yes, they are wrong and right and perfect and imperfect things from our point of view. What is our point of view? Our point of view is a narrow, small, limited point of view. We cannot see further than we can see. We see and hear according to our eyes and ears; our ears cannot hear more than they can, our eyes cannot see farther than they can. So is our view limited. If from our limited point of view we judge God's right and wrong, it is the greatest pity. Then one can say, we must let everything be done as it is done because everything is done from the right point of view of God.

But as individuals we have a certain responsibility. We have a responsibility toward ourselves and toward others, and the moment that the idea of what is just and right is given to us, we are responsible for acting according to that idea. It may be that tomorrow a greater light will be given to us and that we shall act still better. In this way, by acting thus every day, we shall prove a better instrument for the work of God.

8

THE SECRET OF LIFE

I would like to speak this evening on the subject of the secret of life.[1] It is one's attitude that is the secret of life. For upon one's attitude depends success and failure. One's rise and fall both have behind them one's attitude. One may ask what do I mean by the word *attitude*? Attitude is that impulse that is like a battery behind the mechanism of thought. It is not one's thought that is one's attitude, it is something behind one's thought pushing it outward; and according to the strength of that impulse that thought becomes realized. In the beginning of every work it is the attitude that is the most important factor in bringing it to its successful accomplishment.

Now, there are three different sides connected with this subject that one could observe. One side is one's attitude to oneself: whether one treats oneself as a friend or as an enemy, whether one is harmonious with oneself or inharmonious. And remember, it is not everyone who is harmonious with themself, and it is not everyone who treats themself as a friend, although a person may think so. For generally one is one's own enemy; one does not know it, but one proves it in one's doings. One reads in the Qur'an, "Verily, people are foolish and cruel." Foolish because they do not even know their own interest, and cruel be-

---

1. A talk dated Paris, December 1, 1923.

cause they very often prove to be their own enemy. Apart from being cruel to others, people begin their cruelty on themselves. But that cruelty has foolishness as its cause. That foolishness is imprudence. Imprudence means ignorance. The best explanation of ignorance could be found in the example that Buddha has given of ignorance. Someone asked Buddha: "What is ignorance? What is it like?" Buddha said: "A person was clinging to a branch of a tree, his feet not touching the ground; all night he was hanging in the air, and was every moment afraid lest he might fall and hurt himself. He did not know whether there was ground or there was water beneath. He was only afraid for his life, he only felt his own body. And in order to protect his body he was clinging to the tree all night. But with the breaking of the dawn he saw that he was but a distance of two feet from the earth. He could have just let loose that hold he had upon that little branch, if only he had had that trust, that faith, that the ground was just beneath his feet. And this is the ignorance of humans." One might consider oneself very practical and very clever, but at the same time one very often proves to be one's own enemy. As Sa'di, the great writer of Persia, says, "My cleverness, very often thou provest to be my worst enemy." Very often worldly cleverness without that faith and strength and trust is nothing but a delusion. It is the development of the trust in the heart, the development of faith, that first gives one a friendly attitude toward oneself. But how should one become one's own friend first? By bringing one's external being into harmony with one's inner being. For it is when the inner being seeks something else, and the external being does something else, that there is inharmony in oneself. When one's higher self desires one way, and the lower self strikes another way, then there is inharmony. And what is the result of this inharmony? The result of that inharmony is like a volcanic eruption. The two parts of one's own being that should unite together in love strike together, and fire comes out of it. What causes people to commit suicide? What brings that illness and depression and despair? Very often it is that conflict that exists within oneself. Therefore the attitude toward oneself must first be friendly, must first be kindly and harmonious. Even in such things as spirituality one must not go against oneself. I remember when my interest in spiritual lines began, I once asked my teacher: "Murshid, do you approve of my staying up most of the night for my vigils?" "Whom do you torture?" said Murshid, "Yourself. Is God pleased with it?" I had not another word to say. I thought, if I go further, he will say: "Do not do it." Then I shall not be free to do or not do it.

When one thinks about one's dealings with one's friends, with one's relatives, with those with whom one comes in contact in one's everyday life, one finds that one attracts them or repulses them according to one's attitude. Whether one is in business, in commerce, or in whatever walk of life, one either repulses or attracts them, and on that depends one's success or failure in life. The secret of magnetism depends on whether you consider yourself to be a friend or an enemy, a stranger or a friend; and to one who considers anyone else a stranger, to that one even the friend is a stranger. And the one who considers anyone a friend, to that one even a stranger is a friend. If you are afraid of someone who will, you think, harm you, then you inspire that person to harm you. If you distrust someone, and think one day that person will deceive you, certainly you will inspire that person to deceive you. But if you have trust, even in the enemy, the power of your trust may someday turn that one from your enemy into your friend. In everything one does, honesty and dishonesty are reflected in the same way. If the attitude is not right, whatever work one does, whomever one sees, that wrong attitude is reflected upon that person, and that person will respond in the same way. Therefore right-doing and wrongdoing are not only teachings of a religion, some virtue that is forced upon people: they are a scientific and logical truth. For with the wrong attitude nothing right can be accomplished, and with the right attitude nothing can go wrong, even if there are difficulties. I was much interested in the story of a friend from my own experience. A young friend of mine, who was a jeweler, used to take jewelry to the houses of people who like to buy, and in this way he made his business. One day I asked him: "What is the psychology of your business, will you explain?" "Every day more and more I am convinced of the spiritual truth, while doing this business," he said. "In the business of jewelry, there is a very great scope for dishonesty, but," he said that "the day when I have brought some jewels and people have seen them, and I have honestly told them the right price, mostly I have seen that they were sold, and I have profited by it. But," he said, "you cannot be always a saint in business. Sometimes when I feel that a person wants to take something that he really likes I have added a little more to the price. And it seemed that some power was robbed from me, and all day I experienced nothing but the loss of the day." He said: "It is not just one day, but many times; I thought it might be an accident, but whenever that temptation has robbed that sacred power that is in me, then that day I was not successful in my business." What does it show us? It shows us that there is hidden in our heart a wonderful power, a power that can be called divine power, a sacred power, a power that can be developed and cherished by keeping our attitude right. But then it is not always easy to keep our attitude right. The influence of this life on the earth, this life so full of changes, full of temptations, full of falsehood, continually upsets that steadiness of the attitude. Nevertheless, strength lies in the steadiness of the attitude. And any lack in that steadiness is the cause of every failure and disappointment. There is a Hindustani saying, that "A steady attitude secures success." And when we enter the spiritual realm the same rule applies. It is not the prayer that one says, it is not the house where one prays, it is not the faith that one claims, it is one's attitude that counts in religion. It is just as a ticket is taken at the gate of the railway station. They do not ask what position you have, what property you have, what ancestor you had. No, they ask: "Ticket," and you are admitted. That ticket is one's attitude. In order to enter in the spiritual spheres that right attitude is needed, and it shortens the path.

Now the question is how to know the right attitude from the wrong? To know the right attitude from the wrong is as easy as seeing all things when the eyes are open. When one does not see the wrong attitude, it means that one has closed one's eyes. One's eyes do no fail one; one closes them. One does not want to admit to oneself one's wrong attitude, one is afraid of one's own fault. But one who looks at one's own error face-to-face, one who criticizes oneself, that one has no time to criticize others. It is that one who will prove to be wise. But mostly human nature seems to be doing quite another thing. Everyone seems to be most interested in criticizing another. If one would criticize oneself, there are endless faults; however saintly or sagely, there is no end of faults in a soul. And it is only conscientiousness in correcting one's faults, in making oneself better, in taking hold of that right attitude that is the secret of success, and by it one attains to that goal that is the object of every soul.

Now we can add to this subject what the Sufi Movement, especially the Sufi Order, has to teach in this direction. According to the Sufi point of view there is only one teacher, and that teacher is God. No person can teach another person. All one can do for another is to give one's own experience to make that other successful. For instance, if a person happens to know a road, a way, he or she can tell another person: "That is the road that leads to the place you wish to find." The work of the spiritual teacher is like the work of Cupid. The work of Cupid is to bring two souls together; and so the work of the spiritual teacher is to bring together the soul and God. But what is taught to the one who seeks after truth? Nothing is taught. One is taught only how one should learn from God. For it is not the human who teaches spirituality, it is God alone who teaches it.

And how is it learned? When these ears that are open outwardly are closed to the outside world and focused upon the heart within, then instead of hearing all that comes from the outward life, one begins to hear the words within. Therefore, in a few words, if one were to say what meditation is, that also is an attitude, the right attitude to God. Right attitude to God is a direct response to God. For the voice is continually coming as an answer to every call. It is the ears of the heart that should be open and focused upon that source from where the voice is coming. And once that is done, then the teacher within is found; and then there is continual guidance, and one is guided to the extent that one keeps close to that guidance. Then one needs no other guidance than the inner guidance; but first the guidance of a spiritual teacher is necessary in order to come nearer to it. The Sufi Order therefore is the way to that inner guidance. Once a person has come into contact with that inner guidance, then one can get along through life.

Attitude forms a channel for an effort. A right attitude makes a channel for a right effort. The world is a place of tests and trials. If one does not live in the world one has no chance of doing good or bad, and even if one lived a very spiritual life in the wilderness, it would do no good for anybody, not even for oneself, because one has not gone through the tests and trials of the world. One can neither praise the life of a hermit, nor can one condemn it. If one is happy, it is good. Each knows their own life. When one is happy one will give happiness to others also. For instance, some are born to live a hermit's life. In living a hermit's life they do not find any torture or trouble in it. Let them live that life; in that they will prove to be their own friend. In the second step they will be the friend of another. If my friends asked me: Is the hermit's life ideal? I will say: It may be ideal for them, you need not follow it.

* * *

Question: *Is it not that the life of a hermit is selfish?*

Answer: It is very difficult, if we observe life, to say who is not selfish. But at the same time the life of a hermit is not a life that one should make all sacrifices for in order to follow it. I would be the last person to recommend it to anyone. But if one followed it for one's own pleasure and found happiness in it, I would not prevent it. For a Sufi maintains from the first to the last the freedom of soul.

Question: *What should be the attitude to come near to that direct communication with God?*

Answer: The attitude should first be to seek God within. And after seeking God within, then to see God without. In the story of Aladdin in the *Thousand and One Nights* we read that Aladdin went to look for a lantern. That lantern is the divine light within, and that lantern is very difficult to find. And once a person has found that lantern, the next thing to do is to throw that light on the outward life, in order to find God both within and without, both. For instance, a prayer, a night vigil, a form of worship, all these things are helpful. But if someone was not inclined to make peace with their brother and sister, to make harmony with their fellow men and women, to seek the pleasure of those around them, then they have not performed the religious duties. For what can they give to God, who is perfect? Their goodness? Their goodness is very little. Their prayers? How many times will they pray? The whole day they spend for themselves. If two times, three times they pray, it is nothing. If they can do something in order to please God, it is only to please God's creatures, to seek their pleasures. There cannot be a better prayer and a greater religion than being conscientious of the feeling of others, being ready to serve them, to please them in every way, to forgive them, to tolerate them. And in doing wrong, if one thought that one was doing wrong to God, and in doing right if one was thinking: I am doing right to God, one's attitude is right.

All mysticism and philosophy and meditation, and everything that we learn and develop, the end and the sum total of the whole thing is to be a better servant to humanity. The whole thing, from the beginning to the end in the spiritual path is a drilling, a training to be better able to serve humankind. And if one does not do it with that intention, one will find in the end that one has accomplished nothing. There are many who seek wonderworking, or great power to accomplish things. Yes, they may try and perhaps gain this or that power. But the soul will never be satisfied. The true satisfaction of the soul is in honest and humble service to another. If there were two people before me, one with great power of wonderworking who could perform phenomena, and another, humble and kind and gentle and willing to do all they can for their fellow humans, I would prefer this last one. I would say: the first is wonderful, but the other is a sage. The soul of a person is goodness itself, if only that person begins to love it. It is not something that is acquired, it springs from itself.

9

WHAT IS WANTED IN LIFE

Friends, I would like to speak this evening on the subject of what is wanted in life.[1] If this question were asked of several people, each would perhaps make out a list of not less than a thousand things that he or she wants in life. And yet, even after writing this list of a thousand things wanted in life, one rarely knows what one really wants. What one apparently wants in life is not really what one wants in life, for the nature of the outer life is illusion. As soon as one feels that one wants this or that, then the world of illusion will answer, yes, you want me in life, this particular thing is what you want. Because when one finds a lack in life, one only sees the outer lack; one does not find the lack that is within oneself. And coming to the central theme of this question, I would say that if there is anything that we can all be in accordance with—a thing that we lack in life—it is to be tuned with the infinite and to be in rhythm with the finite. In simple words: to be in rhythm with the conditions of life and to be in tune with the source of our existence. I should like to explain more plainly what I mean by being in rhythm with the conditions of life. Our perpetual complaints against all things in life come from us not being in

---

1. A talk given at the home of Baroness d'Eichthal, Paris, November 21, 1925.

rhythm with the diverse conditions of life that we have to face. And when we think that, if this condition would change into something that I wish, it would make my life easier. But that is an inexperienced expectation.

If we were placed in the very conditions that we had just now desired, believing them to be the best, we would not even then say we were quite satisfied; we would surely find something lacking in that condition also. For with all the errors and mistakes and lacks that we find in our external life, we see a perfect hand working behind it all. And if we looked at life a little closer than we generally do, we would certainly find that all the lacks and errors and mistakes and faults add up to something, making life as complete as the wise hand that is working behind it wishes it to be.

There is a Persian saying that the gardener of this garden of the world knows best which plant to rear and which to remove. One might say that this is going too much into what they call fatalism, but I do not wish to take you further in that direction. Now I want to bring you into the sphere of action. In this talk, what I wanted to do was to touch the boundaries of fatalism and then to come into the sphere of action. No doubt people have it in their hands to improve their life's condition, if only they do not lose patience before a desirable condition is brought about, if their courage has not been exhausted, and if their hope has kept along.

And now the question is: How can one come to at-one-ment with the rhythm of life, in other words, with the conditions of life? One's condition of life and one's own desire are generally two conflicting things. If they are not always conflicting, they are mostly conflicting. If desire gives in to the condition, then the condition gets the upper hand. And if the condition is mastered, then no doubt desire has upper hand. But the condition is not always mastered by a conflict, by a struggle. One always needs a precaution in fighting with a condition in life. If harmony can be established peacefully, it is better to avoid battling. If one can harmonize with a condition in life without struggling, it is better than to harmonize with it by struggling with it. Don't be surprised if I were to say that those who complain most about life and those who are very disappointed and very much troubled with life are the ones who struggle most with the conditions of life. Therefore, in coming to at-one-ment with the conditions of life, one need not always use a weapon; one should first try to harmonize with a particular condition of life. And the great heroes, who have really fought through life and gained life's victory in the real sense of the word, have not been those who have fought against conditions. They are those who have made peace with the conditions of life.

The secret of the lives of the great saints in this world, in whatever part of the world they have been, was that they met conditions, whether favorable or unfavorable, with a view to harmonize, with a view to come to at-one-ment with the rhythm of life. A desire sometimes is our friend and sometimes our own enemy. Sometimes in unfavorable conditions desire becomes agitated and loses its patience, and wishes to break the condition; and instead of breaking the conditions, it breaks itself. The great souls have given their hand first to their worst enemy, because the one who makes one's enemy one's friend will make a friend of one's own self. A condition as bitter as poison will be turned into nectar if you can get into rhythm with that condition, if you can understand that condition, if you can endure that condition with patience, with courage, with hope.

When there is a favorable condition, a person is very often afraid that it may pass. But when there is an adverse condition, one does not generally think that it will pass. One thinks that it will last forever. Where does this come from? It comes from fear of the condition. It comes from agitation, from that desire to get out of this condition, and thus one loses even hope, the only source that keeps us alive. When we see the nature of life, and how from morning till evening everything changes, why should we not keep the hope that an unfavorable condition will change and turn into a favorable condition? People get into a habit of expecting the worst. Those who have had some bad experiences in life always think that whatever comes to them, it cannot be good. Nothing good will come to them because they have gone through bad circumstances. They think anybody else can have a better time but them because they were born under an unlucky star, making conditions unfortunate to go through life. In the same way there are many imaginative and intelligent people who read the newspapers day after day and come to the conclusion that there must be a war, there will be a war. Every little struggle they read about only gives them the idea that the world must go to pieces. There are other people interested in astrology who have gone beyond ordinary astrology and are expecting the end of the world, year after year, month after month. It gives people a topic to speak about at the dinner table, and at the same time it gives a shock to those who wish to live a little longer than the world's end.

Many such dangers of the world's destruction have passed. But the prophecy and expectation still remain, and will continue. With all this, what I mean to say is the best thing is to go through every condition that life presents with patience, with understanding, with eyes open, and one should try to rise above it with every little effort one can make.

And now we come to the other side of the subject, and that is being in tune with the infinite. How can one be in tune with the infinite? The nature of being in tune with the infinite is this: comparing our souls to the string of an instrument. It is tied at both ends, one in the infinite and the other in the finite. When one is conscious all the time of the finite, then one is tuned with the finite. And when one is conscious of the infinite, then one is tuned with the infinite. Being in tune with the former makes us limited, weak, hopeless, and powerless. But by being in tune with the latter we obtain that power and that strength to pull through life under all adverse conditions.

The work that a Sufi considers as his or her sacred work has nothing to do with any particular creed, nor has it to do with any particular religion. It is only this simple thing I have just said: to be in rhythm with life's conditions and to be in tune with the infinite.

* * *

Question: *How can you arrive at being in accordance with life?*

Answer: Instead of being frightened by life's conditions, one should meet a condition and observe it keenly, and then to try to harmonize for that time with that condition. And then the next effort is to rise above it if it is an adverse one. For instance, once a young Arab was sleeping in a field and a serpent happened to crawl over his palm and he in his sleep did not know it and held the serpent with all his might. And thereby the serpent was helpless and could not bite. But as soon as he awoke from his sleep he was frightened at the sight of a snake in his hand, and he at once let it go. And as soon as the serpent was out of his hand, the first thing it did was to bite.

One can manage a condition better when it is in one's hand than when it has been lost; then the situation is out of one's hand. For instance, if a person is cross, if a person has lost their temper, the natural tendency is to pay them back in the same coin that they gave out. The outcome is a struggle. It culminates in disappointment. But when the person is cross and they have lost their temper, then they are the weak one, and that is the time that you can manage the person. That is the time that the situation is in your hand—that person is weak, you are strong.

Question: *If one wishes to improve one's position in life, and everything depends upon other people, does one not run the risk of creating by that same action a worse situation for those who are near one? Particularly for those for whom one has an affection? For instance: a man wishes to become very rich, and if he becomes extremely rich and everyone is in a sort of slavery toward him, this slavery will weigh very heavily upon him.*

Answer: Our life in this world is dependent upon one another. And wealth, however powerful it seems to be, is in the end of the examination not so powerful as it appears to be. Its power is limited, and it does not always take away the dependence of one person upon another. The whole thing is to meet one's condition with understanding, not with resignation that says I shall not improve my condition. No, the first thing is to meet the condition as it is, and the second thing is to better the condition; and the less conflict one can employ with it, the better it is. The more one can avoid the conflict in it, the better it is.

For instance, you are traveling through the wilderness and you meet a robber who says: give me your purse or I am going to take your life. I say that in order to meet this situation, the first thing you can do is to reason with him and get out of danger without your having to kill him. What I mean is we cannot always avoid conflict, and we must not turn our back on it if it comes to us. After all, life is a struggle and we must be ready to struggle. Only struggle must not make us drunk so that we lose the way of peace, which is the first to consider. We must not be like a boxer who is always looking for another person to box with: I would like to box, it is my great pleasure.

Question: *What is the other way?*

Answer: The way of tuning oneself to the infinite. That way is by the way of silence, by the way of meditation, by the way of thinking of something that is beyond and above all things of this mortal world; of giving some moments of our life to that which is the source and goal of all of us; in the thought of getting in tune with that source; for in that source alone is the secret of our happiness and peace.

And now as this is my last address here for some time before I come again to Paris, I would like to say a few words about the work of the Sufi Movement. It is a group of students of the seekers after truth who come together to read, to study, to have silence together and think of the same source of which I have just now spoken. And the leader of that group, the Baroness who has been doing her very best to keep this activity alive in Paris, will do everything and will not leave any stone unturned in order to keep this activity alive. May I, therefore, ask the sympathy and cooperation of those who are present here? In all different ways that they can help to further the cause, to further this work that appeals to them and that interests them, that there is this opportunity. And the opportunity they can make by keeping in touch with meetings here and personally with the Baroness d'Eichthal.

There is a saying in Hindustani that there are many friends who are friends when you are present, but there are very few friends who keep friends when you are absent. And now the time has come to recognize friends in my absence. And when they will come here and keep this activity alive, this flame that has been lighted, when I come back and see it kept by my friends, then I shall forget that Hindustani saying, I will no more remember it.

May I also promise, before my leaving, that my thoughts and blessings will be with my friends, more in the absence than they have been in presence. God bless you.

10

LIFE, A CONTINUAL BATTLE (1)

Beloved Ones of God, my subject this evening will be "life, a continual battle."[1] No one in this world, whatever be his or her position or experience in life, will deny the fact that life means a continual battle. And therefore one's success, failure, happiness, or unhappiness mostly depends upon one's knowledge about this battle. Whatever be one's occupation in life, whatever be one's knowledge, if one lacks the knowledge of the battle of life, one lacks the main knowledge that is most important in life.

Now, the question arises of what does this knowledge of life's battle contain. It contains the knowledge of warfare: how to battle and how to make peace. Human nature very often makes the mistake of taking sides, either the side of war or the side of peace. And if you will study the history of nations and races, you will find that it is this mistake that has caused their failure. There have been times when nations and races have developed in their character the knowledge of peace, for instance, people such as the Hindus with their most ancient civilization. But it could not bring the satisfaction that was necessary, for the reason that one side of human nature was neglected and not

---

1. A lecture given at the home of Baroness D'Eichthal, Paris, February 5, 1923.

understood. Now in this present age it seems that the knowledge of battle has developed, but on the other side the knowledge of peace is absent. For the full knowledge of warfare is the knowledge of battle and the knowledge of peace. And this can be learned according to the idea of the mystics by battling one's self and by bringing about peace with one's own soul.

The life of an individual being is not much different from the life of the world. An individual person's home is not different from the world, and an individual's body and mind and spirit make up the whole universe. An individual life can fill the gap between the dawn of creation and the last day.

People do not realize how important is their own life, their self. And it is the study of their own life and their self that is the study of the greatest importance. For instance, a healthy person has waiting at their door several illnesses, several diseases, waiting for the opportunity when they can attack. People with wealth have many waiting at their door to get the occasion to take away from them what they possess. People about whom good is said have many awaiting for a moment when something bad may be said about them. People who have power and position, how many are not waiting for the opportunity to pull them down and see them slide down from the place where they stand. And what does it show? Why is it so? One may give a thousand reasons and yet no proper reason. The best explanation that one can give is that life is a continual battle. The process of creation began like this. According to science, light comes from friction. It is one power against the other power, fighting, and by those two different forces striking each other, comes an effect. And that effect in reality may be called life. And in this lies the secret of both love and hate. One sees in the animal kingdom that animals have as their first instinct the tendency to fight one another. And this tendency becomes modified, and it is its modification and its reduced force that produces in them what we call virtues.

As it is said in the Qur'an that the world was created out of darkness, so one can see that wisdom comes out of ignorance. And the best knowledge is not only the knowledge of all that is good and beautiful, all that is harmonious and peaceful, but also knowledge of the causes that are behind all the conflicts and all the battles that one has to face in life. And the reason why one generally lacks this knowledge is because when one is faced with a battle, one wants to fight instead of first wanting to learn how to fight. And the one who goes into life's battle without first attaining the knowledge of warfare loses in the end. But the one who learns this warfare of life first, learns its reasons and causes, becomes more capable of fighting the battle of life. Christ pointed to this secret when he said "Resist not evil." This means that if one resists or wants to fight a battle every time something in another person appears to you wrong or unjust, you will always lose your power. For the competent general is not the one who always attacks. The competent general is the one who stands in firm in defense. His or her success is more secure than the one who continually attacks. Very often in everyday life one sees that by losing one's temper with someone who has lost already their temper, one does not gain anything, except setting out on the path of stupidity. The one who has self-control enough to stand firm at that moment when another person is in a temper, that one in the end wins the battle. It is not the one who has spoken a hundred words aloud who has won. It is the one who has perhaps spoken only one word.

Now, for this battle in life the first thing that is necessary is to keep the army in order. And what is this army? This army is one's nervous power. Whatever be one's occupation, one's profession, one's walk in life, if one has not the control of one's own nerves, one will be unable to control one's walk in life. Today people study political economy, and other kinds of economy, but the most essential economy is economizing the forces that make one healthy and strong through life. Now this army

Life, a Continual Battle (1)

must be drilled and must be made to work at command. And one will find the proof of this when one can sleep at will, when one can rest and eat and work at will; then that army is really at one's command. Then there are the officers of this army, and these officers are the faculties of mind. These faculties of mind are five: the faculty of retaining thought, the faculty of thinking, the faculty of feeling, the faculty of reasoning and judging, and that faculty in a person that is the principal faculty, the feeling of "I" or ego. Even in a body with strong nerves, when these five faculties that work as the generals of the army are not working in order, if they are not clear, then one cannot expect success in life's warfare. One should further study or practice the art of training these generals of the army in one's own body.

But even with an army and with competent generals, one must have knowledge of what one is battling against. For very often one is battling with one's own real interest. During the battle it is an intoxication; one is battling, but one does not know where one is going, and at the end of the battle, even if victorious, one finds that one's victory is one's loss.

Now, today there seems to be a great seeking and enthusiasm everywhere. There seems to be a new kind of interest aroused in humanity to understand life and truth more. A very large number of people are looking for the best way of gaining the power needed to battle through life, and a small number again are looking for some way of bringing peace to themselves and to others. But both these in their pursuit lack that balance that can be only brought about by understanding, by studying, and by practicing the knowledge of war and peace together. Without knowing about war, one cannot know thoroughly about peace. Without understanding peace, one cannot know thoroughly about war. What is necessary at the present time is the study of life in general, and that means knowledge about such questions as what is the purpose of life, what is really beneficial in life, what is nature, and where is the goal. It is no use trying to practice something before studying it. What does worldly-wise mean? It means expert in this warfare of life, to know how to battle, how to make a peace, why to battle, and what aim is accomplished by peace.

But it must be understood that the battle with oneself is peace and battle with another is war. And if one has not practiced on oneself, one cannot be competent to battle with others. When one finds out the secret that is hidden in this creation, it is only this: that out of one life, the origin and the goal of all, this life of variety has come. That is why the nature of that life from which this world of variety has come is peace, and the nature of this life of variety is war. One can neither be without war, nor can one be without peace. Therefore to say that the war in life must end has no meaning. One might just as well say that the world of variety should not exist. Where there is plurality, there must be conflict. And although conflict seems a tragedy, the true tragedy is ignorance. And therefore instead of wanting to end the battle of life, or instead of opposing peace, what one must do is get the knowledge of life and attain that wisdom that is the purpose of life.

11

LIFE, A CONTINUAL BATTLE (2)

I wish to continue this evening on the subject of life being a continual battle.[1] In this continual battle of life, the one who stands firm through it all comes out victorious in the end. But even with all power and understanding, if one gives up on oneself through lack of hope and courage, one has failed.

What brings bad luck in this life, in this battle? A pessimistic attitude. And what helps one to conquer the battle of life, however difficult, it is? An optimistic attitude.

There are some in this world who look at life with a pessimistic view, thinking that it is clever to see the dark side of things. To some extent, it is beneficial that one also sees the difficult side, but the psychological law is such that once the spirit is impressed with the difficulty of the situation it loses its hope and courage. Once a person asked me if I was looking at life with a pessimistic attitude or if I was an optimist. I said, "An optimist with open eyes." Optimism is good as long as the eyes are open. But once the eyes are closed, then optimism can be dangerous.

In this battle drill is necessary. And that drill is the control over one's physical organs and control over the faculties of mind. For if one is not prepared for this battle, however coura-

---

1. A lecture given at the home of Baroness D'Eichthal, Paris, February 12, 1923.

geous and optimistic one may be, one cannot succeed. Another thing is to know something about this warfare: knowing when to make a retreat and when to make an advance. If one does not know how to retreat and wishes always to advance, one will always be in danger and become a victim of life's battle.

There are many people who in the intoxication of life's battle go on battling, go on fighting; in the end they will meet with failure. Young people, strong and hopeful, and who have had fewer difficulties think of nothing but to battle against all that stands before them. They do not know that it is not always wise to advance. What is necessary is first to fortify the position and then to advance. One can see the same thing in friendship, in business, or in one's profession. A person who does not understand the secret of the law of warfare cannot succeed. Besides this, one must protect one's own from all sides. Very often what one does in the intoxication of the battle is that one goes on and on, pressing forward and forward, not protecting what belongs to one. How many people in the courts and in law cases for perhaps a very little thing, will go on spending and spending money. In the end the loss is greater than the success. Again, how many in this world will perhaps lose more than they gain only because of their fancy or pride. There are times when one must give in; there are times when one must let things loose a little bit; and there are times when one must hold fast the reins of life. There are moments when one must be persistent, and there are moments when one must be easy.

Life is such an intoxication that although people think that they are working for their interest, you will hardly find one among thousands who is really doing so, and the reason is that people become so absorbed in what they are trying to get that they become intoxicated by it, and they lose the track that leads to real success. Very often people, in order to get one particular benefit, sacrifice many other benefits because they do not think of them. The thing to do is to look all around, not only in one direction. It is easy to be powerful, it is easy to be good, but it is most difficult to be wise—and it is the wise who are truly victorious in life. And even the success of those with power and those with goodness has its limitation. If I were to tell you how many people bring about their failures themselves, you would be surprised. There is hardly one person among a hundred who really works for his or her real benefit, although everyone thinks that he or she does. The difference is that one does not think where one's real interest lies. The nature of life is illusive: under a gain, a loss is hidden; under a loss, a gain is hidden. And in this life of illusion it is very difficult for one to realize what is really good for one. And even for the wise much is demanded of their wisdom by life and by its battle. One cannot be gentle enough, one cannot be sufficiently kind. The more to life you give, the more life asks of you. There again is a battle. Yes, no doubt the gain of the wise is greater in the end, although they have many apparent losses. Where ordinary people will not give in, the wise will give in a thousand times. This shows that the success of the wise very often is hidden in an apparent failure. But when one compares the success of the wise with that of ordinary people, the success of the wise is much greater.

In this battle a battery is needed, and that battery is the power of will. In this battle of life, arms are needed, and these arms are the thoughts and actions that work psychologically toward success. For instance, there are people who say to themselves every morning: "Everybody is against me, nobody likes me, everything is wrong, everywhere is injustice, all is failure, for me there is no hope." When they go out, they take that influence with them. Before they arrive at any place, business, profession, or whatever they do, they have sent their influence before them, and they meet with all wrongs and all failure, nothing worthwhile, coldness everywhere. There are others, yes, who know what human nature is, who know that one has to meet with selfishness and inconsideration everywhere. But what do they think of all this? They think it is like a lot of drunken people. They think the others are falling upon each other, fighting each other, offending each other. And naturally sober people who are thoughtful will not trouble with those who are drunk. They will help them, but they will not take seriously what they say or do. Naturally in this world of drunkenness a person who is drunk has a greater fight than those who are sober, for the latter will always avoid it. They will tolerate, they will give in, they will understand; for they know that the others are drunk, and you cannot expect better from them. Besides this, the wise know a secret and that secret is that human nature is imitative. For instance, a proud person will always revive the tendency of pride in his or her surroundings; before a humble person, even a proud person will become humble, because the humble person vivifies the humbleness in that person. Now, from this one can see that in life's battle one can fight the proud with pride, and one can fight the pride with humility, and sometimes gain by it. Besides this, from the point of view of the wise human nature is childish. If one stands in the crowd and looks at it as a spectator, one will see a lot of children playing together. They are playing and they are fighting and they are snatching things from each other's hands, and they are bothering about very unimportant things. One finds their thoughts small and less important, and so their pursuit through life. And the reason for life's battle is often very small when it is looked at in the light of wisdom. This shows that the knowledge of life does not always come by battling. It comes by throwing light upon it. One is not a warrior if one becomes impatient immediately, loses one's temper in a moment, has no control over one's impulses, or is ready to give up hope and courage. The true warrior is the one who can endure, who has a great capacity to tolerate, who has depth enough in the heart to assimilate all things, whose mind reaches far enough to understand all things, whose every desire is to understand others and to help them understand. It must be understood that sensitiveness is no doubt a human development, but if it is not used rightly, it has a great many disadvantages. Sensitive people can lose courage and hope much sooner than other people. Sensitive people can make friends quickly, and they can run away from friends quickly too. Sensitive people are ready to take offense in all things that come their way, and life can become unbearable for them. Yet if a person is not sensitive, then he or she is not fully living. Therefore the idea is to be sensitive but not to abuse it. Abusing sensitiveness is yielding to every impression and every impulse that attacks one. There must be a balance between sensitiveness and willpower. Willpower should enable one to endure all influences, all conditions, all attacks that one meets from morning to night. And sensitiveness should enable one to feel life, to appreciate it, and to live in the beauty of life.

In conclusion to what I have said just now, I would like to tell you that the most advisable thing in life is to be sensitive enough to feel life and its beauty, and to appreciate it, but at the same time to consider that your soul is divine, and that all that belongs to the earth is a foreign thing for your soul. It must not touch your soul. All things come before the eyes. When objects come before the eyes, they come in the eyes. When they are gone, the eyes are clear. Therefore your mind should retain nothing but beauty, all that is beautiful. For one can search for God in God's beauty. All else should be forgotten. And by practicing this every day, forgetting all that is disagreeable, that is ugly, and remembering only what is beautiful and gives happiness, one will attract to oneself all the happiness that is in store.

* * *

Question: *By the cultivation of willpower does one not sometimes mislead oneself? One is not infallible.*

Answer: Yes, there is that danger, but there is danger in everything. There is even danger in being healthy. But that does not mean that one must be ill. What I have said is that we must acquire balance between power and wisdom. If the power is working without the light of wisdom, it will always fail, because power will prove to be blind in the end. But now, you will ask me, what is the use of the wise person without the use of hands and feet, who has no power of action, no power of thought? This shows that wisdom directs, but that one accomplishes by power. Therefore in the battle of life both are necessary.

Question: *In what measure can free will counteract a condition of karma such as ill health?*

Answer: For this I should tell you that the difference between human and divine is the difference between the two ends of the same line. Now, one point represents limitation, the other point represents the unlimited. One point represents imperfection, the other perfection. But if we take all human beings in this world, they do not all stand near the same point. They fill the gap between the one extreme and the other. Although just now the world is going through such a phase of the idea of what they call equality, that the nobility of the soul—even its divinity—is ignored. The whole arrangement of life is just now like this. When there is one vote for everybody in the state, then the same thing is in the home, the same thing is everywhere. But when we come to understand the spiritual life of things, we shall always realize that just as in the piano all the notes are not the same, so all the souls are not the same. One starts one's life as a mechanism, a machine, and can develop to the state where one is the engineer. Therefore the restriction of karma is for the machine. No doubt every soul has to be a machine once, in order to be an engineer later, and one does not turn at once into an engineer; rather one changes gradually from a machine into an engineer. Therefore the influence of karma on every soul is not the same. And at the same time one must realize that it is after all one's ignorance of the divine part of one's soul that keeps one away from God, not only from God, but from the birthright of one's power. But when one becomes conscious of the divine power, then one rises above being the machine, and one becomes the engineer.

Question: *Does not sensitiveness bring surprises for us, which come upon us too quickly for us to avoid the evil they cause?*

Answer: What is sensitiveness? Sensitiveness is life itself. And as life has both its good and evil sides, so has sensitiveness. And if one expects to have all life's experiences, so from sensitiveness all these experiences must come. However, as I have said, sensitiveness must be kept in order if one wants to know and understand and appreciate all that is beautiful and not attract all the depression, sorrows, sadness, and all the woes of the earth. Once one has become so sensitive as to become offended with everybody, and to feel that everybody is against one, trying to wrong one, then one is abusing one's sensitiveness. One must be wise as well as sensitive. One must realize before being sensitive that in this world one is among children, among drunken people. And one should take all that comes one's way as one would take the actions of children and the drunken people. Then sensitiveness can be beneficial. If with sensitiveness one has not developed one's willpower, it is certainly dangerous. No doubt, spirituality is seen in a person who is sensitive to others. No one can develop spiritually without being sensitive.

Question: *How can one distinguish between the difference of the wisdom of the warrior and his or her lack of courage in the battle of life?*

Answer: Everything is distinguished by its result. There is a very well known saying in English: "All's well that ends well." If in the end of the battle the one who was apparently defeated has really won, doubtless it was through wisdom and not through lack of courage. Very often apparent courage leads to nothing but disappointment in the end. Bravery is one thing, the knowledge of warfare is another. The one who is brave is not always victorious. The one who is victorious knows and understands; that one knows the law of life.

12

THE STRUGGLE OF LIFE (1)

No one can deny the fact that life in the world is one continual struggle.[1] The one who does not know the struggle of life is either an immature soul, or a soul who has risen above the life of this world. The object of a human being in this world is to attain to the perfection of humanity, and therefore it is necessary that a person should go through what we call the struggle of life.

Now, there are two different attitudes that one shows while going through this struggle of life. One struggles along bravely through life; the other becomes disappointed, heartbroken, before arriving at their destination. No sooner does one give up the courage to go through the struggle of life than the burden of the whole world falls upon one's head. But the one who goes along struggling through it, that one alone makes his or her way. The one whose patience is exhausted, the one who has fallen in this struggle, is trodden upon by those who walk through life. Even bravery and courage are not sufficient to go through the struggle of life. There is something else that must be studied and understood.

One must study the nature of life, one must understand the psychology of this struggle. In order to understand this struggle,

1. A talk given in Paris, December 12, 1922.

one must see that there are three sides to it: the struggle with oneself, the struggle with others, and the struggle with circumstances. One person may be capable of struggling with him- or herself, but this is not sufficient. Another person is able to struggle with others, but even that is not sufficient. A third person may answer the demands of circumstances, but that is not sufficient either. The thing is, all three things should be studied and learned, and one must be able to manage the struggle in all three directions.

And now the question is: Where should one begin, and where should one end? Generally one starts by struggling with others, and then one struggles all one's life and never comes to an end. And if the person is wise, and struggles with conditions, perhaps that person accomplishes things a little better. But the ones who struggle with themselves first are the wisest, because, once they have struggled with themselves, which is the most difficult struggle, the other struggles will become easy for them. Struggling with oneself is like singing without an accompaniment. Struggling with others is the definition of war; struggling with oneself is the definition of peace. In the beginning, outwardly, it might seem that it is cruel to have to struggle with oneself, especially when one is in the right. But the one who has reached deeper into life will find that the struggle with oneself is the most profitable in the end.

Now, coming to the question of what is the nature of the struggle with oneself, there are three aspects. The first is to make one's thought, speech, and action answer the demand of one's own ideal, while at the same time giving expression to all the impulses and all the desires that belong to one's natural being. The next aspect of the struggle with oneself is to fit in with others, with their various ideas and demands. For this one has to make oneself as narrow or as wide as the accommodation demands one to be, which is a delicate matter, difficult for all to comprehend, and still more difficult to practice. And the third aspect of the struggle with oneself is to make an accommoda-

The Struggle of Life (1)

tion for others in one's own life, in one's own heart, large or small, as the demand may be.

When we consider the question of the struggle with others, there are also three things to think about, the first of which is how to control and govern people and activities that happen to be our duty, our responsibility. Another aspect is how to allow ourselves to be used by others in various situations and positions in life, to know to what extent one should allow others to make use of our time, our energy, our work or our patience, and where to draw the line. And the third aspect is to fit in with the standards and conceptions of different personalities who are at various stages of evolution.

Regarding the third aspect of this struggle, which is with conditions: there are conditions that can be helped, and there are conditions that cannot be helped, before which one is helpless. And again there are conditions that can be helped, and yet one does not find in oneself the capability, the power, or the means to change the condition. If one studies and thinks about these questions of life, and meditates for the inspiration and light to fall on them, so that one may understand how to struggle through life, one certainly will find help and arrive at a state where one would find life easier.

Now, in conclusion to what I have said, I should like to say how a Sufi would look at it, and how a Sufi would set to work. Sufis look upon the struggle as unavoidable, a struggle that must be gone through. They see from their mystical point of view that the more they take notice of the struggle, the more the struggle will expand. And the less they make of it, the better they will be able to pass through it. When Sufis look at the world, what do they see? They see everybody with their hands before their forehead, looking only at their own struggles, which are as big as their own palm. They think: "Shall I also sit like this, and look at my struggles?" That will not answer the question. Their work, therefore, is to engage in the struggle of others, to console them, to strengthen them, to give them a hand, and through that their own struggle becomes easier and makes them free to go forward.

Now the question is: How do Sufis struggle? They struggle with power, with understanding, with open eyes, and with patience. They do not look at the loss; that which is lost, is lost. They do not think of the pain of yesterday; yesterday is gone for them. Yes, if there is a pleasant memory, they keep it before them, for it is helpful on their way. They take both the admiration and the hatred coming from those around them with smiles. They only think that both these things form a rhythm within the rhythm of a certain tempo of music; there is one and two, the strong accent and the weak accent. Praise cannot be without blame, nor can blame be without praise. They do not allow their power to lead them blindfolded, but they keep the torch of wisdom before them, because they believe that the present is the re-echo of the past, and the future will be the reflection of the present. It will not do only to think of the present moment, but to think where it comes from and where it goes. Every thought that comes to their mind, every impulse, every word they speak, to them it is like a seed, a seed that falls in this soil of life and takes root. And in this way they find that nothing is lost; every good deed, every little act of kindness, of love, done to anybody, it will some day rise as a plant and bear fruit.

Sufis do not consider life any different from a business, but they see how the real business can be achieved in the best manner.

The symbol of the mystics of China was a branch of fruit in their hand. What does it mean? It means the purpose of life is to arrive to that stage when every moment of life becomes fruitful. And what does fruitful mean? Does it mean fruits for oneself? No, trees do not bear fruit for themselves, but for others. True profit is not that profit that one makes for oneself. True profit is that which one makes for others. After attaining all that one wants to attain, be it earthly or heavenly, what is the result of it all? The result is only this: that all that one has attained, that one has acquired, whether earthly or heavenly, one can place before others. In the language of the Vedanta, there is a word, *propkar*, which means working for the benefit of others is the only fruit of life.

13

THE STRUGGLE OF LIFE (2)

Beloved Ones of God, I would like to speak this afternoon on the subject of spiritual attainment, and that life proves to be a continual struggle.[1] The only difference is that in worldly life one struggles in the other direction. In worldly life, be it in business or politics or industry, or whatever be your life's path, if you prove to be lacking that power that enables you to struggle along, you will not meet anything but failure. You may be a very good person, a saintly person, a spiritual person, but that does not count. It is for this reason that many in the world lose faith in goodness, in spirituality, because they see this does not mean anything in worldly life. It is absurd for a spiritual person to say that by your goodness, spirituality, and piety your worldly struggle will be helped. No, it cannot be helped. You must have inspiration and power to answer life's demands in life's struggle. By this I want to say to my friends seeking the spiritual path that they must not forget that floating in the air is no good, that standing on the earth is the first thing necessary. There are many who dream, who live in the air, but that does not answer our purpose. When they say that they are doing spiritual work, yet are in bad circumstances, they forget that the language of this path is different, the law of this path is different. It is for this reason that I make these two paths separate: to realize that

1. A lecture given in Geneva, April 7, 1924.

the one thing has little to do with the other. This does not mean that the wicked person will succeed or that success is gained by evil or by an evil character. On the other hand, we should not blame spirituality for failure in worldly things, for worldly things have another inspiration. If it were not so, all great sages would have been millionaires.

Now, coming to the question of the spiritual path. The worldly struggle is an outward struggle; the spiritual struggle is an inward struggle. No sooner does one take the spiritual direction, than the first enemy one meets is one's little self. What does the little self do? It is the most mischievous self. When one says I want to fight it, it says: "I am yourself, you want to fight me?" And when it brings failure, it is clever enough to say that it was someone else. Do all those who failed in life accuse themselves? No, they always accuse the next person. And when they have gained something they say, "I have done it." If they love something and have not got it, they say, "This person has come between." With little and big things it is all the same. The little self does not admit a fault, but always finds it in another. Its vanity, its pride, its smallness, its egotistical tendency, its contentment keeps one blind. The little self does not hinder the worldly path the way it hinders the spiritual path. I remember a Persian verse made by my murshid, that relates to the little self. I shall translate it: "When I feel that now I must make peace with my little self, it finds time to prepare another attack." That is our condition. We think that our little faults are of little consequences, we do not even think of them. But every little fault is a flag for the little self, for its own dominion. This way of battling what is depriving one makes one the sovereign of the kingdom of God. Very few can realize the great power that lies in battling with and conquering the little self. But what does one generally do? One says: "My self is already in conflict with this world, must I also battle with this self?" So one gives the kingdom of this little self to this little self, depriving oneself of the divine power that is hidden in one's heart.

There is in one the false self and the real self. The real self has eternal life in it; the false self has mortal life in it. The real self is wisdom; the false self is ignorance. The real self can rise to perfection; the false self is limitation. The real self has all good; the false self is productive of all evil. One can see both in oneself: God and the other one. By conquering the other one, one realizes God. This other power has been called Satan. But is it a power? In reality it is not. It is and it is not. It is a shadow, and yet it is nothing. If we realize this we see that the false self has no existence of its own. As soon as the soul has risen above the false self it begins to realize its nobility.

But how can we come to the practical aspect of it? How does it show itself? In which form? It rises up in support of its own interest. It defends itself from the attack of others. It feels exclusive toward everyone. It knows itself as an entity separate from friend and foe. It concerns itself with all that is present now, blind to the future and ignorant of the past. It manifests in the form of self-pity. It expresses itself in the form of vengeance. It lives by feeding upon bitterness, and its life is always in obscurity. Its condition is restlessness and discontentment. It has a continual appetite to have all that is there; it is never content, it has no trust in anyone, no thought for anyone, no consideration for anyone. It lacks conscientiousness and therefore manners. The little self considers only its own benefit, its own comfort; giving to others, to those around it, is something dreadful to the little self, for it knows no sacrifice. Renunciation for it is dreadful, worse than death. That is the little self.

When we see it in somebody, we blame that person, we dislike that person, but we overlook the same element in ourselves. There is no soul in the world who can say: "I have this not in me." If only the soul were just, it would see. For often it is the unjust person who blames another. The more just you become, the more quiet you will be in all circumstances. Outwardly you will see faults in others; inwardly you will see the sum total within yourself. For instance, a little child cannot help loving.

If a thief comes, a robber, the child wants to love him, because the child is sinless. Why is it? Because a thief is not awakened in the child. The child comes from heaven, the thief from earth, and no accommodation is there; therefore there is no thief to the child. We accept things because they are in us. If we consider our knowledge, perhaps among the thousand things we have experienced, most of them have been told to us by others, and we have believed them at once. As soon as a person tells us something about someone wicked, we say: "Now we know, we were quite sure of it." The most wonderful thing is that when a person says: "This person is good," then everyone thinks: "Is it really true? Do we really know all about that person? Is it possible to be good as that?" Good seems to be something unnatural.

Now coming to the question: Is it necessary that one struggles? Why should one take the spiritual path? Is that tyranny over oneself? No, for it is by doing this that one molds one's character, one makes one's personality. In this resides all religion. When one begins to think: "I must not bring harm to, or hurt anyone I meet, worthy or unworthy, friend or foe," only then does one begin one's work in the spiritual direction. Spirituality is not in wonderworking. Spirituality is attained by good manner, by right manner. Where is the shrine of God? In the human heart. As soon as one begins to consider the feeling of another, one begins to worship God. That feeling is not what gives profit, but what other way is there of worship to God? One might say: It is difficult to please everyone. No doubt, it is. It becomes more difficult still if one has in oneself the inclination to please everyone. There is a story of a murshid, who was going with his murids to some village. He was keeping a fast; the murids had also taken the vow of fasting. They arrived at a peasant's house, who with enthusiasm and happiness had arranged a dinner. Of course, when it was brought to the table, the murshid went and sat down, but the murids did not dare because they had taken a vow of fasting. Yet they would not mention it to the murshid, as spiritual persons never mention such things. As to the murshid, they thought, "Murshid has forgotten the vow." (Murshids are forgetful.) After the dinner was finished and they went out the pupils said: "Did you not forget your vow of fasting?" "No," said the murshid, "I had not forgotten, but I preferred breaking my fast to breaking the heart of that man, who with all his enthusiasm had prepared that food."

If we just think of everyday life, we see that in overlooking all the little things we lose an opportunity of doing some good. Every moment of life is an opportunity of being conscious of human feeling. In prosperity, in adversity, in all conditions, it costs little; only the thought is necessary. A person may be good within, but at the same time not be conscious of little things. There is no greater religion than love. God is love; and the best form of love is to be conscientious of the feelings of those with whom we are in contact in everyday life. The further one goes, the more difficulties there are; one finds greater faults as one advances in the spiritual path. It is not the number of faults that increases, but the sense of them, of finding them, that becomes so keen. It is like a musician: the more they know, the better they play, the more faults they hear. The one who does not find faults is in reality becoming worse. There is no end of faults. If one thinks of this, it makes one humble. Before realizing this aspect of truth, there is an aspect of metaphysics that does not make one humble: the profane thought, God is in me. Yes, God is in the depth of the heart. But the intellect is of no use if the doors of the heart are not open. It is the realization of our numberless faults that makes one humble, and effaces the little self from one's consciousness. It is in the effacement of the little self that real spiritual attainment lies.

Now, coming to the question: What is real spiritual consciousness? Spiritual consciousness is consciousness of the spirit. Before one is aware of that consciousness, the little self is covering it. When this is moved aside, then what is there? Then there is spirit. Call it whatever you may, it is what it is.

14

REACTION

Beloved Ones of God, I would like to speak this evening on the subject of reaction.[1] Every condition, favorable or unfavorable, in which a person is, and every person, whether agreeable or disagreeable, in whose presence a person is, causes one to react. Upon this reaction depends one's happiness and one's spiritual progress. If one has control over this reaction it means that one is progressing. If one has no control over it, it shows that one is going backward. When you take two persons, wise and foolish, the wise person reacts more intensely than the foolish one. If you take a dense person and a fine person, a fine person naturally reacts more than the dense one. If you take a just person or an unjust person, naturally the just person reacts more than the unjust one. If you take a spiritual person and a material person, naturally a spiritual person reacts more than the material one.

And yet it is lack of mastery when one has no control over one's reaction. A person who is fine, spiritual, sensitive, wise, and just, and yet is without control over their reactions, is incomplete. And this shows that even becoming fine and just and spiritual is not sufficient. For all these things, though they

---

1. A private lecture given at the home of Baroness D'Eichthal, Paris, December 10, 1924.

make one finer and more sensitive, at the same time weaken one in the face of the disturbing influences of the crowd. This shows that a person who is just, wise, spiritual, and fine, and yet weak, is not perfect. The balance in life lies in being as fine as a thread and as strong as a steel wire. If one does not show that durability and strength to withstand the opposing and disturbing influences among which one always has to be in life, one certainly reveals a weakness, a lack of development.

In the first place this reaction gives people a certain amount of vanity. They feel they are better than the one who disturbs them. But they certainly cannot say they are stronger than the one who disturbs them. When one cannot stand the conditions around one, one may think that one is a superior person in not standing for the conditions, but in reality the conditions are stronger when one cannot stand them.

If we are born on earth, if we are destined to walk on the earth, we cannot dream of paradise when we have to stand firm in all the conditions that the earth brings before us. When people progress toward spirituality, they must bear this in mind, that together with their spiritual progress they must strengthen themselves against disturbing influences. If not, they should know that with every desire to make progress, they will be pulled back against their will by conditions, by circumstances.

There are four different ways in which a person reacts: in deed, in speech, in thought, in feeling. A deed produces a definite result, speech produces effect, thought produces atmosphere, feeling produces conditions. And therefore no way in which a person reacts will be without effect. A reaction will be perceived quickly or slowly, but it must be perceived. And very often a reaction is not only agreeable to oneself, but to others also. A person who answers an insult by insulting the other stands on the same level; the one who does not answer stands above it. And in this way we can rise above things against which we react, only if we know how to fly. It means flying above things instead of standing against them, as a material person would. How can one call oneself spiritual if one cannot fly? That is the first condition of being spiritual.

The whole mechanism of this world is action and reaction, in the objective world as well as in the world of people. Only in a person there is the possibility of developing that spirit that is called the spirit of mastery, and that spirit is easily and best developed by trying to get control over one's reactions. Life offers us abundant occasions from morning till evening to practice this lesson. Every move, every turn we make, we are faced with something agreeable or disagreeable, harmonious or inharmonious, either a condition or a person. If we react automatically we are no better than a machine and no different from thousands and millions of people who act automatically. But if we can trace in ourselves a divine heritage, a heritage that is called mastery, it is found in controlling our reactions against influences. In theory it is simple, it is easy. In practice it is the most difficult thing there is to master, to conquer. And when we think of its usefulness, we shall find that there is nothing in the world that is more necessary and more important than this development. If there is any strength to be found in the world, it is that strength is within ourselves, and the proof of having that strength is when one is able to control one's reactions. This preserves dignity, this maintains honor. It is this that sustains respect, and it is this that keeps a person wise. For it is easy to be wise, but it is difficult to continue to be wise. It is easy to think, but it is difficult to continue to be a thoughtful person. Very often people have asked me if there is any practice, any study, anything that one can do in order to develop willpower. And I have answered, "Yes, there are many practices and many ways, but the simplest and best practice that one can do without being taught is to have a hand over one's reactions." I always interpret the meaning of the words, "I cannot endure," "I cannot stand," "I cannot sustain," "I cannot have patience," as being, "I am weak." By speaking thus we only admit, using other words, that we are weak. And friends, can there be any person in the world who can be a worse enemy to us than our own weakness? If the whole world were our friend, that one enemy, our weakness, would be enough to ruin our life. But once this enemy is conquered, we can stand against all those who will come in conflict with us.

Now, the question is, how should one set to work in this direction? One must also take into consideration one's physical condition in this. The nervous system must be in a proper condition. It is from nervousness that one goes from bad to worse. And even good people with good intentions may prove to be otherwise because they may have good intentions, but they cannot carry them out, because their nerves are weak. What is needed is the habit of silence, of concentration, of meditation. Those who go on continually talking or doing things and do not meditate for a while, do not take a rest, cannot control their nervous system, cannot keep it in order. If there is anything that can control the nervous system, it is right breathing. And when that right breathing is done, with a concentration of thought connected with it, then a great fortification is made in the nervous system. All the strength of the mystics, of the Yogis that you have heard of, has come from these practices that puts the nervous system in hand. Besides, there are many things that cause unhappiness, and by holding the nervous system in hand, it can be avoided.

And when we see it from a higher point of view, this can be done by denying the impulses that arise suddenly and that want their answer. What is called self-denial is really this, that one must control one's thoughts and wishes and desires and passions. But that does not mean retirement from the life of the world. It only means taking oneself in hand.

* * *

Question: *Can one begin with that control in advanced age of life or must it be done when one is young?*

Answer: It is never too soon to begin control, and it is never too late to improve it.

Reaction

Question: *Ought not the proper control over oneself be a part of good education given to children?*

Answer: Of course, I think that if from childhood that education is given, wonderful results can be brought about. There was a time in India, one sees very little of it just now, but in the ancient times, when youths were trained in *asana*, a certain way of sitting, a certain way of walking, and a certain way of standing. By that they first achieved a control over their muscles and over their nerves. It would be of immense value if education today adopted the two things. One thing is the study of controlling the reaction and the practice of it in sports and gymnastics.

Question: *Is it not much more difficult to control one's reaction when one suffers unjustly from someone whom one loves than from someone to whom one is indifferent?*

Answer: The control of the reaction will always give a certain amount of pain. But at the same time, it is by suffering that pain that one will get the power to rise above it. But of course, if it is not understood rightly, one might endanger oneself. But the danger is in both cases. On one side there is a pit, on the other side there is water. For instance, there may be a person who, by being afraid to get hurt or be oppressed by someone, is always keeping their thoughts or feelings suppressed, who if they had expressed it would have become a worse person, but if they had not expressed it, would have suppressed it, and would have been ruined. Therefore, discrimination must be developed, a thought must be developed in order to analyze the reaction, to understand it before it is expressed. Because one must know, "That which is in my hand now, shall I not throw it out? By throwing it out, shall I do something wrong? Where shall I throw it? Shall I throw it on my head? What shall become of it?" One must know what one has in one's hand. If in order to avoid breaking another person's head, he has broken his own head; he has done wrong too.

Question: *Then what must one do?*

Answer: One must first weigh and measure the impulses that come to one. Instead of throwing the impulse out automatically, one must first weigh it, analyze it, measure it, and utilize it to the best advantage in life. A stone is not only used to break another person's head or to break one's own head, but it is also used to build houses. Use everything where it will be useful, where it will be of some advantage. All such things as passion and anger and irritation, one looks upon as something very bad, as an evil. But if that evil were kept in hand, it could be used for a good purpose, because it is a power, it is an energy. In other words, evil properly utilized becomes a virtue, and virtue wrongly used becomes an evil.

Question: *Can you give an instance of the way in which an impulse of anger can be utilized?*

Answer: For instance, when one is in a rage and when one really feels like being angry, if one has controlled that thought and has not expressed it in words, that gives one great power. Otherwise the expression would have had a bad effect upon one's nerves. By controlling it, it has given one strength that will remain with one. A person who has anger and control is to be preferred to the person who has got neither. A person came to me and said—thinking that I would be very pleased with it—"I have been a vegetarian for twenty years." I said, "What made you become a vegetarian?" He said, "It takes away anger and passion and all the evils that make a person go wrong." I said, "That is a wrong way of becoming a vegetarian. If by being ill a person becomes virtuous, that virtue is worth nothing."

Question: *Does self-control not take away spontaneity?*

Answer: Self-control gives a greater power of spontaneity. It develops thought-power, it makes one think about every impulse, which otherwise would have manifested automatically.

Question: *Should one not feel first?*

Answer: One should know about it. At every impulse one should be awake so that one holds that impulse in hand and knows what it is. In other words, hold the word between the lips before it drops out.

Question: *Is impulse before it is controlled wrong in itself or is it good?*

Answer: When we think about the origin of impulse we go in quite a different direction of thought; then we have to think of what direction it is facing, also the direction of the mind, whether it is in illumination or in darkness. The mind is sometimes illuminated, sometimes in darkness. One should think about the condition of the mind at the time. There is another thing to be considered in this connection. A person may have good intentions and their mind focused on good ideas. And then another with evil intentions and wrong ideas says or does something that automatically turned the mind of the first person to the wrong, against the person's own will. There is a word in the Bible, "Resist not evil."[2] Sometimes evil comes like fire thrown by a person into the mind of another, a mind that did not have fire in it. A fire then starts there, and in reaction that mind too expresses that fire. To resist evil is to send fire in answer to fire, in other words, to partake of the fire that comes from another. But by not partaking of it one has thrown the fire out. The fire falls on the person who threw it.

2. Matthew 5:38.

Question: *In what way do you look upon those saints in the East and West who have risen above all such feeling; whether there will always be very few or will their number increase?*

Answer: With the evolution of humanity their number will naturally increase, and we must all try for the increase of that number.

Question: *What kind of breathing should be taught to children from twelve to sixteen years of age for them to learn control?*

Answer: If the child from twelve to sixteen years can breathe clearly and rhythmically and deep enough, that is something.

Question: *The sages and saints, if they should let go of their control, would they have the same impulse as ordinary persons have?*

Answer: Limitation goes as far as perfection. The thing is this, that one carries a limitation further than one can imagine. As long as the saints and sages have to wear this limited garb, which is this material body, they have their limitations just the same. But at the same time, they increase and they develop that power that makes them control their impulse, which makes them control their reaction.

Question: *Is it possible that there exist persons who have only good impulses?*

Answer: When the word *good* comes, it is very difficult to analyze it. Because good is not something that is stamped as something that is good. What is good at one time, the same thing is not good at another time. What is good in one situation, in another situation the same thing is bad. Besides, what a person considers good just now, the same thing, after three days, may be the worst thing for that person. Therefore, those who think, those who know, never defend the good that they consider good for the moment. Because they think, "What is good in my estimation may not be good in the estimation of another. And what I consider good just now, perhaps after a week the same thing I may not consider to be good." It is therefore that they judge no one, they only try to do what they consider good for the moment.

15

THE DEEPER SIDE OF LIFE

Friends, I have the unexpected pleasure to comply with the request to speak before you some words on the deeper side of life.[1]

When we consider life deeply, we can very well divide it into two parts and call one the lighter side of life and the other the deeper side of life. The importance of both these sides may seem at moments as equally great. When a person is thinking of the lighter side of life, at that moment that side is more important; the other side, of which the person is not conscious, seems to have no great importance. But then there are other moments that come in life, perhaps after suffering, or after a loss or some other experience, when a person suddenly awakens to a different realization of life. And when one is awakened to that, the deeper side of life seems to have more importance than the lighter side. No one, neither clergyman nor mystic nor any authority can say which side is more important. It depends upon how we look at it. If we raise its value, though it may be a small thing, we shall attach a greater value to it. There is no such thing in this world with a constant value attached to it. If there is such a thing, it does not always stay in the same

---

1. A talk given on board the S.S. *Volendam*, Holland-America Line, bound for New York, December 2, 1925.

position. If such a thing as money can change, then what is there in this world that does not change in importance! And when we picture these two parts, the lighter and the deeper side of life, we see that we picture them in our present experience.

We are traveling together, some from one country, others from another country, coming from different directions of the world, yet we are gathered together. By what? By destiny. More clearly, by a common destination where we all wish to go, which has us for a few days together in this ship. And now it is our happy disposition, our favorable attitude to one another, our desire to be kind, friendly, sociable, serviceable that alone makes us understand one another and that will help us to make one another happy. And it brings us far closer than destiny has brought us. The same is the small picture of life. When we consider the life of a community, a nation, a race, of the whole world, what is it? Is it not a large ship on which all are traveling whether knowingly or unknowingly, all moving, all changing. Therefore, it is only traveling.

There are two types of traveler. There are travelers who do not know where they are coming from and where they are going to. When they open their eyes they realize they are in this ship, coming from somewhere and in a ship that is moving and is going somewhere. There are many people like this living in the world today. They are so absorbed in their everyday activity that they are ignorant of where they come from and where they are going. Imagine the difference between these two travelers: those who know where they come from and know why they are traveling and who will prepare themselves, sooner rather than later, for the place where they are going. The second type is made of those who do not know where they come from, only where they are, and only know of their activity in their immediate surroundings. Those who do not know where they are going to are not prepared to make arrangements, to face their destination; they do not know what is in store for them. Therefore, they are not prepared for it.

The Deeper Side of Life

Buddha was asked one day by his disciples, what he meant by ignorance. And he answered with this story. He said that a person was clinging in distress to the branch of a tree in the utter darkness of night, not knowing if beneath his feet there was earth or a ditch or water. All night long he trembled and wept and was clinging fast to that branch. And with the break of dawn he found that he was not one foot away from the earth beneath his feet.

If I were to say how ignorance can be defined, it would be as fear, doubt, passion, confusion. Where do all these come from? They come from our ignorance of one side of life, and that is the deeper side. We may be clever in making the best of what we call the lighter side of life, whether in a profession, art, industry, or business. But that is not all. We know not, with all our efforts from morning till evening, what we shall arrive at, what we might gain by it. If we consider wealth, position, fame, name, or anything else, it only confuses us, since life is moving. It is all moving. We cannot hold it. A person may have riches one day and be poor the next; a person may be successful one day and yet perhaps sooner or later will meet with failure. Such powerful nations as Russia and Germany—nations that took hundreds of years to become strong, to build themselves up—who could ever have thought that they would fall down in a moment's time? But when their time came, it did not take but one day to turn from east to west. If such great powers are subject to falling in a moment and their whole construction can be broken, if that is the nature and character of life, then no thoughtful person will deny the fact that there must be some mystery behind it, some secret of which he or she would like to find the key. At least a person would want to know what life is and what is behind it?

Those who have studied life and thought long enough about this subject have arrived at the same point as the thinkers who lived as much as eight thousand years before. Buddha has said and has realized the same things that a really wise person would realize today. And this shows us that wisdom is the same in all ages. We may be evolving or going backward, but wisdom never changes and will always be the same. The same realization will come to those who will think deeply and try to realize what life is. I do not say by this that in order to realize life it is necessary for a person to follow a certain religion. I do not mean to say that a person has to be so great or so good, so pious or so spiritual. I mean to say that the first and most necessary thing is that we must become observant. We should look at life more keenly than we do, instead of living superficially. It costs us nothing. It only takes us away from our everyday occupation for a few minutes. Life always gives an opportunity of thinking, however busy we may be, if we care to know its secret. It is not necessary that we leave our occupation, our work in life, and go in the forest and sit in silence and meditate upon life. We can meditate upon life in the midst of life if only we want to. What happens is that one begins one's life with action, and the more one becomes active, the less one thinks. Besides, one's action becomes one's thought. But if one thought of what exists besides the action and thoughts that are connected with everyday life, if one also gave thought to the deeper side of life, one would have more benefit.

People often fight and argue and discuss. Over what? Over a reason. When two persons dispute, each of them has a reason. Each one thinks his or her reason the right one. They may dispute for years and yet will arrive nowhere because the reason of each is different. Therefore, to think more is to see behind the reason. And the moment one has begun to see behind the reason, one will look at life quite differently. Then one finds that where one puts blame, perhaps behind that blame there is something to praise, and where there is something to praise, there is perhaps a reason for blame. One will begin to see what is behind all things and that will give one the proof that the whole of life is a kind of unfoldment. The deeper you look at life, the more it unfolds itself, allowing you to see more keenly.

If I were to say that life is revealing, it would not be an exaggeration. It is not only human beings who speak; if only the ears could hear, even plants and trees speak, and all nature speaks, in the sense that it reveals itself, reveals its secret, its nature. In this way, when we communicate with the whole of life, then we are never alone; then life becomes worth living.

The thoughtful of all ages have considered the source of creation to be one and the same. Scientists today will tell you that the cause behind creation is motion, vibration. But they will only go so far in saying it is motion. But if from motion or vibration this manifestation has come into our view, then that motion is not lifeless. If that motion is life itself, then it is intelligent, although it is not intelligent in the sense we understand the word. We know the most limited sense of it; we call the limited brain "intelligence." We say that one thing is intelligent because it is living and another thing where we do not distinguish life we say is an unintelligent thing, an unintelligent being. But a scientist from India, visiting the West, has pointed out that even trees breathe. If that is true, then the trees are living. And if today it is proved that trees are living, it will also be found that stones are living, that all we see is living. Then one will realize that it all comes from one source, which is the very life of all things, and not only life but intelligence also, what religion calls God. Whatever we call it, it is the same. The difference is only in name.

The difference in religious faiths, where does it come from? From looking superficially. People debate about things that in essence are the same. The difference is only in words. And it is a keen observation of life that in time awakens in us that sight that, when once light is thrown upon life, life begins to reveal itself. As the great poet of Persia, Sa'di, has said that, "Even the leaves of the tree become as sacred pages of the sacred book once the eyes of the heart are open."

* * *

Question: *What do you think is the best means to bring about better understanding and tolerance between those of different beliefs?*

Answer: I think that the efforts that are made by missionaries of different faiths to convert those who do not belong to their faiths, their efforts are not of great importance today. The efforts we can make today must be to bring about an understanding among the followers of different religions by way of writing or speaking or preaching *the* religion instead of *a* religion, which means by trying to explain the truth of Christianity to the Buddhists in the realm of Buddhism, to the Christians Buddhism in the realm of Christianity. To compare with their own teachings, not in order to make differences, but to make them understand that it is all the same thing, that the effort of every great teacher was to make humanity come to this understanding. It has resulted in dividing in communities. One says, "My church is the only thing that will save you." The other says, "My temple or pagoda is the only thing worthwhile." The great teachers had no desire to further the cause of any particular religion, community, or church. Rather they wanted to bring about that religion that is the religion of humanity, that stands above all divisions. That service is of greater importance; it does not take away from religion, but puts a new light on the religion a person has and makes a person more tolerant by understanding the ideal of others.

Question: *There are some who consider the lighter side of life more important, others the deeper side of life. Would there be a possibility for those who consider the lighter side of life to develop so that they may realize the deeper side of life more and more? By practical thought, not by words or dogmas, which are not well understood by people, but by practical thought that leads to a proper understanding of the deeper side of life?*

Answer: As it is necessary to have repose after action, so it is necessary to have a glimpse of the deeper side of life after having performed one's everyday duties. Religions, therefore, have taught prayers. Also there were churches where people used to go every day to be in a right atmosphere and to be silent. And now religion has become a secondary thing and people's lives have developed with more struggles; naturally, one hardly has time to go to a solitary place or into a church and be in silence. Those few who have the time and who care to continue with their religion, go once a week to a service. Therefore, if I would suggest a way at the present time, it is the way of esotericism, the esoteric way, which means on the one hand studying, on the other hand practicing, and also meditating, doing these three things. You will ask, "What should one study?" There are two kinds of studies. One kind is to read the teachings of the great thinkers, and to keep them in mind, to study metaphysics, psychology, and mysticism. And the other kind of study is the study of life. Every day we have the opportunity for studying, but it should be correct study. When one travels in a tramcar, in the train, with a paper in one's hand, one wants to read the sensational news, which is worth nothing. But to read human nature that is before one, people coming and going, if one would continue to this reading, one would begin to read human beings as letters written by the divine pen, which speak of their past and future. To look at the heavens and nature and all things we see in everyday life deeply and to reflect upon it and want to understand, this is a kind of study that is much greater, incomparably greater than the study of books. And then there is practice, a practice that the Yogis and Sufis in the East have done for many, many years. And it is their thousands of years experience that they have passed on as a tradition from teacher to pupil. Manners of sitting, manners of standing, of breathing properly, being in silence, manners of relaxing, concentrating, of feeling inspirational, joyful, more peaceful. Of course, for such a practice the help of a teacher is necessary. And the third thing is the practice in everyday life, to practice the principles one has esteemed in life, to uphold the ideal one has always held in one's heart. These things and many other things, such as one's attitude to others, one's manner to others, everything one does from morning till evening would one care to look, all these things help one's development till one arrives at a stage when one can see the deeper side of life naturally. In my experience I have seen numberless people unhappy, depressed, in great despair, wanting to commit suicide, who after having done this, in three, four, six months time I heard them say that life is worth living after all.

Question: *What do you think is the ideal life for the average person?*

Answer: I think the ideal life is at least to try to live up to one's ideal. But in order to have an ideal one must awaken to an ideal. Not everyone possesses an ideal; many people do not know of it. It is no exaggeration to say that the wars and disasters we have gone through, the unrest that all feel, and the disagreement among people that is sometimes seen and sometimes not seen, it all is caused by one thing, and that is the lack of ideal. We are progressing commercially, industrially. But in all walks of life progress will be hindered one way or the other if the ideal is destroyed. If there is anything that can be said as the means of saving the world, it is the wakening of the ideal, which is the first task that is worth considering. Besides, for the average person to consider just one thing, that "I must live a life of balance," would be of a great importance. And it is not very difficult. When one is busy with work, one should realize that recreation is necessary. When one tires oneself, it is necessary to take repose. When one thinks too much it is necessary to rest the mind at a certain time, during which one must try not to think. But life is an intoxication, it is like a drink, whatever be one's motive, whether one is compelled and thrown into it or not. It is all an intoxication, all drinking, going at it with all one's might and thought and feeling till either one has accomplished one's desire, or one is destroyed. If we use balance in everything we do, we shall get the key to live a life of greater happiness.

Question: *Buddhism teaches reincarnation.*

Answer: Yes, it does, but all other faiths also.

Question: *Would it be possible to find a common ground between Buddhism and Christianity?*

Answer: The common ground on the dogma of reincarnation is rather a difficult one. The reason is that the message of Jesus Christ was given to the children of Beni Israel, to those prepared to understand God as the king, the master of the day of judgment, as the one who was all justice and all power. And the message that Buddha gave was to the people of India, who were more metaphysical and scientific. The simple people of India had their gods and goddesses and their religion, and they were satisfied with it. But the intellectual class was not satisfied with the gods and goddesses alone, and with the religion of devotion. They were scientific, logical; they had their own philosophies. Buddha's mission, therefore, was to make the people of India understand, beyond what religious devotion can teach. Therefore, he did not give the essential wisdom in the form of religion, but in the form of philosophy. The common belief was of reincarnation. It spared the master very much by not attacking that particular belief, but by building on that belief a wonderful structure. Some Buddhists today, whose insight is great, ask, "Why did Buddha give this theory? Why did he not give the reason for it?" When I was in San Francisco, I was very interested when a Buddhist came to see me. He was a great preacher of Buddhism in Japan. There was another man who had read many Buddhist books. I was eagerly waiting to hear from this Buddhist priest. But he did not think it necessary to say. In order to make him speak I said I would so much like to know the Buddhist teaching about reincarnation. The one who had read many books said, "It is reincarnation that is the principal thing in Buddhist religion, that one is born again, and so it goes on, and that is what constitutes karma. That is action." But I was eager to hear from the priest. After this man had finished his explanation, I again asked the Buddhist preacher if this is right. And in his gentle way of speaking, he said, "What this gentleman has said is his belief." He said no more. The words of the great teachers are as the notes of the piano. Some notes are of a lower octave, some are higher. In order to play all octaves it is necessary to play the higher notes as well as the lower notes. If there is such a thing as reincarnation, the answer is yes and no. Why? Because in both answers there is a meaning, both answers are true. When you look at life as one life, then you do not divide persons as separate entities. Then you cannot say that this person has incarnated as another. If there is the same spirit, it is the same one who is all, and each one is nothing. Either you look at life in that way, or you look at life by noticing each person as a separate entity. Naturally we say, as everything has to be something, after it is destroyed it must exist, it has an existence in some form. The destruction or death is only a change. Something cannot be nothing. If it is nothing to our eyes, it is because we do not see. Everything must exist in some form or another. Therefore, the theory of reincarnation teaches that there is nothing that will be nothing, that everything will be something, must be something. But then the other conception is that, if the source is one, the goal is one, then all that we see is phenomena, as long as we do not see deeply. When once we see deeply, then no longer shall we distinguish separate entities; then one sees one life, one being. Then there is no reason to think about reincarnation. Then the same thought of Buddha was the teaching of Jesus Christ, only given to Hindus in another form. The religion of the master was the same, whether that master was called Buddha or Christ.

16

LIFE, AN OPPORTUNITY

Beloved Ones of God, my subject for this evening is life, an opportunity.[1] When one looks at the world today and at its condition as it is just now, one begins to wonder if one understands this idea of "life, an opportunity" today better than those who lived before us. In spite of the stage of evolution that we experience, and the scientific advancement that the world has made, the war that humanity went through not long ago shows that never in the history of the world was such a great catastrophe caused by humankind.[2] It seems as if the whole evolution of humanity had been intended to prepare and to create such means of destruction that the greatest part of humanity has been ruined by it. And when we think of the distrust that exists today among nations and how one nation has allowed another nation to be ruined, we begin to feel that we understand the idea of "life, an opportunity" much less than those who lived before us.

When we come to education, year by year the study in the schools and colleges is becoming more difficult; to pass their examinations students have to work so hard that it seems that by the time they have got a degree, their nerves are shattered

1. A talk given at the Engineering Societies Auditorium, New York, May 18, 1926.
2. World War I.

and their finer forces are scattered, and they are less capable of making use of their education.

When we look at the political world, we see the same: each political party is striving for its own welfare, just as each individual is trying to get the better of another. Among nations, the same principle is at work, each nation making several parties running after the object that they each profess to accomplish.

When we come to domestic life it seems every day to be more reduced. Life today is becoming more and more a hotel life. Very few in the world today experience and enjoy what is called home life, or are even capable of appreciating it, because they do not know it. Those who lived before us were much happier, for they knew the simplicity and affection of home life and the joy and pleasure of home. The gaiety today is not like those enjoyments that the most intelligent and wise had in ancient times. They used to enjoy poetry and higher music. Today jazz has become most popular. In every hotel, in every place, there is a jazz band. It is the same with all other entertainments. When you go to the theatre you will find the plays more and more narrow in pitch, there is no depth, no height, no ideal. There is realism, showing life as it is, but that does not inspire or uplift humankind. What is needed is to show life better than it is, so that people may follow that example. Besides that, the tendency of the writer, of the poet, of the artist, of the musician is to appeal to the most ordinary person, to the person of the lowest evolution, "the man in the street." If all these different things that educate people—theatre, books, poetry, and art—if they pull people down to the lowest stage of evolution, it means going downward instead of going upward. When a person writes good music or poetry with higher subjects, there is no market for it. Whenever a person brings something higher that person is told "It is not wanted, it will not take." It seems that education, high ideals, everything, is becoming commercialized. And by being commercialized, it is lowered. And at the same time, if you stood in the midst of the crowd and looked at the people hurrying by, you would think that never before have people tried so hard to make the best of life's opportunity.

The opportunity of life must be considered from a different point of view. The wiser we become, the more our outlook changes, the more we look upon things differently. In the first place, there are four different stages in one's life: childhood, youth, middle age, and advanced age, and each of these four stages shows a great opportunity. For instance, in childhood the consciousness is in paradise. The child, living in the same world of woe, treachery, and wickedness as the grown-up is happy because it is not yet awakened to the other aspect of life. It only knows the best of it, the beauty of life. And therefore, the same world is the Garden of Eden for the child till it grows and is exiled from the Garden of Eden. Before that, it enjoys a paradise on earth. It is unaware of the wickedness and of the evil and ugliness of human nature. It still maintains in itself the heavenly air and angelic innocence and the tendency of appreciating all beauty and loving every being. As it grows, it gets away from that tendency. Nevertheless, the child shows by its words and actions and by every tendency that angelic essence in its soul. This is the opportunity for every child to experience kingliness in life. And this opportunity is taken away by parents who send the child to school too early and burden it with study. We need not have this anxiety of preparing the child for studies so that it will be able to answer in school. That natural kingliness that God has given to it, that joy and beauty for which it is born and which it longs to have are thus taken away. This period of life should be made free of anxiety and worry. The parents burden the child with studies, but after all what do these studies lead to? In the first place, the child's strength and intelligence are lessened by being burdened with unnecessary studies before the mind is developed. And this tendency is increasing to such an extent! Now people say, "We must also teach a child concentration." But they have forgotten that a child is born with concentration. It is the grown-up whose concentration is weak. Every soul is born with concentration. It loses this tendency as it grows up.

The other day I was traveling in England and someone invited me to see a school where concentration was taught. They brought before me ten or fifteen children, and each child was asked to look at a blank curtain and say what was there. One child looked and looked and said, "A lily." Another child said, "A rose." The teacher asked a third child to tell her what was there. The child answered, "I don't see anything." I thought, "That is much better; he says what he sees." And so the teacher asked ten or twelve children questions about what they saw. It was a lesson of hypocrisy, of becoming imaginative. It never helps a child, because the child's concentration is already there. If a child is kept as a child, that is enough. We want to make the child a grown-up person, but it is only happy when left with its own wishes to run about, to be cheerful. The child should not have this burden. We have made it for ourselves, but it is not born with us. We are not made to take this burden, to make life miserable for ourselves and others. If life were not so complex, there would not have been the need for war and the difficulties such as we have today. Because we have spoiled ourselves, we want more and more; and yet we make it so difficult to get what we want, that in the end we do not get it at all. And at the same time, by wanting more than is necessary, we make life miserable, and the life of others also.

The amount of study that is put upon youth is the greatest wrong done to them today. And the culture of youth seems to have disappeared. They are not inspired. We have not thought about what is necessary for them in their youth. They are not inspired with lofty ideals, nor with those impressions that make them do great things. There is a kind of uniformity to all youths. There is no admiration among youth of a hero; no stimulus is given to youth to become a wonderful or an inspired person, or a great poet or musician. Because there is this uniform education, each child does not get that nourishment for its soul to become that for which it was born. And besides that, youth is the opportune time when a beautiful manner, high aspiration, and lofty ideals can be taught. And it is youth that has that enthusiasm to take everything that comes, assimilate it, and express it in return. But when this time is only spent in working hard all day long and trying to pass examinations, and little time is left for recreation and other things, that does not suffice for one's life's purpose.

Those who understand these ideas realize that youth is the greatest opportunity that comes in life; it never comes again. Life's spring never returns; it comes only once. And when that opportunity is taken away and a youth is not inspired by what it ought to be inspired by, it is just like keeping a plant without watering it. For that is the time for it to be watered, that is the time for it to be reared, and that time should not be neglected.

There are thousands and millions of young people in the colleges who have had no good manners taught to them, no inspiration given to them. When they are grown up, they can show that they have passed examinations, and that they have gained a lot of knowledge. But at the same time, the good ground for that knowledge that ennobles the soul is the time of youth because at that time the mind is receptive. The child, with all its enthusiasm and capacity for concentration, can grasp everything that is good and beautiful.

The inspiration of those great musicians and poets who have done great work in the world was created during their youth. Either they saw an example, a living example that impressed them, or someone told them, or they studied something that was just like sowing the seed in their heart. For that is the only time that destines the child to become great in life. And if this time is past, it will never come again. Whether a person wants to be a businessperson, or a politician, a professional, a scientist, or a musician, it is in youth when it must be started, when it must be inspired. At that time the ground is fertile. And when that time is gone, the chance does not easily come again.

Besides the training in various professions and occupations, there remains another capacity that is neglected in youth: the cultivation of the heart quality. Today every effort is made to train youths to become intellectual, what they call learning. But there is a difference between intellect and wisdom. It is not necessarily the same. As we confuse pleasure and happiness, so we confuse clever and wise. But the clever is not necessarily wise. Wisdom is a different thing from cleverness. So intellect is different from wisdom. Intellect is that which one learns by impressions and studies and that one gathers in the form of the knowledge of names and forms. Wisdom is something that is gathered like the honey from the flower, like butter from milk. And therefore, wisdom is gained from within and also from without. This combination of within and without makes it wisdom.

Today there is hardly one person in a hundred who has cultivated the heart quality. Although instinctively the heart quality is always there, every effort is made to blunt that quality because what is learned today is intellectual. Now I shall tell you what I mean by the heart quality. There is intuition, there is inspiration, and there is revelation. All these things come from the culture of the heart or from the heart quality. A person may be most cultivated, may have studied much, and at the same time may not be intuitive. A person may learn all the technique of music and poetry without having the heart quality. Heart quality is something that must be developed within oneself. And when no attention is given at the time of youth to developing that particular quality, what happens when a person is grown up? They will be selfish, proud, mannerless, and not ready to sacrifice. They think these qualities guard their interest best, and one calls such a person someone who has common sense, a practical person. Imagine! If everybody is a practical person of common sense, what could one expect from life except constant conflict as there is today.

Besides, religion, or the devotional side in nature, is also dying out for the reason that people do not need religion because there is no heart quality. Even if they went to church or to a place of worship, their piety is intellectual. People can only enjoy something intellectual. When there is a mathematical explanation of something it is wonderful; but when it comes to feeling blessed and uplifted, to feeling the raising of the consciousness toward the higher spheres, that they cannot experience because they live in their intellect.

There are two principal experiences of life: one experience is called sensation and the other exaltation. What is generally known and experienced by the average person today is what is called sensation: all beauty that one sees, of line, of color, all one sees with the eyes or that one tastes and touches. It is living in sensation that makes people material. And after some time, they become ignorant of spirit.

Exaltation, which is a greater bliss, a higher pleasure, and which makes one independent of the outer life for one's happiness, does not seem to be known by the majority. And now one might ask, what do I mean by exaltation? The soul can experience four things, four different experiences that are all in reality the longing of the soul. Mistakenly people do not experience those four experiences, but instead experience something else. For instance, it is a constant yearning of the soul to experience happiness, and instead of that it becomes connected with what one calls pleasure. But pleasure belongs to sensation, happiness to exaltation. Pleasure is the suggestion, happiness is reality.

And then comes knowledge. Every soul yearns for knowledge, that knowledge that will give exaltation. But the soul cannot be satisfied by knowledge one gathers from books, by learning, or by the study of outside things. For instance, the knowledge of science, the knowledge of art, are outside knowledge. They all are different studies and they all give one a kind of strength, a kind of satisfaction. But it does not last, for it is another knowledge that the soul is really seeking. The soul cannot be satisfied unless it finds that knowledge, but that knowledge does not come by the learning of names and forms. On the contrary, it comes from unlearning. Do not be surprised, therefore, if you read in some books of the East that mahatmas went into the mountains and sat there for many years. I do not say that we should follow that example; but I want to say that we can appreciate what they have brought from there. They went there to explore life, and that aspect of life that is unseen and remains unexplored. They sat there for years in meditation. They lived on vegetables, on leaves and fruits, on what they could find in the forest. They contemplated. And what they gathered is not a knowledge learned from this world, but a greater knowledge that can be learned from within. One has seen pictures of Buddha, with closed eyes, sitting cross-legged. What does that symbol convey to us? That there is a knowledge that can be learned by not only closing the eyes but also the mind from the outside world. Closing the eyes does not make the concentration any better. Most people go as far as closing the eyes, but do not go further. If the eyes are closed and the mind is pondering over things, that is not concentration. Those who can concentrate can do it without having to close the eyes.

Once I saw, when traveling in the East, a person working in a telegraph office, and as busy as he was in the office, his concentration continued. I said, "That is very wonderful, that with all this work, you can keep to your concentration." He smiled and said, "That is the way of concentration."

And the third thing one experiences in life and the soul yearns for is happiness. That can be gained also by getting in touch within oneself.

And the fourth thing is peace. It cannot be gained by outer means, by outer comfort and rest alone. It can only be gained when mind is at rest.

After youth comes the stage of middle age. Middle age is the time when one has gathered knowledge, when one has experienced life, when one has gone through joy and sorrow, when one has learned lessons from one's profession, from one's occupation, from one's home, from every side of life. It is the opportunity to make the best use of what one has gathered by experience. But what generally happens is what the Persian poet Saʿdi says, "O my self, you have come to middle age, and yet you are no better than a child." If one has not learned by that time all one ought to learn, one has indeed lost one's life's opportunity. Because it is that age when one has earned not only money, but experience and knowledge; and the more one has learned, the richer one is at that time, and the better one knows how to make use of what powers one has, the more successful and fruitful one becomes.

Besides, that is the age when one begins to know life's obligations, and if one does not know them by then, one has not learned anything. To know one's obligation toward those who look up to one, who surround one, who expect some help, some advice, some service from one—that is the time when one must be conscious of these things. It is the beautiful age when the tree comes to full blossom, when it begins to give fruit to the world. Not only is this the time for the singer whose voice is in full blossom, not only is this the time for the artist or the thinker when they can express thoughts in their fullness, but for every person that age is the promise of the ripened mind expressing itself to the best advantage. And if that opportunity is not taken, one has missed a great deal in life.

And advanced age also has its own blessings. People do not appreciate the blessings of every period of life. Therefore, they appreciate one and dislike another. In the East, especially in India, great respect is given to age. And there is every reason that that ideal should be known. That is the age when one is the record of all one's life, whether one has been sympathetic, kind, wise, foolish—whatever one has been—advanced age brings the record of it. One can read it in someone's face, in their features, in their atmosphere, one can read what they have done. Their opportunity is greater to inspire, to bless, to serve those who want their service or who want to be directed. They can show others better manners, a better way of looking at life. But when people do not realize their opportunities, they will act like a child in middle age, while in childhood they were given the work of an old person, and in youth they were burdened like someone of middle age.

If we only knew that every moment in life, every day in life, every month, and every year has its particular blessing. If we only knew life's opportunity. But the greatest opportunity that one can realize in life is to accomplish that purpose for which one was sent on earth. And if one has lost that opportunity, then all one has accomplished in the world, whether one has gathered wealth, whether one possesses much property or has a great name—it does not matter what—one will not be satisfied. Once one's eyes are opened and one begins to look at the world, one finds that there is a greater opportunity than one had never thought before. In the first place, if one only knew what thought can do. One is as poor as one is, as limited as one is, as troubled as one is, but at the same time there is nothing in this world that could not be accomplished by one if one only knew what thought can do. And at the same time, it is ignorance that keeps one away from what one ought to accomplish. One should know how to operate one's thought, how to accomplish certain things, how to focus one's mind on the object that should be accomplished. If one does not know, then one has not made use of one's mind, then one has lived as a machine. If one knew the power of feeling, and realized that the power of feeling can reach anywhere, can penetrate anything, one could make anything one might wish.

There is a Persian story of Shirin and Farhad. Once Shirin, the woman whom Farhad admired, in order to test his love, said, "Farhad, do you love me? If you love me, you will have to make a way through the mountains." Farhad said, "Yes, I was waiting for that test." He went to the mountains full of the feeling of love that he had for her. Every time he broke the rock with his hammer, he said the name of Shirin. And the strength of the hammer was a thousand times greater because it was joined with the feeling of the heart.

Today people have forgotten the great power there is in feeling. It can break rocks. There is nothing that cannot be accomplished by the power of feeling. But generally there is no feeling; feeling has become drowned, it no longer exists. Life's greatest opportunity is to realize the power of feeling and to express it. But a still greater opportunity of life is to free oneself from the captivity of limitations. Every person is a captive in some form or other; every person's life is limited in some form or other. But one could get above this limitation by realizing the latent power and inspiration of the soul.

Kabir, the great poet of India, says that, "Life is a field and you are born to cultivate it. And if you know how to cultivate this field, you can produce anything you like. All the need of your life can be produced in this field. All that your soul yearns after, all you need is to be gotten from this field, if you knew how to cultivate it, how to reap the fruit." But if this opportunity is only studied in order to make the best of life by taking what we can take, by being more comfortable, that is not satisfying. We must enrich ourselves with thought, with that happiness that is spiritual happiness, with that peace that belongs to our soul, with that liberty, that freedom for which our soul longs, and attain to that higher knowledge that breaks all fetters of life and raises one's consciousness to look at life from a different point of view. Once one has realized this opportunity, one has fulfilled the purpose of life.

17

OUR LIFE

We, consciously or unconsciously, call to us that element that makes us what we are.[1] What we experience in life, therefore, has come either from what we have already called to us in the past or from what we call in the present. It is very difficult for a person to hear this for the first time and to accept it immediately, for no person in this world is desirous of calling for something that he or she does not wish to have. But the modern philosopher Emerson has said, think beforehand of what you want. The principle of the whole creation is based on this. Even the fruits and flowers, the plants and trees, in order to be what they are, call for that element that makes them so. If fragrance belonged to the flower, then every flower would have fragrance. But it is only a certain flower that has fragrance; it is that flower that calls for it. Each flower has a different color. Why? Because each flower calls for it. Every seed or herb that has medicinal value shows that its peculiarity belongs to it; and it calls for it.

The life of little insects will also show us proof of the same fact. Their green or blue or red color and beautiful or ugly form is based on, is constructed on, what they have called to themselves. Little insects moving among beautiful flowers, which are to be found in the green, show beauty in their color, in their

1. The typescript for this talk is dated November 5, 1925.

construction; for they live in beauty and so they call for beauty. Insects living in the mud show again a different quality. Why? Because they call for it.

There is the past of the rose behind it, and since the seed of the rose had conceived those properties that the rose shows, it has maintained as its heritage that fragrance and color; but at the same time it takes from the air and the sun that sustenance that makes it the perfect rose. In other words, there is perhaps in the same garden another plant, a flower that is without fragrance. It has the same sun, it has the same air, it is in the same space. But it is the rose that calls for the properties that make it a rose; that other flower, being in the same place, does not call for it, it only calls for those properties that keep it as it is. Is it not so, if it is said symbolically, that one creeps on this earth, the other walks gently, the third runs, and the fourth flies; and they are all on the same earth, under the same sun? No quality can exist without being maintained by what it attracts every moment of the day.

As our physical body depends upon physical sustenance for its existence, and as our mind depends on the sustenance of its own sphere, so each quality has its food, a food that it calls for and on which it lives. As the body may cease to exist if its sustenance is not given to it, so every quality, however great it may show to be in a person, may cease to exist if there is no sustenance within reach. If we keenly observed this life around us, we would find a thousand proofs of this. In how many born with genius, how many with a tendency to write poetry, how many with an inclination to sing, how many with a desire to do some good, see their qualities vanish; they themselves could not find their qualities once they are starved of that food on which they live.

The more we study science, be it natural science or chemistry, the more we shall find that each being and each object by its peculiarity shows that it is so because it has called for that element to become so. Human beings, who are the finished specimen of the creation, show this doctrine in its fullness. Their success, their failure, their sorrows, their joys, all depend upon what they call and what they have called to themselves. Many will say, is it not that people experience what was meant for them to experience? That is the idealistic point of view, and a good point of view to take; it is also consoling. Yet when we come to the study of metaphysics, we shall find that the secret behind creation is what the Hindus call the dream of Brahma. Since each being represents Brahma, the creator, so each being, in its part, is a creator of its own life. It is ignorance of this fact that keeps one back from progressing toward perfection; and it is the knowledge of this that alone can be called a divine knowledge; for if anyone has ever arrived at a higher realization, it was by this knowledge.

There is another side of it to be considered. One may say that there are many undesirable things that one should never have desired, but one did not desire them as one sees them now, but as one saw them before; it was in another form that one desired them. Very often happiness shows itself in the guise of unhappiness; very often pain shows itself in the guise of pleasure. The one who does not seek after pain will seek after pleasure, but does not know that perhaps behind that pleasure the pain was hiding. A seeker after success may not see failure hiding behind it; and at the same time the very seeking for success would lead the person to failure. For that success was in appearance; in reality it was a failure. Life is a comedy, and the more you look at it, the more you can smile at it; smile not at other persons, but smile at yourself. It is always different from what one thinks it to be, whether you look at pain, at pleasure, at happiness, at success and failure, or at any other thing.

There are two ways of calling that which makes up one's self. One way is calling that which is outside of one's life to make one's life complete, be it wealth, power, position, or anything else. But there is another way of calling, and that is to call the very self. By calling one's real self, one naturally harmonizes one's spirit. And it may become so harmonized that with both friend and foe one would feel harmony. Once one has communicated with one's self, once one has called one's self, one's real self, one naturally becomes harmonized with pain and pleasure, and one becomes contented with success and failure. For in spite of all the different experiences of our external life, there rises in the bottom of our heart a harmony and a peace and a power that keep one centralized. In order not to be wet in the rain, we cannot stop the rain; all that we can do is have an umbrella that is waterproof. We cannot, by developing ourselves materially or spiritually, stop the natural consequences of life. When we are in the midst of the world we are exposed to all agreeable and disagreeable experiences that life gives us. If there is a way of making life easy for ourselves it is only this way: by harmonizing within ourselves so that we can harmonize with all the different conditions and experiences of life. If we complain, there is no end to our complaint; in order to have no complaints we must not complain. But we should be conscious of the fact that all that we experience is called by us, and all that we shall experience will be called by us also. Thus at each step in our life we must be wise in order to distinguish, among all the things we desire, those that we should call to ourselves and those we should not. It is no use mourning over the past—it is passed. It is just as well to forget the past except for beautiful impressions and good memories. It is the present for which we are responsible; for it is the present that will build our future. The present is the reflection of the past, and the future is the re-echo of the present. The most essential thing, therefore, is that by centralizing our thought within ourselves, by finding our real self, we must so harmonize that the future may become harmonized. There is a prayer in the East: "We give thanks for all we have experienced; the only thing we ask is make our end the best of all."

18

COMMUNICATING WITH LIFE

Beloved Ones of God, I would like to speak on the subject of communicating with life, that from the point of view of the mystic, life in all its aspects is communicative if one only knew the secret of communicating with it.[1] As long as one is ignorant of this secret, one is deaf though one has ears and blind though one has eyes. There are stories of sages and saints who spoke with trees and plants and rocks and mountains and seas. People take them as legends, but it is as true as anything else in this world of variety. It is not only true of the past, but it can always be and always is possible if one knows how to communicate with life. In the lower creation we recognize a faculty that we call instinct: the tendency that makes the bird fly and the fish swim without learning. Besides, this instinct also appears in the form of intuition among the lower creation. Many scientists today say that animals have no mind, but in reality all creatures have a mind; even trees and plants have a mind. Those who live close to nature, and those whose life work is agriculture, always living in solitude with the animals, know the fact that animals often give a warning of illness or of death, of a storm or a flood. They have intuition. The mechanism of the human

---

1. A lecture given at the home of Mr. and Mrs. White, Burlingame, California, April 10, 1926.

body and mind is finer still, and humans are capable of a greater intuition. And yet it seems that animals perceive things even before humans do. The reason is that people are so absorbed in their outer life, in their object in life, that it is very difficult for them to believe in intuition. And therefore their intuitive faculty becomes blunted, and they prove to be less intuitive than the lower creation. Those living close to nature in the solitude, peasants living a country life, have a greater intuition than those intellectual people living in the midst of worldly life. This shows that the life we live today in large towns is all an unnatural life, lived in an artificial atmosphere, eating artificial food, adopting artificial ways of living. So one loses that heavenly quality, the divine heritage of the human that is shown in the intuitive qualities. Fine persons seem to have more intuition than gross ones, women seems to have a greater intuition than men. The reason is that woman is by nature respondent. It is the receptivity of her nature that makes her more intuitive. Sometimes a man reasons and argues, but a woman says, "Yes, but I feel it, I feel it is to be so." And her feeling proves to be right. She cannot give a reason for it. She says, "I feel it."

In every person there exists to a greater or lesser degree a faculty of perceiving impressions, and that is the first step toward intuition. The finer the person, the greater that person's perception. But everyone at times feels, as an impression, the conditions of the place, the character of the people one meets, their tendencies, their motives, their desire, their grade of evolution. If you ask, "Why do you feel like this?" the person cannot always give an explanation. Sometimes the person will say, "From the features," or "from the atmosphere," or "from what someone has said." But in reality it is a feeling that is beyond description. A fine, sensitive, intelligent person always gets an impression on seeing another.

The next stage is intuition. By intuition one feels the warning of a coming danger, the promise of success, the warning of a failure; if any change is to take place in life, one feels it.

But very often, by not having self-confidence, one loses that intuitive faculty. One fears that one's intuition is wrong; and in this way one loses self-confidence. If one thinks that, "Maybe my intuition is not right, and by following my intuition I will fail," then one takes another way. That is the way of reasoning, of logic. Naturally one's intuition becomes blunted after some time. If one has not made use of that faculty it disappears, and someone who is capable of perceiving intuitively then loses that faculty. Another wonderful thing about intuition is that one is blessed with intuition according to one's sincerity. If a person is earnest, sincere, sympathetic, kind, that person is blessed with intuition. And if these qualities are lacking, intuition will be lacking too. Also those who have no intuition have difficulty in attaining to the spiritual ideal, for spiritual belief does not come from outer experience, from reason and logic; it is a belief that springs from within in the form of intuition. And if intuitive faculty is not developed, that person's belief is not strong. In the first place a person who lacks intuition lacks belief too. And if a person has belief, that belief will not be strong enough because it is not built on a sound foundation.

And the next step in the path of intuition is inspiration. Poets, writers, musicians, thinkers, philosophers are able to make use of this faculty. Others have it but they do not know how to use it. In art, poetry, or music, one can create it in a few moments by inspiration that which one could not otherwise create in ten years. It is a natural flow. You have no difficulty in working it out. Inspiration comes already arranged; there is very little to be done by the brain and by the mind. Besides, everything that comes through inspiration is living, and is most beautiful, most harmonious compared to the art or poetry or music that is the outcome of the brain. Music works from older times, such as by Wagner and Beethoven, are still living. And no matter how often you hear them, you always thirst for them. Modern music has not that appeal. And it is the same thing with ancient art. There is something living in that art, and today with all the progress made in art, that something is missing. It is the same with poetry. In Persia we had great poets such as Hafiz and Rumi and Saʿdi, whose works are today studied and highly esteemed by millions of people in the East. They consider that without these works there would be no humane culture. Their work is the foundation of humane culture in the East. Many later poets have tried to produce the same kind of works as those of Rumi and Hafiz, but they have not yet succeeded even after many centuries. It seems that inspiration is lost. Whenever inspiration comes it is living and life-giving, and it will always last and one will never get tired of it.

One might ask, "What is the theory of inspiration? Where does one find it? Where does it come from?" My answer is that there is one treasure house where all the knowledge collected and experienced and learned and discovered by human beings is stored. And that treasure house is the divine mind, a mind with which all minds are linked. There is no experience we have that does not remain or that is not recorded in that treasure house. Every good or bad experience we have, every new thing we learn, every discovery we make, it is all stored in that treasure house. But one might ask, "How does one find it? If we have a large store, perhaps hundreds and thousands of things, it is difficult to find anything we want at a moment's notice." The power of mind, the power of the will is such that if one has sufficient power of will one can find anything one wants to find. It is said that someone with great willpower wanted to buy a certain piece of furniture. In the first street the person went to after leaving home he saw in the showroom the very piece of furniture he wanted. In other words, he was taken to it. What you really want is attracted to you and you are attracted to what you want. And it is the same with poets, musicians, thinkers. When they are deeply interested in what they are doing, then they only have to wish, and by the automatic action of the desire their wish becomes a light. And this light is thrown on the divine storehouse, and it is projected on the same object that they want to find. Such is the phenomenon of will and inspiration, that no sooner inspired souls are moved by the beauty and harmony of life and wishes to express their soul, the light of their soul shines on that particular object or on that particular knowledge. And it comes instantly to their mind, expressing itself outwardly through their mind. And all that is brought from within in this way is perfect, is harmonious, is beautiful, and has a wonderful effect.

In ancient times the shah of Persia expressed the desire to have a history of Persia written. But he was told, "We have lost the records, and it would be very difficult to trace back the accounts of the kings who lived before." However, there was a poet, Firdausi, who said, "I will write the history of Persia." He was an inspired poet. People were amazed. They asked, "How will he do it?" But he sent his soul, so to speak, into the past, and his soul became a receptacle of the knowledge of the past and he expressed it in the form of poetry. This book is called the *Shah Nameh* of Persia, and it was brought by inspiration.

Many think that science is based upon the knowledge of facts proved by reason and logic, and very few know that its beginning was intuition. All scientific discoveries in their beginning spring from intuition. Then reason finds its place, logic helps. The discoveries are analyzed and made intelligible to others as such, but in the beginning they come from intuition just the same. If the great inventors of America, such as Edison and others, had been great mechanics only, it would not have been sufficient. There is intuition at the back of it.

Today there is a tendency not to admit that side of life. People think it is not solid enough to rely upon intuition or inspiration. I was surprised the other day in Paris hearing a great writer say, "Is there such a thing as inspiration?" I thought, "Now here is a great writer who has made a name for himself, and still he does not know if there is such a thing as inspiration." By continual material strife, and by continually ignoring God-spirit, people have become so materialistic that they do not think that such a thing as inspiration exists. Besides, this man became famous without believing in inspiration. That was all he wanted. But when I learned more about the work of this person, I found that his works were nothing but superficial. There is no depth to them, there is no height, and a very narrow pitch. And that is what takes these days. Even when you see in the United States modern plays you will find the same thing. There is hardly a play where you will find any depth. And if you ask why it is so, the answer is: "In order to please the man in the street." That means, "We must keep everybody back because the man in the street must be pleased." A newspaper reporter one day said to me when I spoke to him about philosophy, "How very interesting! But say, how shall I put it before the man in the street?" Therefore, the general education is to keep everyone on the level of the street. In the stage magazines it is all at a narrow pitch; it does not touch at the depth. Then where is the hope of progress if inspiration is ignored, intuition blunted? The trend of mind today is toward facts, void of truth.

The next step from inspiration is what is called vision. It is more than inspiration. One need not see a vision only in a dream; one can also have a vision when awake. There is nothing to be frightened about in this. It is only clearness of the inner sight. Knowledge comes in a flash, and a problem is solved; a philosophical problem, or a certain hidden law of life, of nature, has become manifest in a very clear form. Or one has got in touch with something or with someone at an unimaginable distance. People have misunderstood the meaning of vision, and many have pretended to be visionary. But in reality the development of the inner vision shows great progress of the soul.

And if one goes still further in the path of intuition one comes to what we call revelation, which means that every thing and every being reveals to one its secret. One finds that every leaf has a tongue to tell its legend. One finds that every soul is a living book that reads its own story. One finds that every condition of life is turned inside out before one the moment one begins to look at it. One feels that one is at home on earth and in heaven, that both the here and the hereafter become manifest to one's soul. As Sa'di has said, "Once a person begins to read, every leaf of the tree becomes a page of the Bible."

And now in conclusion, how does it happen that one experiences or one perceives intuition or inspiration, that one sees vision and gets revelation? There is a story of the apostles who instantly knew many languages. But this does not mean that they knew French or English, German or Spanish. It means that they knew the language of every soul, that every soul began to speak to them, that they began to communicate with every person. The meaning of revelation is the understanding of the language of the soul, that every soul is always speaking if one can hear it. That it is not always from the noise of the world, from the voice of people that one hears, but even the silent trees and the still mountains speak to us when we are able to hear them. It is a language of vibration, a language imperceptible, and yet a fine mind can grasp it. And the only explanation of it is that it is a music. For musicians, music is a language that tells them something. The high and the low note, the flat and sharp—it is all expressive, and it all tells the musician something—it all has a meaning. A person who is not a student of music does not know the language. That one will enjoy music but he or she does not know the language.

But then there is the language of life, for life is music also. Each person is a note in that music, and that makes the symphony of life. One person is in tune, the other person is out of tune; one soul is sounding the right note, the other a false note. In this way every person makes or mars the music. Revelation comes from the understanding of this music. You cannot learn it, you cannot teach it. But you can tune your heart to that pitch where it begins to live and begins to enjoy the music of life. And in this way revelation is perceived: when the heart has become awake and living so that it can perceive meaning of the vibrations coming from every soul and every condition.

The great prophets and teachers who have brought religion to humanity, who have inspired humanity with a higher ideal, who have guided humankind toward spiritual attainment, they were the revealed souls, the souls who had revelation. And what they gave to the world is their interpretation of the revelation they felt. But no sooner do composers put their music on paper than much of it is lost. And when the prophet gives teachings in the form of words, much is lost too. Then there are some who say, "This is something sacred, and there is my belief." And they keep to those words. But there are others who want to know the spirit of it. That these words that have come down to us are only interpretations of the revelations the prophets had. And if all the people in the world knew the spirit, then there would not be so many different religions, there would not be so many different creeds. They would all adhere to that one truth. That there are so many creeds, so many different religions is because they do not understand religion. If one understood religion, then there is only one religion, interpreted differently by the different teachers of humanity. And their revelation comes from the music of life that is interpreted in a human tongue.

19

THE INTOXICATION OF LIFE (1)

There are many different things in life that are intoxicating, but if we would consider the nature of life, we would think that there is nothing more intoxicating than our life itself.[1] In the first place, we can see the truth of this idea by thinking of what we were yesterday and comparing it with our condition today. Our unhappiness or happiness, our riches or poverty of yesterday are like a dream to us; it is only our condition today that counts. This life of continual rise and fall and of continual changes is like running water, and with the running of this water one thinks, "I am this water." In reality one does not know what one is. For instance, if someone goes from poverty to riches and if those riches are taken away from them, they lament; and they lament because they do not remember that before having those riches they were poor and from that poverty they came to riches. If one can consider one's fancies through life one will find that at every stage of one's development, one had a particular fancy; sometimes one longed for certain things and at other times one did not care for them. If one can look as a spectator at one's own life, one will find that it was nothing but an intoxication. What at one time gives one great satisfaction and pride, at another time humiliates one; what at one

1. A talk given at L'Hotel Splendide, Montreux, Switzerland, June 21, 1921.

time one enjoys, at another time troubles one; what at one time one values greatly, at another time one does not value at all. If one can observe one's actions in everyday life and if one has an awakened sense of justice and understanding, one will find oneself doing something that one had not intended to do, or saying something that one would like not to have said, or behaving in such a way that one asks oneself, "Why was I such a fool?"

Sometimes one allows oneself to love someone, to admire someone; it goes on for days, for weeks for months, years (although years may be very long); and then perhaps one feels, oh I was wrong, or something that is more attractive comes along; then one is on another road and does not know where one is anymore nor whom one loves. In the action and reaction of one's life one sometimes does things on impulse, not considering what one is doing and at other times, one has, so to speak, a spell of goodness and one goes on doing what one thinks is good; at other times a reaction comes and all this goodness is gone.

Then in business and in professions and commerce, one gets an impulse—I must do this, I must do that—and one seems to have all strength and courage; and sometimes one continues on, and sometimes it lasts only a day or two and then one forgets what one was doing and does something else. This shows that in one's life in the activity of the world one is just like a little piece of wood, raised by the waves of the sea when they rise up and cast down when the waves go down. Therefore the Hindus have called the life of the world *bhavasagara*, an ocean, an ever-rising ocean. And in life one is floating in this ocean of the activity of the world, not knowing what one is doing, not knowing where one is going. What seems of importance to one is only the moment that one calls the present; the past is a dream, the future is in a mist, and the only thing clear to one is the present.

The attachment and love and affection of people in the world's life are not very different from the attachment of the

The Intoxication of Life (1)

birds and animals. There is a time when the sparrow looks after its young and brings grains in its beak and puts them into the beak of its young ones, and they anxiously await the coming of the mother who puts grain in their beak. And this goes on until their wings are grown, and once the young ones have known the branches of the tree and they have flown in the forests under the protection of the kind mother, they never again know the mother who was so kind to them.

There are moments of emotion, there are impulses of love, of attachment, of affection, but there comes a time when these pass; they pale and fade away. And there comes a time when one thinks that there is something else one desires and something else one would like to love. The more one thinks of a person's life in the world, the more one comes to understand that it is not very different from the life of a child. The child takes a fancy to a doll and then it gets tired of the doll and takes a fancy to another toy. And when it takes a fancy to the doll or the toy it thinks it the most valuable thing in the world; and then there comes a time when it tears up the doll and destroys the toy. And so it is with people, their scope is perhaps a little different but their action is the same. All that one considers important in life, such as the collection of wealth, the possession of property, the attainment of fame or rising to a position that one thinks ideal—any of these objects before one have nothing other than an intoxicating effect, but after attaining the object one is not satisfied. One thinks that there is perhaps something else one wants, that it was not this that one wanted. Whatever one wants one feels is the most important thing, but after attaining it one thinks that it is not important at all, and wants something else. In everything that pleases one and makes one happy, one's amusements, one's theatre, one's moving pictures, golf, polo, tennis, it seems that it amuses one to be in a puzzle and not to know where one is going. It seems that one only desires to fill up one's time, and one does not know where one is going or what one is doing.

The Intoxication of Life (1)

And what one calls pleasure is that moment when one is more intoxicated with the activity of life. Anything that covers one's eyes from reality; anything that makes one feel a kind of sensation of life; anything that one can indulge in and be conscious of some activity, it is that that one calls pleasure. Human nature is such that whatever one becomes accustomed to, that is one's pleasure, be it eating, drinking, or any activity. If one becomes accustomed to what is bitter, bitterness becomes one's pleasure; if one becomes accustomed to what is sour, then sourness gives one pleasure; if one becomes accustomed to eat sweets, then one likes sweets. Some people get into the habit of complaining about their life and if they have nothing to complain about then they look for something to complain about. Others want the sympathy of other people, in order to complain that they are badly treated and look for some treatment to complain about. It is an intoxication.

Then there are those who fall into the habit of theft, they derive pleasure from it, and it turns into a habit, so much so that if another source of income is offered, they are not interested, they do not want it. In this way people become accustomed to certain things in life, and these things become a pleasure, an intoxication. There are many for whom it becomes a habit to worry about things. The least little thing worries them very much. They cherish whatever little sorrow they have; it is a plant they water and nourish. And so many, directly or indirectly, consciously or unconsciously, become accustomed to illness, and the illness is more an intoxication than a reality. And as long as one holds the thought of that illness, one, so to speak, sustains it, and the illness settles in one's body and no doctor can take it away. And this sorrow and illness are also an intoxication.

Then one's environment and condition in life create for one an illusion and give one an intoxication so that one does not know the condition of the people around one, the people of the city in which one lives and of the country in which one lives.

The Intoxication of Life (1)

And the intoxication not only remains with one in one's wakeful condition but it continues in one's dreams, as the drunken person too will dream of the things that have to do with drunkenness. If one has joy, if one has sorrow, if one has a worry, or if one has a pleasure, the same will be one's condition in one's dream. And day and night the dream continues to exist; with some the continuation of the dream lasts the whole life, with others only a certain time.

But people love this intoxication as much as the drunken person loves the intoxication of wine. When a person is seeing something interesting in their dream and somebody else tries to wake them, even on waking they feel for a moment that they should go back to sleep and finish that interesting dream; though they know that it was a dream and that someone is waking them they still wish to sleep and to finish that interesting dream. This intoxication can be seen in all different aspects of life, even in the religious, philosophical, and mystical aspects. People seek after subtlety and wish to know something that they cannot understand; they are pleased to be told something that their reason cannot understand. Give them the simple truth, they will not like it. When teachers like Jesus Christ came to earth and gave the message of truth in simple words, the people of that time said, "This is in our book, we know it already." But whenever there is an attempt to mystify people, telling them of fairies and ghosts and spirits, they are very pleased; they desire to understand what they cannot understand.

What people have always called spiritual or religious truth has been the key to that ultimate truth that humans cannot see because of their intoxication. And this truth nobody can give to another person. It is in every soul, for the human soul itself is this truth. And if anybody can give, they can only give the means by which the truth can be known. The religions, in different forms, have been methods. By these methods people have been taught by the inspired souls to know this truth and to be benefited by this truth that is in the soul of man. But instead of being benefited by a religion in this way people have taken only the external part of the religion to be their religion and have fought with others, saying, "My religion is the only right one, your religion is false."

But there have always existed some wise ones, as it is said in the Bible that the wise of the East came when Jesus Christ was born, to see the child.[2] What does this mean? It means that the wise have existed at different times, and it has been their life's mission to keep themselves sober in spite of this intoxication from all around and to help their brothers and sisters to gain this soberness. Among those who have been wise by their soberness there have been some who had great inspiration and great power and control over themselves and over life within and without. And it is such wise ones who have been called saints or sages or prophets or masters.

People, in the world, through their intoxication, even in following or accepting these wise ones, have monopolized one of them as their prophet or teacher and have fought with others, saying my teacher is the only true one. And in this way they have shown their intoxication and drunkenness. And as drunken people would, without any thought, hit or hurt another person who may be different from them, who thought or felt or did differently, so mostly the great people of the world who came to help humanity have been killed, crucified, hurt, or tortured. But they have not complained against it, they have taken it as a natural consequence. They have understood that they were in a world of intoxication or drunkenness and that it is natural that a drunken person must hurt or harm them. That has been the history of the world in whatever part of the world the message of God has been given.

In reality there has been the message from one source and that is God and under whatever name the wise gave that message it was not their message, it was the message of God. Those

2. Matthew 2:1.

whose hearts had eyes to see and ears to hear, they have known and seen the same messenger because they have received the message. And those whose hearts had not eyes or ears have taken the messenger to be what is important and not the message. At whatever period that message came and in whatever form the message was garbed it was only that one message, the message of wisdom.

And it seems that the drunkenness of the world has increased and increased to such an extent that the great bloodshed and disaster that the world has recently gone through was something the likes of which cannot be found in the history of the world. That shows that the drunkenness of the world has reached its summit, and no one can deny that even now the world is not in a sober condition, that even now the traces of that drunkenness can be found in the unrest of this time, even if the great bloodshed, is, for the moment, over.

The Sufi movement originates from the word *sophia*, "wisdom," the message of wisdom. And its aim is the same that was at all periods of the world's history the aim of the message—to bring about that soberness in humanity, to bring about that love for one's neighbor. No doubt, politics or education or business are the means of bringing people of different races or nations into contact with one another, but spiritual truth and the understanding of life are the only means of bringing about that feeling of kinship in the world, which nothing else can bring.

This message does not work to form an exclusive community, as there are already so many communities fighting against one another. But the object of the message is to bring about a better understanding between different communities in the knowledge of truth. It is not a new religion; and how can it be a new religion when Jesus Christ has said, I am not come to give a new law, I am come to fulfill the religion.[3] This is the combination of the religions.

3. Matthew 5:17.

The chief aim of this movement is to revivify the religions of the world, in this way bringing together the followers of the different religions in friendly understanding and in tolerance. All are received with open arms in the Order of the Sufis whatever be their religion, to whatever church they belong, whatever faith they have—there is no interference with it. There is personal help and guidance in the methods of meditation. There is a course of study to consider the problems of life, and the chief aim of every member of the Order is to do the best in their power to bring about that understanding, that the whole humanity may become one single family in the parenthood of God.

20

THE INTOXICATION OF LIFE (2)

It is not only what one eats or drinks that provides a certain amount of stimulancy but also what one smells, what one sees or hears—even those have an influence and effect on one's being.[1] And the stimulus that one experiences through food and drink is really a small intoxication. But it is not only the food that one eats and the water that one drinks and all that one sees and hears and touches that intoxicates, but even the air that one breathes from morning to evening is continually giving one a stimulus and an intoxication. And if this is true, is there then one moment when one is not intoxicated? One is always intoxicated, only sometimes more so than other times. But this is not the only intoxication. One's absorption in the affairs of one's life also keeps one intoxicated. Besides that second intoxication from work and affairs in which one's mind is absorbed, there is a third intoxication, and that is the attachment that one has with oneself, the sympathy that one has with oneself. It is this intoxication that makes one selfish, that makes one greedy, and very often unjust toward others. The effect of this intoxication is that one is continually busy feeling, thinking, and acting in terms of what would be in my interest, what would bring me a certain profit? And in that one's whole time and life become

---

1. A talk given at Musée Guimet, Paris, December 2, 1923.

fully involved. It is this intoxication that makes one say, "This is my friend, and that is my enemy; this one is my well-wisher, and that one is against me," and it is from this intoxication that the ego, the false ego of a person, is made. And it is this third intoxication that keeps one continually in the thought of attaining that which is for the profit of oneself. But just as intoxicated people do not really know what is profitable to them, so selfish people in their selfishness never know or understand what is really to their benefit. And in the moments of soberness people wonder, "If this is intoxication, then what is reality? I would like to know what reality is." But to know reality it is not only the eyes and ears that are necessary, but soberness too is needed to hear and see better. One might ask, "Why should we call this intoxication if it seems to be the normal state of every person?" Yes, it may be called the normal condition only because it is the condition of everyone. But intoxication is intoxication. Intoxication is not satisfactory.

And then there is an innate longing for a certain satisfaction that one does not know, yet for which one seeks, and that satisfaction is the continual longing of one's soul. No active person with any wisdom will deny the fact that often every effort a person makes for happiness seems to bring a disappointing result. That shows that the effort was made in the wrong direction. But apart from making an effort to find reality one must first realize what this intoxication is. And the first step in the path of truth is to know that such a thing as intoxication exists. Take the intoxication of childhood: imagine what attention, what service, what care the child demands. At the same time it does not know who takes the trouble, who takes care of it. It plays with its toys, it plays with its playmates, it does not know what is awaiting it in the future. What it wants, what it is pleased with, is what is immediately around it. It does not see any farther. No child has ever known in its childhood what value its mother or father or those who cared for it had, until when one arrives at that stage when one begins to see for oneself. And when we observe the condition of youth, that again is another intoxication, that time of blossoming, of the fullness of energy, the soul in that springtime never thinks that there can be anything else. The soul never thinks that this is a passing stage. The soul at that time only thinks that it is full of intoxication. It knows nothing apart from itself. How many errors a youth commits, how many follies, how many thoughtless and inconsiderate things it does of which it afterward repents, but about which it never thinks at the time. It is not the fault of the soul, it is the intoxication of that time of life. The person who is intoxicated is not responsible for it; such a one is intoxicated. Neither is the child to be blamed for its not being responsible or appreciative enough, nor the youth for being blind in its energy. It is natural.

This intoxication remains as a person goes on in life; there is only a change of wine. The wine of childhood is different from the wine of youth, and when the wine of youth is passed, then some other wine is taken. Then according to what walk of life one follows, one drinks that wine that absorbs one's life, whether collecting wealth or acquiring power or looking for a position. All these things intoxicate one. And even if one goes further in life, intoxication still pursues one. It may be the joy found in music or a fondness of poetry, it may be a love of art or a delight in learning—it is all intoxication.

But now a person may ask, "If all these different occupations and things of interest are like different wines, then what is there in the world that can be called a state of soberness?" It is wine, indeed, from beginning to end. Even those who are good and advanced spiritually and morally, they also have a certain wine. One has to take wine all along the way, but it is a different wine. A highly advanced artist, a great poet, an inspired musician will admit that there are moments of intoxication that come to them as a joy, as an upliftment, from their art, music, or poetry, and it makes them exalted and as if they were not living in this world.

The higher intoxication cannot be compared with the lower intoxication of this world, but it is still intoxication. What is joy, what is fear, what is anger, what is passion, what is the feeling of attachment, and what is the feeling of detachment? All these have the effect of wine, all have their intoxications. Understanding this mystery, the Sufis have founded their culture upon this principle of intoxication. They call this intoxication *hal,* and *hal* literally means "condition" or "state." And there is a saying of the Sufis that one speaks and acts according to one's condition.

One cannot speak or act differently from the wine one has had. With those who have drunk the wine of anger, whatever they say or do is irritable, is irritation. With those who have drunk the wine of detachment, in their thought, speech, and action you will find nothing but detachment. With those who drink the wine of attachment, you will feel in their presence that all are drawn to them and they are drawn to all. Everything a person does and says, all that person does and says, is according to the wine that he or she has taken. And that is why the Sufi says: "Heaven and hell are in one's hand, if one only knew their mystery." For Sufis the world is like a wine cellar, a store in which all sorts of wines are collected. They have only to choose what wine they will have and what wine will bring them that delight that is the longing of their soul.

I had once an experience in India, which was my first impression and a deep impression indeed, of this aspect of life. When walking in the district of the dervishes, where the dervishes live in solitude, I found ten or twelve dervishes sitting together under the shade of a tree, in their ragged clothes, talking with one another. As I was curious to hear and see a path of different thoughts and ideas, I stood there watching this assembly and what was going on there. These thinking souls, sitting on the ground without a carpet, at first gave the impression of being poor and helpless, sitting in disappointment, having nothing by way of possessions. But as they began to speak with one another, that impression did not remain, for they addressed one another by saying: "O King of kings," and "O Emperor of emperors." At first I was taken aback on hearing these words, but after giving it a little thought, I wondered, what is an emperor, what is a king? Is the real king and emperor within or without? And the one who is the emperor of the environment without is dependent on all that is without. The moment he is separated from that environment, he is no longer an emperor. But these emperors sitting on the bare ground were real emperors. No one could take away their empire, for their empire, their kingdom, was not an illusion; their kingdom was a real kingdom. An emperor may have a bottle of wine in front of him, but these emperors had drunk that wine and had become real emperors. Do we not see in our everyday life persons who say: "I am ill, I am sorry, I am miserable, I am wretched"? Put them in a palace and put a thousand doctors and nurses around them, they will still be wretched. And some may be in great suffering and pain and yet they say: "No, I am well, I am happy." All is well, all goes right, for those are who are right. Does it not show to us that we are, that we become, the wine we drink? Those who are drunk with the wine of success know not failure. And if circumstances made them fail nine times, the tenth time they will succeed. Those who have drunk the wine of failure may be given all the possibility of success, but they have drunk the wine of failure, they cannot succeed.

But with all this there is one subtle feeling every soul has, a feeling that cannot be explained in words, a feeling that makes one more comfortable in one's armchair at home than when perhaps ten thousand people are standing before one paying one homage. One may be loaded with wealth, but the moment when all the pearls and jewels are set aside and one sits down alone and takes a rest, that is the time when one breathes a free breath. And what does this teach us? It teaches us that one may have everything in the world, may have what has the greatest value in one's eyes, but yet there is something hidden that one is seeking. When one has that, then one is happy. One might explain this same idea with perhaps more examples: that one does not want to have a person, however beloved, around one all the time; one sometimes wants to have a moment away from even the dearest person in the world. However proud one is of one's thoughts, the thoughts may be great, deep, and good, yet the greatest joy is the moment when one is not thinking. One may have the finest feeling of love, tenderness, and goodness, but there are moments when there are no feelings. That moment is more exalting.

What does this show? This shows that the whole life is interesting because it is all intoxicating. But what is desired by the soul is one thing only and that is a glimpse of soberness. What is this glimpse of soberness, and how does one experience this glimpse of soberness that is the continual longing of the soul? One experiences it by means of meditation, by means of concentration. But if it is a natural thing, why has one to make an effort for it? The reason is that one enjoys this intoxication so much that afterward one becomes addicted to drink. And that is the condition of every soul in this world. Every soul becomes addicted to drinking the wine of life, and at the same time there comes a moment—if not in the early part of life, then later, if not when one is happy, then when one is unhappy—when one begins to look for that soberness that is a continual longing of one's soul.

The Sufi culture therefore is a culture designed in order to experience that soberness. It is no doubt very difficult to explain how this soberness is attained, and yet after having explained this subject of intoxication, it is not so very difficult. For it is as simple as saying that the way to give up drink is to keep the drink away and let one be without a drink for a time. And therefore, as I have said, there are three principal wines, three principal intoxications: the intoxication of one's self, the intoxication of one's occupation, and the third intoxication is what the senses feel every moment. Now, these three wines cannot all be taken away at once. It would be just like taking away from those who live on wine their life's sustenance. But one can give those persons a certain time and see that during that time they keep sober and only take two wines, not three. And at another time they take only one, not two. And as people advance in meditative life, they may arrive to that stage that the three wines on which they live may all be withheld, and yet they still feel they can live and so they will become convinced that they can exist without these three intoxications. Verily, this conviction of existing independently of these three wines, which brings one the realization of eternal life, is the central theme of the divine message and the essence of all religions.

21

THE MEANING OF LIFE

After a great enquiry is made regarding the depths of life one finds that the seeking of all souls is only for knowing the meaning of life.[1] Scientists look for it in their search in the realm of science, and artists find it in their art. Whatever different interests people may have, whatever they are interested in, their only inclination behind it is to find the meaning of life. And this shows that it is the nature of the soul, that the soul has come here for the purpose that it may realize, that it may understand, the meaning of life. Therefore through either a material way or a spiritual way, every soul is striving for what it longs for all the time, each in its own particular way. And this one can see even in the life of an infant. The desire of an infant to look at a thing, to tear it to pieces and see what is in it, shows that it is the soul's desire to look into life, to understand life.

No doubt the effect and the influence of life on earth is intoxicating, and through this intoxication people become so absorbed in themselves and their own interest that they, so to speak, lose the way, the way that was inborn in them. And not only in people, but even in the lower creation one finds the same attitude. In animals, in birds, the deepest desire is not looking for food or seeking for a comfortable nest—the

---

1. A talk given in Rome on November 15, 1923.

deepest tendency is to understand the nature of life, and this tendency culminates in the human being. One sees in the life of the youth the continual asking of its parents questions such as, "What does this mean?" "What does that mean?" and this shows a continual longing to know the meaning of life, a longing that continues all through life.

And what does this teach us? It teaches us the principle that the source and goal of the universe are one and the same, that the Creator created all this in order to know its own creation. But how does the Creator see and understand its creation? Not only in its highest and deepest aspect but also through every thing and every being the Creator is continually knowing and understanding its creation. For instance, if a person were to ask me, "What is art? Is it not made by humans?" I would answer, "Yes, but made by God also, through humans." And if that is the case, then what is this whole mechanism of the universe doing? It is working. Working for what purpose? Working for the understanding of itself. And what is this mechanism of the world—is it living or is it dead? All that we call living is living, and all that we call dead is living too. It is for our convenience that we say "thing" and "being." In reality there are no things, they are all beings. Only it is a gradual awakening from that witnessing aspect to the recognizing aspect. And no science, however material, will deny the truth of this, for the truth is to be realized from all things—from religion, from philosophy, from science, from art, from industry, it is to be realized from all things. The only difference is that one takes a longer way and the other takes a shorter way; one goes round about, and the other takes a straight path. There is no difference in the destination, the difference is in the way: whether one goes on foot or whether one drives, whether one is awake or whether one is asleep and is taken blindly to the destination not knowing the beauties of the way.

Destiny may be divided into two parts: one part is the mechanism that works the destiny, and the other part is the soul that knows. Therefore the mechanism is the machine and the soul within it is the engineer who is there in order to work this mechanism and to produce from it what is to be produced. There are many methods, there are many systems, there are many ways people adopt in order to know and understand; and the mind is the vehicle, the tool by the help of which, by taking this as a medium, a person experiences life in the accomplishment of this purpose. And it is therefore that in Sanskrit the mind is called *mana*, and from the word *mana* the English word *man* is derived. And that means that a person is the mind, not the body. And as the soul has its tool, according to the readiness of its tool it experiences and it knows life. It is the condition of mind that enables the soul to see life clearly. The mind is likened to water; when water is troubled there is no reflection to be seen; when the water is clear then it shows the reflection. But in the pursuit of material gain, which is what a person values the most (as it is said in the Bible, "Where your treasure is, there will your heart be also"[2]), people have become absorbed in material life and have lost the benefit of life. When, as at the present time, one defines civilization as commercial or industrial progress, that becomes the ideal of every soul; and it becomes difficult for a soul to keep that tranquility in order to accomplish that purpose for which the soul was born. Do I mean by this that industrial or commercial development is not necessary for the life of humanity? Not at all, as long as it does not ruin or hinder the life's purpose for which a person was born. Otherwise, in spite of all their progress, people have wasted their life, they have not attained the purpose for which they were born.

There are superstitions in the East, and also in the West, that animals such as horses, dogs, cats, and birds give warning of when a person is about to fall ill or die, and many have found that there is some truth in these superstitions. If one were to ask and investigate the truth in this, where lies the truth in this,

2. Matthew 6:21.

why is it then that humans do not understand and perceive life as the animals do? The answer is that the animals live a more natural life, they are nearer to nature than humans, who are taken up in their artificial life. A thinker will not deny for one moment how many things one thinks and does and says are far from what is true, from what is natural. The more one can be one with nature and one with the deeper life, the more one realizes that humans are in a continual agitation against reality. I do not mean in doing wrong or evil, but even in doing good. If animals can know this, then humans are more capable of knowing it, and it is this knowledge alone that is the satisfaction of a person's life, not all the external things, as it says in the Bible, "The spirit quickeneth, the flesh profiteth nothing."[3] Where is a person's wealth? It is in their knowledge. If it is only in the bank and not in their knowledge they do not really have that wealth, it is the property of the bank. All good and great things, values and titles, position and possession, where are they? Outside? No, outside is only that which one knows by the knowledge within, and therefore the real possession is not without but within. Therefore it is the self within, it is the heart that must be developed, it is the heart that must be in its natural rhythm and at its proper pitch. When it is tuned to its natural rhythm and pitch, then it can accomplish the purpose for which it is made.

There are five different ways by which the knowledge of life is perceived. One way is known to many of us, though to woman perhaps more than to man, and that is impression. Very often a person comes into the house or one meets a person, and before one has spoken to that person one gets a kind of impression, either or unpleasant, a certain knowledge of that person's being. Sometimes at the sight of a person one feels, "Keep away"; sometimes at first glance one feels drawn to that person, without knowing why. The mind does not know, but the soul does. It is not only that one gets an impression of a

---

3. John 6:63.

person whom one meets, but if one is sensitive to impressions, one can also feel the impression of a letter that comes to one from a stranger. And there are many who say that they know someone's character, or physiognomy, or phrenology, but if they have not the sense of impression in their heart, even if they read a thousand books on physiognomy or phrenology, they would never get the impression in their heart. And what does it show? It shows that true knowledge, from beginning to end, does not belong to the material realm.

And then there is another way, that is the intuitive way, by which one knows before one does something whether it will be a success or whether it will be a failure. There are some more intuitive people who feel this before doing anything, before undertaking anything, and it is not rare; it is very often found to be the case that people know before doing anything what the result will be.

But then there is a third way, and that is the dream or the vision. Some will say that dreams have meaning, and there are many who will say that there is no meaning in a dream. But in point of fact there is nothing in this world that has no meaning, there is no situation, no action, no word that has not its meaning. All that one does with intention and all that is done without intention has a meaning behind it, if one only can understand it. The reason why one should see more clearly in a dream than when awake is that when one is in a dream one's mind is naturally concentrated. For when one is in the waking state all that is perceived through the senses calls one's attention at every moment. No doubt the impression or intuition of a true dream is not manifested to every soul and it is manifested to one soul more than to another; and neither does everyone live always in the rhythm and tune in which to receive impressions and intuitions. No, at different times one's impression differs, and it shows that in accordance with one's evolution one is able to experience the knowledge of life. The more evolved one is spiritually, the more naturally one receives from within the knowledge of life.

And the fourth way in which one perceives the knowledge of life is what may be called inspiration. It may come to an artist, it may come to a musician, it may come to a poet. At the time when it has come one can write or compose or do something that afterward one will be surprised at and wonder whether one really did it, or if someone else did it. If it were not for that inspiration that same poet might strive for six months and would not be able to write that verse that was written in three minutes' time. And what is the explanation of it? Is it by the development of one's mind that one receives inspiration? No, it is by the receiving quality of one's mind, it is the purity of one's mind, it is one's absorption in the art, the direction in which one has devoted one's life. The great souls whose inspirational works have become immortal, where have they got them from? They have got them from inspiration. And how did they get this? They got it by forgetting themselves, by being absorbed in the object of their love. That is the meaning of sacrifice, sacrificing to the beauty of the ideal. One has to place the ideal before one, that is the way to get it.

And then one step further there comes realization, which may be called revelation. When the soul is tuned to that state then the eyes and ears of the heart are open to see and hear the word that comes from all sides. In point of fact every atom of this world, either in heaven or earth, speaks, and speaks aloud. It is the deaf ears of the heart and the closed eyes of the soul that prevent one from seeing it and hearing it. There is a verse of a Hindustani poet that says, "O self, it is not the fault of the Divine Beloved that you do not see that one, that you do not hear that one. That one is continually before you and is continually speaking to you. If you do not hear it and if you do not see it, it is your own fault." It is for this purpose that every soul has been created, and it is in the fulfillment of this that one fulfills the object of God. When that spark that is found in every heart, that spark that may be called the divine spark in one, is blown upon and the flame arises, the whole life becomes illuminated and one hears and sees and knows and understands. A Sufi poet said that every leaf of the tree becomes like a page of the sacred book when the heart is open to read it and when the soul has opened its eyes.

22

THE INNER LIFE

There is one aspect of life that is known to us, which we call our everyday life.[1] The consciousness of doing all that we do in our everyday life is called the outer life. And there is a part of our life of which we are very often unconscious, and it is that part of our life which may be called the inner life. To be without inner life means to be without one arm or one leg or one eye or one ear; but even this simile does not sufficiently illustrate the idea of the inner life. The reason is that the inner life is much greater and nobler and much more powerful than the outer life. Humankind gives a great importance to the outer life, being absorbed in it from morning till evening, and not being conscious of another aspect of life that may be called the inner life. It is therefore that all that matters to people is what happens to them in their outer life; and the occupation of the outer life keeps them so absorbed that they hardly have a moment to think of the inner life. The disadvantage of not being conscious of the inner life is incomparably greater than all the advantage that one can derive by being conscious of the outer life, in which one always is.

The reason for this is that the inner life makes one richer, and the outer life, poorer. With all its riches and treasures that the

1. Lecture given in September 1922 in Katwijk, the Netherlands.

earth can offer, humankind is poor. And very often the richer one is, the poorer one is; for the greater the riches, the more the limitation one finds in one's life. The inner life makes one powerful, whereas the outer life and its consciousness makes one weak. It makes one weak because it is the consciousness of limitation. The consciousness of the inner life makes one powerful, because it is the consciousness of perfection. The outer life keeps one confused. However intellectual or learned people may be, they are never clear. Their knowledge is based upon reasons that are founded upon outer things, things that are liable to change and destruction. That is why, however wise those people may seem to be, their wisdom has limitations. What today one thinks right, after four days one thinks perhaps wrong. The inner life makes the mind clear. The reason is that it is the part of one's being that may be called divine, the essence of life, the pure intelligence. The phenomenon of it is that wherever the light of pure intelligence is thrown, things become clear. The absorption in the outer life, without what the inner life gives, makes one blind. All one says, thinks, or does is based upon outer experiences; and no one can realize to what extent the power gained by the inner life enables humankind to see through life. There exists the belief in the third eye. In reality, the third eye is the inner eye, the eye that is opened by one's wakening to the inner life.

Therefore, inner life, in other words, may be called the spiritual life. One can see it in the forest, that it is the rain from above that makes the forest beautiful, which means that what the forest needs is not all that it has, but it needs something that comes from above: the light, the rain. It is the sun and rain that make the forest complete. And in the desert there is no rain, and therefore, it is only one aspect; there is the earth, but there is no water, water from above. The water that gives life to the forest, that water is not to be found in the desert. The desert is unhappy as a person in the desert is unhappy, looking for a shade from the hot sun, because the desert is longing. And the person in the desert is longing too, for something that person cannot find. Whereas in the thick forest there is a joy, there is an inspiration, the heart is lifted up, because the forest is the picture of the inner life. It is not only the earth, not only the trees and plants, but because something that it needs has been sent upon it. And so it is with humanity. Those who are solely occupied with the things of the world are in the outer life; in the midst of the world they may be, but they are in the desert. But it is the inner life that produces in them, not artificial virtues and not human-made qualities, but such virtues that can only rise from the inner life besides the insight that makes the eyes see more than the mortal eyes can see.

And now the question is, how are we to be sure that this is an inner life? What proof is there? And the answer is there is not one moment in our life when we do not see the proof of inner life, only we do not look for it. All different communications, such as telegraphy and the telephone and new communications that are coming—radio and X-rays and all new inventions that make a person wonder how much humanity has accomplished—if one saw that all these machines and all these inventions are nothing but a little imitation, a poor imitation of what this human body is, of the human being—if only one knew what the human being is! Humankind is the center of joy, of happiness, of peace, of power, of life, and light. The phenomenon that can be vouchsafed to humanity is much greater than any other machine, if only one had the patience and perseverance to explore one's self. Only what we do is explore the others. When it comes to analysis, one thinks it is a great study to analyze things; and when one analyzes human nature, one calls it psychology. People analyze all others except themselves, and therefore, true psychology is never reached, because the real psychology is to analyze oneself first; and when one's self is analyzed, then one is able to analyze others.

If one only knew that besides what one says or does or thinks, and the effect of what one says, does, or thinks that is manifest to one, there is another action of the same that creates something in one's life that makes one's world. And perhaps in a week or in a month, or perhaps in a year or ten years, that which one has created one day comes before one as a world, as a world created by oneself. Such is the phenomenon of life. How insignificant a human being appears to be, just like a drop in the water; and at the same time, what effect one creates by every thought, by every feeling, by every act! And what influence it spreads, and what influence it has on the lives of the others! If one only knew, one would find that the outer life and the results of all one thinks, says, or does in the outer life are much smaller, incomparably smaller than the results produced by everything one thinks, says, or does in the inner life. It is therefore the inner life that makes humankind more responsible than the consciousness of the outer life. The responsibilities of the outer life, compared with the responsibilities of the inner life, are much smaller. For the moment they might appear to be heavy burdens, but they are nothing compared with the responsibilities one has with one's inner life. If one sees what one creates, the responsibility is much greater. As they say, in the Eastern language, of the chukar,[2] the donkey seems to be much happier than the chukar, which is the most intelligent bird. Those in the outer life seem quite pleased, because their responsibilities are less, their outlook small, their horizon narrow, and what they see of the world very little. But when the horizon is opened, when the heart has penetrated through the barrier that divides the here and hereafter, when one begins to see behind the veil, and all that appears on the surface becomes a screen behind which something else is hidden, then one experiences life quite differently. The view of the one who stands on the top of the mountain is quite different from the view of the one who stands at the bottom of the mountain. Both are human beings, both have the same eyes, but the horizon of one is different from the horizon of the other. Inner life, therefore,

2. A Eurasian partridge.

means the widening of the horizon and the change of direction of seeing.

In the English language they call a mystic a seer; *seer* means the "one who sees." In the East there is a quotation of a great Yogi, who says, "In order to see what is before you, you must see within yourself." And this means that within yourself there is a mirror, and it is that mirror which may be called the inner world, the inner life. It is in this mirror that all that is before you is reflected. But when the eyes are looking outside, then one has turned one's back to the mirror that is inside. But when the eyes are turned inside, then one sees in this mirror all that is outside reflected. Therefore, all seeing by this process is so clear and manifests to such fullness that, in comparison, the vision that one has before one's eyes is a blurred or confused vision. Two people may live together for twenty-five years, for forty, fifty years, and may not be able to understand one another for the lack of the inner life; and the inner life would enable them to understand one another in one moment. When they said that the twelve apostles began to understand the language of all nations,[3] did they learn the grammar of all nations at that moment? No, they learned the language of the heart. The language of the heart speaks louder than words can speak. If the ears of the heart were open to hear that language, the outer words would not be necessary.

With all the progress that humanity is making, it still is most limited; and the more you see the limitations of this process, the more you find that it is limited because of the absence of the inner life. When you see, in the traditions and histories of the past, how many thieves there used to be, and robbers and murderers, and how many murders there were committed, one thinks what a horrid time it was. And yet when one thinks more about it, one sees that the time at present is much worse, and the time of robbers and murderers was much milder. One or two persons in a village were murdered; now towns and

---

3. Acts 2:1–11.

countries are swept away. One war has swept away such a large number of humanity.[4] Imagine if another war comes—what will be the result? They say people have progressed, they are more thoughtful. But, with all thoughtfulness, we have progressed to cause all the destruction and disasters that we find in a much greater degree. Does it mean that humanity is not progressing? It is progressing, but in which direction? Downward.

The condition of going in the path of the inner life is to be free first, in order to walk in that path. If the feet are pinned and the hands are nailed by beliefs, by preconceived ideas, by thoughts that one has, then people stand; they have every desire to go, but they are not going because they are holding on to something. Certain beliefs that they have—what they believed or what they thought—they are holding on to them; they are not going on, they are not going forward. And therefore, many with many good qualities and high ideals, and with religious tendencies, with devotional temperament, with all the spiritual qualities that one may have, can still stand in the same place. Either their ideas are holding them as pins or nails in the feet, or the hands are somewhere leaning on the railings and holding it, and they are not going further.

What the inner life requires first is the freedom to proceed. The old meaning of freedom is very little understood, although everyone is seeking freedom. They say so much about freedom, but one can be free of all things except one thing, and that is the self. That is the last thing one thinks about. The conception of freedom is quite different at this time. Therefore, while seeking freedom people become anything but free, because they are caught in the trap of their own selves. That is the greatest captivity there is, and there they remain, as a jinn in the bottle. Besides that, the inner life requires sacrifice. As people consider their learning, their qualification, everything in their life is in order to be better qualified to gain all that they can in the world: power or possession or wealth or anything. And sacri-

---

4. World War I.

fice is quite a contrary way to gain; therefore, one develops in oneself the nature of gaining instead of sacrificing. Besides, sacrifice requires a large mind, sacrifice requires deep sympathies, sacrifice requires great love; sacrifice is the most difficult thing. The inner life is something that is within oneself. It has been called a chamber of divine light in one's own heart. And the door remains closed until an effort is made to open it, and that effort is a sacrifice. In biblical terms there is a word—*self-denial*—but it is always misinterpreted by people. Self-denial, as people think generally, is to deny all that is good and beautiful, all that is worth attaining. Really, self-denial is not to deny all that is good and beautiful to the self, but to deny the self—and that is the last thing one wishes to deny. And the automatic action of this denial opens this door to the inner life.

And now, coming to the path of sages. The sages who have realized the inner life have realized it by the contemplative method. Humanity, from its infancy, is unaware of something within that is more than a faculty. By experiencing life through the outer senses, this faculty, which is the faculty of inner life—I use the word *faculty* because it expresses it a little better—this faculty, by not using it, becomes closed, just as if a door of a chamber of joy and light and of life is closed. And as from infancy one has not experienced the joy and the life and the light of this chamber, which may be called a celestial chamber in the human heart, one remains unaware of it, except for the feeling that one sometimes has and that one remains unconscious of. And sometimes when one is deeply touched, or sometimes when one has deeply suffered, sometimes when life has showed its hideous face, at such times or after an illness or by the help of meditation this feeling, which is unconsciously working there as a longing to unfold itself, this feeling becomes manifest. In what way? In love for solitude, in sympathy for others, in a tendency to sincerity, in the form of inspiration of all that is good and beautiful.

It may manifest in the form of emotion, love, affection; in the form of inspiration; in the form of a revelation, vision, art, or poetry or music. In whatever form one allows it to express itself or one happens to be busy with, in that form it begins to manifest. And therefore, it is all spiritual when this door of the chamber of the heart is once open. If one is a musician, then one's music is celestial; if one is a poet, then one's poetry is spiritual; if one is an artist, then one's art is a spiritual work. Whatever one may do in life, that divine spirit manifests. One need not be a religious person, one need not be a philosopher, one need not be a mystic. Only that which was hidden within and which was keeping one incomplete in life, begins to manifest to view. That makes life perfect; that enables a person to express life to its fullness. Every attempt made today to better the condition of humanity by politics, by education, by social reconstruction, and by many other ways—all these, with excellent plans, can only be fulfilled if this something that was missing was added to them. But in the absence of this, all efforts of many, many years will prove to be fatal. For this something that is missing is the most essential of all things. The world cannot remain a world without rainfall. The world cannot progress without a spiritual stimulus, a spiritual awakening. If that is not the first thing—it is natural that it is not the first thing—still it can be the last thing; and if it is not even the last thing, then it is a pity.

Now, I should like to explain what reason I will give for the awakening of the meditative souls, how are they awakened, how would they experience the inner life. In the first place, the adept values the object of attaining the inner life more than anything else in life. As long as one does not value it, so long one remains unable to attain to it. That is the first condition: that one values the inner life more than anything else in the world—wealth or power, position, rank, or anything. It does not mean that one must not be in pursuit in this world of things one needs; it means one must give the greatest value to something that is really worthwhile. The next thing is that when one begins to give value to something, one thinks it is worthwhile to give time. Because today in the modern world, they say time is money; and money means the most valuable thing. If that which is money, if that which is precious, one gives to something one considers most worthwhile—more than anything else in the world—then no doubt that is the next step toward the inner life. And the third thing is that the condition of the mind is relieved of the pressure that always is in a person's heart while thinking that, "I have not done what I ought to have done toward my fellow human being"—be it one's father or mother, child, husband, wife, brother, friend, whoever it is—or "What I was expected to do toward the persons with whom I am put, or in the condition I am in, I have not done it." If that pressure is troubling the mind, then that mind is not yet fit. A person will give time to contemplation and spiritual life; but at the same time, if the mind is disturbed, the heart is not at rest, feeling, "I have not done my duty. I have a debt to pay to someone." It is a most essential point that the adept considers that any debt to be paid in life does not remain unpaid. When we look at life, is it not a marketplace? The give-and-take is to be seen in everything, and for what one has not paid just now, the bill will be presented afterward. People think: "I have gained without paying." They must wait till they realize that they will have to pay it with interest added to it. In what form one takes, in what form one gives, one is seldom aware of it. In giving service, kindness, sympathy it may be that one gives service, sympathy, kindness, money, all that one has, to the north; and from the south it comes, it comes back. When once one takes from the west, to the east one has to pay. Only people do not know in what form they have to pay, in what form they take. Very often they do not know when they take, what they give; but in give-and-take, every moment of their life is occupied. And with all the injustice of the word, it all adjusts itself in the end. It is the clear idea of this condition that shows that it all balances. If there was no balance of this, the world would not exist. This ever-moving world, turning round and round—what holds it? What makes it stand? It is the balance. It is not only the world that is going on, but everything is going on, the whole of life in its own way. What keeps it existing? It is the balance that holds it. We do not know that balance, being occupied by our worldly life. But when the inner eye is opened and one sees life keenly, one will find that it is a continual balancing process going on, and we are as particles of one mechanism that is constantly busy keeping this balance. When once the heart is at rest by the thought that one has paid, or one is paying one's debts, then one has come to a balanced condition. That balanced condition brings about a balance in one's life. That balance creates a condition in which the heart, which is likened to the sea, becomes then not a restless sea, as it is in the storm, but a calm sea, undisturbed water; and it is that condition which enables one to experience the inner life even better.

Do we not see in our everyday life the presence of persons who have not that tranquility, that peace, that calmness, and what influence it has—a terrible influence upon themselves and a disastrous influence upon others. One realizes it in one's everyday life if one sees it. One may be sitting in the office with someone, one may be standing in a place, one may be staying in the house where other people are standing or sitting, and one can realize by a person's atmosphere whether that person has reached a state of balance, tranquility, calm, and peace, or whether that person is in a state that is not rhythmic, not balanced. This again gives us an idea that what we call happiness and unhappiness is one's state: a balanced state or unbalanced state. When people are in a normal state in which their minds and hearts ought to be, in that state they are in a normal state; they need not seek for happiness, they are happiness itself, they radiate happiness. When that state is disturbed, they are unhappy. It is not that unhappiness comes to them, but they themselves are unhappiness. In Hindu terms, a Hindu idea is that *self* means "happiness," the depth of the self is happiness, which means all this structure which is outside—the physical body, the breath, the senses of perception, all these that make a person—all these stand outside; but their inner being can only be called by one name, and that is happiness. It is natural, therefore, that all are seeking after happiness, not knowing where to get it, always seeking for it outside of themselves. Therefore, instead of finding that happiness that is their own, they want to take away the happiness of another. And what happens? That neither can they get the happiness of another, nor can they give it. By trying to get it from another, they cause sorrow to the other, and the sorrow comes to them. There are very few robbers who go in the houses of others and steal; but there are so many robbers of happiness, and they seldom know they rob others of happiness. But the robbers of happiness are more foolish than the robbers who are after wealth, because when the robbers of wealth are successful they get something; but the robbers of happiness never get something, they only give sorrow to others.

Inner life, therefore, must not be considered, as many have thought it to be: a life that is in the forest or in the cave of the mountain or a retired life. Yes, there is a need for certain people who seek for solitude. They prefer to be away from the midst of the world, those whose inspiration is stimulated by being alone, who feel themselves when they are by themselves. But this is not a necessity of attaining to that happiness. One can be in the midst of the world, and one can stand above the world. Life has many woes, and the only way of getting rid of it is to stand above them all. And it is this that can be attained by one and only one thing, and that is the discovering of the inner life.

23

THE INNER LIFE AND SELF-REALIZATION

Beloved Ones of God, my subject this evening is the inner life and self-realization.[1] It is by the inner life that self-realization is achieved. Life can be divided into two parts. One part of our life is attending to our worldly necessities, toiling, earning money, serving in different capacities in order to live ourselves and in order to look after our families. That is one side of life. And the other side is to think that there is something besides the worldly life, that there is a higher ideal, a greater happiness, that there is a deeper insight into life, and that there is a greater peace. That is another life. By inner life I do not at all mean a religious life, for a person may be religious and at the same time be very worldly.

There is a story of Aurangzeb's reign in India, that he had announced a royal command that everyone inhabiting in his dominions must attend each of the five prayers of the faithful. And there was a sage, but no one knew that he was a sage; he lived in solitude, and he also received this command. But he forgot it, or he did not think about it. And then the police were sent to bring him to the house of prayer. Naturally, he came and joined the congregation. But once the man who leads the prayer for the others began to lead the prayer, this sage ran

---

1. A talk given at the Fine Arts Building, Chicago, May 5, 1926.

away from the congregation within five seconds. The police went after him, and he was again brought before the judge, for he had not only violated the first law, but disturbed the whole congregation, by running away. He said to the judge, "I would like to know what is meant by the leader of the prayer." The judge said, "According to religion your thoughts should be united with the thoughts of your leader." The sage said, "That is what I did. The leader's thought went to his house. He had forgotten his keys at home. So I could not stand in the house of prayer. I ran for the keys. Wherever the leader's thought led me, I ran there." They found out in the end that it was so. This was a great sage and to him was known all that was going on in the minds of others. Therefore, to be religious, to be orthodox, or to be pious does not necessarily mean to be spiritual. To be spiritual is quite different than being "prayerful," as they say.

And now I shall come to the question: How does one proceed in the inner life? One first takes the inner life as a journey, a journey to a desired goal. And there are certain conditions on this journey that one should first know. In the first place, the journey is hard, because there are no electric trains. It is a journey we have to make on foot. This at once changes the character of the journey, makes it different from a traditional journey. There is no equipment as we have today. Therefore, we have forgotten the journey of the past, how one would have to go through the wilderness, over mountains, crossing rivers, swimming to get to the other side, risking all sorts of dangers on the way—that is the kind of journey one has to make in spiritual attainment. The outer journeys are made easy today, but the inner journey has kept its difficulties. And the first condition of this journey is conscientiousness of the customs of this journey. The first thing is that as soon as one has to walk long distances, one gives up unnecessary burdens. And so we have to give up many things in this life in order to make this journey. We unconsciously make our life so heavy for ourselves, and since outwardly it may not seem difficult to have it be heavy, yet when we begin to journey inwardly we realize how difficult it is to carry a heavy load. When we have to walk on foot, every little responsibility we take upon us, every little habit, all weigh upon ourselves, little things that in everyday life we never think about. We become addicted to comforts more and more, intolerant of our environment more and more, sensitive to jarring influences more and more. Instead of becoming stronger we become weaker every day. And when it comes to journeying and facing the difficulties that will come in the journey, it becomes very difficult. You must remember that everyone at every time of the world's history who has tried to go farther in the spiritual path has met with difficulties. The moment one starts on this path, one has more difficulties than the average person; and greater and greater temptations that perhaps had never come before appear on one's way. The moment one takes this path, temptations of all kinds come. One is tested and tried at every step one takes. Besides, one is taken to task. If one does not do it oneself, one is taken to task very seriously. Others are not taken to task so seriously. And this is natural. If a child breaks a glass one overlooks it, one says, "Why! It is natural." But if the maid breaks a glass one asks, "Why did you do it? Did you not see it?" For a grown-up person is responsible. The one who takes the spiritual path, then, is responsible. Therefore, there is a greater exacting; one has to answer for everything one does, either to oneself or to life.

Besides, friends, we have in our lives many debts to pay, debts that we don't always know. We only know our money debts. But there are many others: the husband to wife, and the wife to husband; mother to child, and child to mother; the debts to pay to our friends and acquaintances, to those close to us, near to us, to those who stand above us, and those who are dependent upon us. There are so many different kinds of debts we have to pay; and yet we never think about them. In ancient times, even those not taking the spiritual path, for instance, nobles and warriors, had the law of chivalry, and they were very much about paying debts. The way ancient people thought about their mother was that, "My mother has brought me up from my infancy, from my childhood, sacrificed her sleep, rest, and comfort, and loved me with the love that is beyond any other love in this world, and has shown in life that mercy that is the compassion of God." And the child thought so much about the debt it had toward its mother. Someone went to the Prophet Muhammad and asked him, "Prophet, you said there is a great debt to be paid to the mother. Suppose I gave all that I have earned, will that pay her back?" The Prophet said, "No, not in the least. If you served her for your whole life, even then you cannot pay the debt of what she has done for you in one day." He said, "Why? How?" The Prophet said, "When she brought you up, she thought that even when she is gone you would live; she has not only given her service and heart and love to you, but also her life. That you will live after her, that has been all her thought. And what is your thought? If you are a kind and good person, your thought is, "As long as my poor mother is living, I will care for her to the end; one day she will die, and then I shall be free." It is a different thought compared to her thought.

This is only one example I give. But there are many other debts, to our neighbors, to strangers, to those who depend upon us or who expect from us some help, some counsel, a word of advice, some service. They are all debts we have to pay. There is also much to pay to God, but God can forgive. But the debt to the world, that debt must not be forgotten before entering on the spiritual path. The spirit feels a great release when it pays its debts as it goes on further. Do we think of these simple things these days? As soon as a thought is given to the spiritual path, the first question is, "What occult books shall we read?" We never think about these little things and how much depends upon them. When we think of spiritual things, we think, "If I only could get the key to that path." But there is a condition that must be fulfilled, and that condition is our consideration for every soul.

And now one may ask, "What if they don't deserve it, if they are not worthy of it?" That is not our concern, whether they deserve it or not. We do not think about it. When there is money to be paid to a moneylender it must be paid, whether the lender deserves it or not. And so it is in the spiritual path. Those to whom we have to pay we have to pay, in the way of attention, service, respect. All that is due to anyone, we have to pay. And in the first place, apart from spiritual realization, we feel such a release after having paid our debt to everyone to whom it is due. This also opens up for us the light of the soul, making the way straight and illuminating the way, so that this confusion one always feels in oneself when striving to progress spiritually disappears. If not, there is always this confusion.

And now we come to understand what is the next step necessary on the spiritual path, and that is to develop our tendency to trust. A person who wants to go along the spiritual path must have a greater desire to trust than the average person. No doubt, the world is going from bad to worse today. Promises have no value. One values a ten-cent stamp much more than a word of honor, because that is sure. Since this is the state of the world, it is difficult for a person to develop the tendency to trust. But once you begin to tread the spiritual path, trust is the first thing necessary. Very often a person says, "Well, I would like to trust people, but people are not worthy of trust." Yes, I say that is a practical way to think about it in business, but when it comes to another life, social life or the life of spiritual attainment, there you should not look at it in this way. There you only can develop the tendency of trusting others by being ready to undergo every loss. It is not always foolish to trust. On the contrary, it is the wise who trusts more than the foolish one. Besides, it is not a weakness to trust, it is a strength; and those who have less trust are weak, and every day makes them weaker. Those who do not trust outsiders then cannot trust their own relatives, their own friends, and then that distrust develops to such an extent that they do not trust themselves. That is the end.

There is a story of a great Sufi, who in his early life was a robber. Once there was a man traveling through the desert in a caravan, and he had a purse full of coins and he wanted to entrust them to someone because he heard robbers were about. He looked around and saw a tent at some distance. And he saw a man sitting there looking most dignified. So he said, "Will you please keep this purse, for I am afraid that if the robbers will come they will take it." The man said, "Give it to me, I will keep it." When the traveler came back to the caravan he found that robbers had come and taken all the money of the others. He thanked God that he had given his purse to someone to keep. When he returned to the tent he saw the robbers and this most dignified man all sitting there, dividing the shares of each. Then he realized that this was the chief of the robbers. He thought, "I was more foolish than all the others, for I gave my money to a thief. Who can be more foolish than me?" And then he was frightened and began to step back. But as soon as they saw him begin to return, this chief called to him and said, "Where are you going? Why did you come here?" He said, "I came here to get my purse back, but I found that I gave it to the same party from whom I wanted to keep it away." The man said, "You gave me your purse, is it not so? You trusted it to me, and it was not robbed from you. How can I take it away? Did you not trust me? How can you expect me to take it from you? Here is your purse, you take it." This act of trustworthiness impressed the robbers so much that they followed the example of their chief. They gave up robbery. It moved them to the bottom of their being to feel what trust means. And in his later days this chief accomplished great spiritual work. This shows, friends, that by distrusting perhaps we avoid a little loss, but the distrust that we have sown in our heart, that is a still greater loss.

And the third step in the inner life is to find someone in life in whose guidance we can trust. You might find a spiritual teacher who may be as great as an angel, and yet if you have no trust, that teacher can do very little for you. Besides, if you found a spiritual guide who did not prove trustworthy to you, your loss would be smaller than the loss of that teacher. The loss of that teacher is greater. Nevertheless, the whole of spiritual progress under the guidance of a teacher depends upon the extent you have trust in the teacher's guidance. If there is no trust, all the teachings and practice of occult laws will amount to nothing. This is the one thing.

The people in the United States who are seeking after truth must know the place of the teacher in their lives, the importance of a spiritual guide and his or her guidance, and learn to value it and consider it sacred. And if that is not there then nothing is there. Then a person is a lost sheep. And this tendency of going from one thing to another, from one teacher to another, is an offense to the teacher, to God, and to oneself. By this one accomplishes nothing.

Dear friends, in my youth my interest in the spiritual path was great, and I came in contact with the teacher in whose hand I was destined to be initiated. And one thing my teacher said was, "No matter how great a teacher comes, once you have taken this initiation, this blessing from my hands, your faith may not change." Having had a modern education, I wondered how to think about this. I did not doubt, but I thought, "What does it mean?" And with every step further in my life, I found out that this alone is the right way. When the mind is disturbed, and a person is distrustful and goes first to one teacher and then to another method, what can one find in that person? There is no ideal there. In a university education one may study under one professor and then under another, and so on. That is all right for a university. That is another kind of education. But when it comes to spiritual education, idealism is necessary.

In a village there was once a young peasant who was known to be a great seeker after truth. A great teacher came to that village, and it was announced that "Whoever will come in the presence of this teacher, for those the doors of heaven will be open, and they will be admitted there without having to account for their deeds." So the peasants were very excited about it, and they all went there in the presence of the teacher except for this young man who was known to be a great seeker after truth. The teacher said, "Everyone from the village came to me, except that young man. I shall go to him myself." So he came to the cottage of this young man and said, "What is it? Is it that you are antagonistic to me, or that you doubt my knowledge? What is it that kept you from coming to see me?" And he said, "There was nothing that kept me back except one thing. That was the announcement. I heard the announcement that, 'Everyone in your presence would be admitted to heaven, without question.' And I don't seek that admission, because although I had a teacher once I don't know where he is, in heaven or in hell. If I went to heaven and he was in the other place, it would be different for me. Heaven would become hell for me. I would rather be with my teacher. It does not matter where he is."

That is the ideal the seekers after truth have about their spiritual teacher. And it is with that idealism that they are able to go further and gain the confidence of their teacher. Today the tendency is different. Pupils begin to weigh and measure the teacher before they have started on the spiritual path. They want to know whether the teacher fits in with their idea or whether the teacher does not fit in with their idea; they do not come to learn. But when it comes to teaching it is a different idea altogether. This is what is keeping thousands of people back: they say they are seeking a teacher, but they think they are teachers themselves.

And when we go still further still, it is not only the faith and devotion one has for one's teacher, but also the effacing of one's self. Because the teacher's work is like that of a goldsmith who melts the gold and then turns it into an ornament. Therefore, the teacher has to test and try, mold and melt before he or she can use the pupil for a better purpose. If a pupils cannot give themselves to that molding, then they will have a difficult time. For instance, the king of Bukhara once went to Afghanistan, giving up his kingdom to get spiritual guidance. And the first thing the teacher gave him to do was to dust all the rooms of the pupils. The pupils were poor and rich, all kinds, but none was a king. They all felt so sorry for this man who once was a king and who now had to dust the rooms, a kind of work he had never done before. They said nothing, but one day they could not keep this feeling from coming to them, "It is a pity, this man should do this work. He is so nice and kind and gentle, such a fine man, to have to do this work!" They came to the teacher and said, "Teacher, will you not give this work to one of us? It pains us to see this man who has been a king, who lived in palaces, who is now dusting rooms." "My pupils," said the teacher, "you must wait. I don't think the time has come." They said, "It gives us a great pain." "Well," he then said, "I will tell one of you what to do, and then we shall see." One day this young man was taking a little basket, the wastepaper basket, and one of them pushed it so that it turned over and everything went on the floor. And the king had to gather it up. So the king looked at the man and said, "Well, if I was what I was before, I would have showed you what it means, such mischief." And then the king gathered it all up and went away. And this report reached the teacher, who said, "Did I not tell you, the time is not yet there." Then again someone did a similar thing. And the king stood and looked at him and wanted to say something, but did not. And the report went to the teacher and he said, "Not yet." A third time something of a similar kind was done. The king did not even look. He went his way. And the teacher said, "Now, the time has come."

One might ask, "Is it not a weakness to be so passive?" Yes, if one were so passive from weakness it would be weakness. But if one is so passive from thought then it is a strength, for it requires great strength to dominate one's own self. One's self has a silent influence as is shown in the story of Daniel. It was the power of his self. Friends, it is easy to tame a lion, but difficult to tame one's self. One's self can be horrible, more horrible than a lion. One may say, "How gentle, how melted, how thoughtful I have become," but then there may be moments that one acts quite differently, to one's astonishment. And to really dominate that crude nature is a melting process. Then when the gold is melted one can turn it to any ornament one likes.

And when we go still further in the spiritual path, it becomes the path of power, of concentration. The mind is just like a restive horse that will not stay quiet, that cannot be controlled. And once one begins to practice concentration, one finds even more difficulty in making one's mind obey. As long as one does not try, one does not know, but the moment one begins one realizes how very difficult it is to concentrate one's mind.

There is a story of Farid who was sent to the forest by his mother because he wanted to meditate, to communicate with nature, and wanted to find God. He developed the nature of concentration. Then he came to a teacher who asked him, "Is there anything in your domestic life that you love or like?" He answered, "I have no friends. I have always been in the wilderness. But at home there is a cow. That is the one being I like." The teacher said, "Well, I will ask you to think of this cow." He said, "Yes." All other pupils had different objects to concentrate and meditate upon. While they were doing their work, they would sit for five minutes, and then they would go out. In this way they were practicing. One day, when the teacher wanted to speak before his pupils, he said, "Where is the new pupil?" They said, "We have not seen him all these days when we were playing together. The teacher said, "Perhaps he is sitting where I told him to practice." The teacher went himself and asked him to come. The first time he called him he did not answer. The second time he answered in the same sound as the cow.

The teacher said, "Come out." He said, "I cannot come out the door, I have long horns." The teacher showed it to his pupils; he said, "This is called concentration. You are all playing. If he can turn into a cow by concentrating upon the cow, then there is nothing he cannot turn into."

That is the secret of all things. What is meant by concentration is to change the identification of the soul, so that it may be able to lose the false conception of identification and identify with the true self instead of with the false self. That is what is meant by self-realization. Once a person realizes the self by the proper way of concentration, by the way of contemplation, of meditation, that one has understood the essence of all religions. Because all religions are only different ways that lead to one truth, and that truth is self-realization.

* * *

Question: *What part of God do animals express? Animals and vegetables, in what does their soul differ from man?*

Answer: The difference is in their bodies and minds. That the soul is the ray and as the ray it is one and the same. But the body adorns itself in accordance with the fineness of that soul, whether greater or smaller, or with more or less intelligence. Apart from the degree in which animals and vegetables differ from humans, among people you will find the same. Some have vegetable quality, some animal quality, some human, and some angelic quality. Among Hindus there used to be a custom that when they married, their friends used to take their horoscope to the Brahmin. But he saw little in the horoscope. For he was a psychologist and he focused on the question as to what category the both persons belong. Was it angelic, human, animal, or still denser? Then he found out if there was a vast distance between the categories, and then he saw that it was not the right thing to marry. Therefore, they used to say, "The planets are not right." In this way he avoided many disasters by knowing psychology and not thinking about the pose and position of the stars.

Question: *One who is of lower evolution cannot love a higher object. When two beings love one another who are not equal, and yet the one who is lower loves the other who is of higher evolution, it is the higher object in this case that the lower loves and will not the person who is highly evolved lose love of those of lower evolution?*

Answer: In a few words, what I would like to say is this, that when a person of higher evolution loves a person of lower evolution, perhaps the love becomes greater, the heart larger, the feeling more intense, the love reaches far. People would be surprised; at the same time it is so. Who could ever think of Christ having such love and such friendship with the fishermen with whom he had his dinner; and with those he met he poured his love on them, and those who were of the same evolution as he, he despised them, disliked them. The higher you advance, the greater is your love, and it is to be spread somewhere. You just spread it. And now the question of a person of lower evolution who cannot love a person of higher evolution, there are some reasons for it. In the first place a person is very often blind to appreciate a beauty that they cannot reach. And therefore, a person may have within their neighborhood the most beautiful personality, a saintly soul with all virtues and goodness, and yet may not appreciate them because that person is not evolved enough to appreciate them. It is therefore that it is said in *In an Eastern Rose Garden* that a person of lower evolution cannot love a person of higher evolution. And sometimes if those who are lower love someone higher, it is because of that one's power, which holds them. Those lower are bound by it, but not from the bottom of their heart: they cannot resist it. But at the same time, they have no love because they cannot admire the beauty that rises above their view.

Question: *Why should it be necessary in order to arrive at spiritual attainment to seek the guidance of a personality other than oneself?*

Answer: If a person is self-sufficient, if a person is satisfied and guided by the light from within, that person should not seek any personality. But I have never seen a child born having learned all the language, that never needed help from his mother or father. And as it is necessary for an infant to learn from someone, so to learn the heavenly language it is necessary to learn from someone who knows it. But at the same time, if one is satisfied with one's inner light, that is the best thing to be.

Concentration is focusing of mind on form. Contemplation is focusing of mind on an idea. Meditation is raising of the consciousness.

24

THE INTERDEPENDENCE OF LIFE WITHIN AND WITHOUT

Beloved Ones of God, I would like to speak this afternoon on the subject of the interdependence of life within and without.[1] It is the lack of this one knowledge that makes one live in confusion, in a mist. One asks for the cause of everything, and one does not know the cause. The first thing to understand in connection with this subject is that the individual is a mechanism as well as an engineer. There is a part of one's being that is merely a mechanism, and there is another part of one's being that is an engineer. If the part of one's being that is a mechanism overpowers, in other words, covers that part in one that is the engineer, then that person becomes a machine, working under the influence of all that it comes in touch with. The influences of the finer world and the influences of the grosser world—influences of all kinds—acting upon that person, keep him or her in working order every moment of the day; whether that working is in one's favor or disfavor, whether against one's will or according to one's will. If it is according to one's will, it is a good accident; if it is against one's will, it is a misfortune. Will has a great part to play in life. But if the will is hidden under that mechanism, then it has no more power over that

1. A public lecture given in Suresnes, France, August 16, 1925.

mechanism. The mechanism works automatically, influenced by different forces coming from the finer and grosser worlds.

Why are there in this world so many people who think they have something wrong with them, and why are there so very few who think that all is well? Even among ten thousand people there is hardly one person who says: "All is well with me." But the rest, all the rest say: "Something is wrong with me." And it is very easy to blame it on destiny and call it misfortune or ill luck. But it cannot be remedied by calling it by all these names; on the contrary, it grows with the years. Besides, the more the mechanism takes hold of a person's life, the more that part that is called the engineer is suppressed; it never has a chance. A person with little will, with few desires and wishes, is pushed downward by the force of this automatic working of life. A person calls this automatic working "conditions" or "circumstances." A person may see some reason for it and may find an answer when it is seen from a logical point of view. But it is never satisfactory; it does not give the fullest satisfaction because there is behind it the feeling that one can find some solution and some other meaning in every problem.

Everything one sees, hears, perceives through any sense or experience has a distinct and definite effect upon one's soul, upon one's spirit. What one eats, what one drinks, what one sees, what one touches, the atmosphere in which one lives, the circumstances that one faces, the conditions that one goes through—all have a certain effect upon one's spirit. Sometimes out of bad experiences there is a benefit derived. Sometimes out of good experiences there is some loss. And sometimes out of good experiences there is some good received, and out of bad experiences something bad.

For instance, a person who has a bad experience in friendship and because of it what develops is a kind of coldness, a kind of pessimistic view of life, a kind of indifference. The person shows despisement, hatred, prejudice, an unwillingness to associate with anybody in the world. Out of the experience that person has derived the bad side. There is another person who has been disappointed but who has learned something. That person has learned how to be tolerant, how to be forgiving, how to understand human nature, how to expect little from others and how to give more to others, how to forget oneself, and how to be open to sympathize with another. It is one and the same experience that makes one go to the north and another to the south. The effect of the experiences of life is different for each person. A certain drug or herb has a certain effect on a person (favorable to one and unfavorable to another) and so with the outer experiences of life. On one person it has a certain effect, on the other it has quite a different effect. We are put into the world in a condition where we are always subject to outer influences. It is as if a soul were thrown into life with susceptibility to move to the south, north, east, or west, and absolutely dependent on which way the wind blows, with the soul turned accordingly. If there were not this little spark in our soul that may be called the engineer, and that we recognize as free will or self will, we would never think for one moment that we are a being. There would be no difference between things and beings. And the more we realize the existence of will in us, the more we are conscious of it, the more we are able to stand in the north wind or south wind or west wind or east wind—whichever side it comes from, we can stand it. Even from a material point of view, the strength that enables a person to stand on the earth, on this ever-moving earth, is not the person's mechanical body, it is the will. And if a person lost the will that holds the body, that person could not stand on the earth.

Since we do not know what the will is or where it is, we very often overlook its existence in us and become absorbed in the causes that are outside of us, causes of all things that bring us joy and distress. The outer conditions move the spirit, and the condition of the spirit moves the outer conditions of life. Never, therefore, be surprised that good luck and ill luck rise and fall; both are directed by the will behind them. And the human being, accustomed to looking at all things according to reason and logic, sees them in another form than they actually are. The sages and the wise therefore wish to find this faculty that is called the will, and on finding it, they work with it. And when one becomes able to work with it properly, one gains mastery of it. Very often a thinking person asks whether there is free will or there is destiny, for it seems that these two things cannot exist at the same time. These two things are likened to what we call light and darkness. In reality there is no such thing as darkness, just less light or more light. Only when they are compared do we distinguish them as light and darkness. In the same way one can look at free will and destiny, that destiny is always at work with free will, and free will with destiny. They are one and the same thing. It is a difference of consciousness. The more you are conscious of your will, the more you see that destiny works around it, and destiny works according to it. And the less conscious you are of that will, the more you see yourself subject to destiny. In other words, one is either a mechanism or the engineer. If one is a mechanism, then in one there is a spark of engineer. And if one is an engineer, then the mechanism is a part of one's being.

In spiritual realization we do not need to renounce things. Self-denial, as described in the Bible, has a different meaning: it means to deny one's self its false conception of itself, in other words to take away from the self that false conception it has of itself—that is true self-denial. When once one recognizes that part of one that is called *will* as a divine spark in one's heart, and blows on it with the hope of turning it into a flame and then into a blaze, it is then that one gives oneself life, a life that may be called the birth of the soul. It is not true that there is no destiny. There is the plan of an individual, and there is a plan that may be called the divine plan. But mostly the plan of an individual is not different from the plan of God. It is not true, however, that destiny does not change; as we change our plans, the creator changes its plans also.

For instance, take an artist who paints a picture on a canvas, and while painting the picture and drawing lines, and giving different colors to it, looks at it, and, inspired by the picture that has already been made, feels like changing the lines, the colors, and could even change it to such an extent that it no longer remains the same picture that the artist had first made in thought. So it is with an individual, and so it is with God. All that we make inspires us to complete it. We make a wrong thing over a right thing, a good thing over a bad thing. Its effect upon us is to complete it in some way, and therefore we complete our good fortune or our ill luck. If we make an ill luck for ourselves, we complete it; we may be against it, but still we make it complete; that is the tendency of a human: to complete what he or she has made. One may not know it, but when the will is hid behind the mind, one sees oneself in the hand of conditions. And then what little power the will has is used to fulfill the mission of conditions around one, and to complete that destiny that may be called good luck or ill luck. In conclusion, it is in the consciousness of the self-will and in the understanding of the definite plan that one really wishes to complete and to fulfill that one can find life's ultimate purpose.

25

INTEREST AND INDIFFERENCE

I would like to speak this afternoon on the subject of interest and indifference.[1] Very often spiritual people speak about indifference, giving preference to indifference; and many who have not reached that stage begin to wonder if interest is preferable, or if indifference is preferable to interest. And very often people lose their interest because they think in principle indifference is the best thing. But in reality it is a subject that one must study: what is gained by interest and what is accomplished by indifference, all there is to be gained by interest, and all there is to be lost by indifference. And one must first find out if one wants to gain or lose. If one is hungering after gain, one must have interest. But if one feels a relief in losing, one must have indifference. In other words, either keep your coins locked in the safe or throw them away and feel relieved. Both things are nice, it is only as we wish.

Interest can be divided into four parts. The first is the interest in the self. Even if one is not interested in anybody or anything, one is certainly interested in oneself. No person is loveless. When a person boasts that "I love no one," then you can be sure that person loves him- or herself. The love must be used somewhere; it can just as well be used upon oneself.

---

1. A public lecture given in Suresnes, France, June 20, 1926.

And then there is the interest in another. It has a different character again because it is chiefly based upon sacrifice. The third interest is in a science or art, or in the obtaining of a material object, wealth or power or possessions. This interest has nothing to do with the person; it is for something that is to be gained and this needs sacrifice also. And the fourth interest is the interest in spiritual things. That again brings one to the interest in oneself, but that is the higher self-interest. The first selfishness is the lower selfishness, the other is the higher selfishness. And when we come to indifference, it can also be divided into four classes. There is indifference to oneself, as when a person says "Well, I don't care whether I eat or don't eat, or how I look. I don't care what people say. I am not interested in myself; I have something else on my mind." That is one indifference. And the next indifference is to a person or to persons. You don't mind whether they live or die, you don't mind what happens to them, whether they love you or hate you, whether you profited by them or not. If they are happy or if they are unhappy, it is just as well.

And the third aspect of indifference is when one says: "What do I care whether I am rich or poor, whether my rank is high or low, whether I gain this thing or that thing in the world, I am quite indifferent to it." Then there is a fourth kind of indifference, as when a person says: "What does it matter if I pray or do not pray, if in the hereafter it is good or bad. What does it matter if I am received in paradise or not, it matters little." That is the fourth kind of indifference. And remember that the people we see in everyday life, each one has one or the other, either interest or indifference—either one of the four kinds of indifference or one of the four aspects of interest I have mentioned just now.

One might ask which is desirable and which is undesirable. I say all that is natural is desirable, and all that is unnatural is undesirable. When one is interested in something but says "I do not want to interest myself in it even though I am taken captive by it, even though I am tempted by it, I am attracted to it," that is not right. Or when a person feels "I should look after myself, feed myself, clothe myself; I must look as nice as I can. I must live as nicely as I should," but then says in principle it is not good to pay attention to oneself, that also is wrong.

When a person says all earthly things are unimportant and are of no value compared to the spiritual principle, that we should not take notice of them, we must think otherwise, and yet at the same time is inwardly attracted to things of the earth, then that person should not say such things. That person's interest is preferable to his or her indifference. One should evolve as one naturally evolves. One should not think that to take an interest in the things of the world is wrong because in principle it is better or greater to be without worldly interests. That is not right. But if one is indifferent to them by nature, and even if the whole world says one is indifferent, it does not matter. One should say "I am indifferent to your opinion too."

People often say that by indifference I mean a philosophy, for it is the Yogis, ascetics, adepts, and mystics who say that indifference gives a great power. But I must add that interest gives a great power, too. The whole of manifestation is a phenomenon of interest. All that we see in this world of art and science—the new inventions, the beautiful things of art and of science, the beautiful houses, and all this world that humans have made—where has it come and from what has it come? It has come from the power of interest. The power of interest is behind it, and it is that power that has enabled humans to create it.

And when we go still further, it is the interest of the Creator that has made this creation. Even the Creator would not have been able to create if there had not been interest. The whole creation and all that is in it is the product of the Creator's interest, the Creator as spirit, or as a human being, as a living being. It is the interest of the bird to build its nest, and so it is the interest of humans to make all that they make.

And imagine if humans did not have this faculty of taking interest, the world would never have evolved. Therefore, the secret of manifestation and the mystery of evolution is to be found in interest. But at the same time I do not deny the power of indifference. The power of indifference is greater still if the indifference is not artificial. When a person chooses indifference because it is a good thing in principle, then it is not a virtue. Besides that, there is no power, because a person is captive: on one side drawn by interest and on the other side wanting to show indifference. Therefore, it is wrong on one's part; one neither accomplishes something by the power of interest, nor does one gain the benefit that can be derived from indifference.

And now from the point of view of metaphysics, I should like to explain why the power of indifference is greater than the power of interest. Because motive has a power and at the same time motive limits a power. People are endowed at birth with much greater power than they ever imagine, and it is motive that limits this power. Any motive, every motive, and yet it is the motive that gives a person power to accomplish something. If there were no motive, there would be no power to accomplish it. But when you compare the original power of a human with the power that one finds in motive, it is just like the difference between the ocean and the drop. The motive makes the power as a drop. Without the motive the power of the soul is like an ocean. But at the same time, that ocean-like power is of no use without a motive; as soon as you want to use it for a purpose, it becomes less.

And now coming to indifference. Indifference releases that limitation automatically. With indifference a limitation is released; it is broken and the power unconsciously becomes greater. You will see this even in worldly things, there are people who run after money and there are people after whom money runs. I do not mean that they are necessarily spiritual people. Sometimes they themselves do not know it. There are some who are worshippers of beauty. There are others before whom beauty worships. There are some who wish to hold power, what little power they can get. And there are others upon whom power is pouring though they do not want it. We see so many examples in this world of how interest often limits a person's power and indifference makes it greater. But at the same time indifference should not be practiced unless it springs naturally from your heart.

There is a saying in the Hindi language that interest makes kings, but indifference makes emperors. There is a story of a great sage who lived near Delhi. One day, Emperor Akbar, hearing his name, wanted to go and pay him homage. This sage was sitting on a rock with his legs stretched and arms folded. The emperor had Birbal, his wise prime minister with him. The prime minister did not like the way the emperor was received by this sage, for the sage knew that he was an emperor, yet he remained in the same position in which he was sitting. So Birbal, in sarcasm, asked the sage how long he had been sitting this way? What was the answer of the sage? "Since I have taken my hands back." This means that "As long as my hands were forward, in need, my legs stood up. But since my hands are like this, my legs are stretched; it does not matter if a king comes or the emperor comes, it does not matter who comes. In other words, as long as I had interest, my legs were in order. Since the time I had no interest anymore, I sit in any way that I like to sit." No matter who comes to the sage, he is what he is, regardless; that is the indifference of the sages.

But now I should like to explain how this indifference comes to them, how is it practiced. There comes a day in one's life, sooner or later, the day when one no longer thinks about oneself. How I eat, how I am clothed, or how I live, how anybody treats me, does anybody love me, does anybody hate me? Every thought that is concerned with oneself goes away. That day comes, and it is a blessed day when it comes to a person. It is that day that one's soul begins to live, to live independently, to live independently of fear. As long as one is bound to the thought that, "I am treated badly or wrongly, or people do not love me or like me, or people do not treat me justly or fairly"—one is poor. Whatever one's position in life, one is poor, and the moment one begins to forget about it, one's power becomes great.

From a worldly aspect there are those who look after themselves, who are self-conscious, who think of themselves, who are concerned about themselves. One can see the good points in that person, but at the same time that is all that one can admire. One can see something good in them, but there are others who have given up the thought of themselves. You cannot help respecting them. The respect comes by itself as soon as they have emerged from that thought of self. And when one has lost the interest of holding and possessing others, then one's charm is such that, without one's holding and possessing and owning, all becomes one's own. You can feel that person to be above the average person in the world. And when you look from the point of view of sages, no one really belongs to oneself. In the East they say that it displeases God when parents think that their children are their own. God is never pleased with that idea of owning, that "I possess this." All are creatures of God. God has created and providence has brought about situations in which we are connected with them as parents, as master, as servant, as friend in whatever relation we may be. And when we think that we possess them, we own them, we hold them, God is not pleased. And when human beings are not pleased either they then arrive at that stage where one does not possess, does not own anything, or anyone. That is also a stage of indifference.

And then one comes to the stage of indifference where all the rank and position and honor and power—even they do not matter very much, because all of these are also false claims. In order to occupy a certain position, in order to keep some rank or position for oneself, one has to deprive others of it. And when one has reached that stage when a position or a rank makes no difference to one, then one has reached a still higher stage. And when one arrives at that stage when even paradise has no more attraction for one, when one is willing to meet whatever the hereafter may bring, then one's point of view becomes the point of view of a sage, of a master.

Now a question arises: How can one learn indifference? By learning interest. If you do not learn interest in your life, you cannot learn indifference. A person who is born with no interest in life is but an idiot. The child who does not stick to the toy that it has in its hand and will not keep it, that child has no promise of progress. It is natural for the child to hold on to the toy and claim it as its own. That is the first lesson for it to learn. It is normal for a child to say "This is mine," about a toy to hold on to it, keep it. In that way one develops interest; interest in one's well-being, in one's welfare, in one's progress in life, so that one can accomplish one's purpose in life. All this is natural and normal—interest in other persons, in their affairs, in those one loves and likes; it is this that develops the character, then there is interest in things of the world. By this interest one helps the world; by interest one contributes one's service to the world. If one had no interest, one would not contribute one's service, one would not render one's service to the nation or to the cause of the world.

Therefore, evolution is going step-by-step and not making a hurry. And indifference is to be attained by developing interest and by developing discrimination in one's interest. Instead of going backward one should go forward in one's interest. And one will find that a spring will naturally rise in one's heart; when the heart in the path of interest has touched the zenith, then the fountain of indifference will break out gradually, and when that natural breaking out of indifference comes, one should follow it, so that in the end one may know what interest means and what indifference means.

26

FROM LIMITATION TO PERFECTION (1)

Beloved Ones of God, my subject this evening is from limitation to perfection.[1] The rocks, the trees, the animals, and humans all in their turn show an inclination to seek perfection. The tendency of rocks is to form into a mountain reaching upward, and the waves are ever reaching upward as if they were trying to attain something that is beyond their reach. The tendency of birds is the same. Their joy is flying in the air and going upward. And the tendency of animals is to stand on their hind legs, and when they stand on their hind legs they are most pleased. And the human being, who has finished creation, has this tendency from infancy to stand up. An infant who is not able to stand moves its little hands and legs, showing the desire to stand up.

This all shows the desire for perfection. The law of gravitation is known to the world of science in a half measure, in a half way: that the earth attracts all that belongs to it. It is true. But the spirit also attracts all that belongs to it. That law of gravitation has always been known by mystics. Therefore, from two sides is the law of gravitation working, from the side of the earth, which draws all that belong to the earth, and from

---

1. A talk given at the Engineering Societies Auditorium, New York, May 24, 1926.

the side of the spirit, which attracts the soul toward it. Even those unconscious of this law of gravitation are also striving for perfection, being drawn by this law, with the soul being continually drawn to the spirit. They are striving for perfection just the same. In small things of everyday life a person wants more and more and more. Even if one has made a name or fame, one is never satisfied with what one has. One always wants more and more, be it a higher rank or position. One is always striving for it; one is never satisfied with it. This shows that the heart is a magic bowl, however much you pour into it, that much deeper it becomes. It is always found to be empty. Whatever one strives after, one strives after more and more. One is never satisfied. The reason is that one is unconsciously striving for perfection. Those, however, who strive consciously after perfection have a different way. Nevertheless, each atom of the universe is meant to struggle and strive to become perfect one day. In other words, if a seer, a thinker, of an evolved soul happens to be in the mountains, that one will hear the mountains cry continually, "We are waiting for that day when something in us will awaken. There will come a day of wakening, of unfoldment. We are waiting silently for it." If the seer went to the forest and saw the trees standing there, they would seem to be saying that they were waiting patiently. You can feel it; the more you sit there the more you feel, you get the feeling of the trees, that they are waiting for that time when there will be an unfoldment. So it is with all beings. But at the same time, humans, being so absorbed in their everyday actions and greed, seem to be unaware of that innate desire of unfoldment. It is their everyday occupation, their avariciousness, their cruelty to other beings, that keeps them continually engaged with things, busy with things. Therefore, they cannot hear that continual cry of their own soul to awaken, to unfold, to reach upward, to expand, and to go toward perfection.

But now one might ask, "What do I mean by perfection? Is it possible for a human to reach perfection?" When one sees how limited the human is, one never can think for a moment that a person is entitled to perfection. There is no end to one's limitedness, and one cannot even comprehend what perfection means, and one becomes pessimistic when it is a question of perfection. And yet, we read in the Bible the words of Christ that, "Be ye perfect even as your Father in heaven is perfect."[2] This shows there is a possibility of it. All philosophies, all religious and sacred teachings, are intended to bring about that realization that is called perfection. Any philosophy or religion that does not show this path to perfection fails, has been corrupted; there is something missing in it. But if you look at religion as one and the same religion in all ages given by different masters of humanity inspired by one and the same spirit of guidance, one and the same light of wisdom, they have all given the same truth. It is only when it is interpreted differently to suit people of different ages, periods, and races that it differs. But the underlying truth of all religions is one and the same. And whenever a religious preacher teaches that perfection is not for humans, that one corrupts the teaching that is given in all religions. That one has not understood. That one professes a certain religion, but does not understand it. For the main object of every religion is striving toward perfection.

I have met several people seeking for knowledge who have said, "What we want in the world today is greater harmony, greater peace, better conditions. We don't want spiritual perfection. What we want is what we need today." And my answer has been the same as Christ has said in the Bible that, "Seek ye first the kingdom of God, and all these things shall be added unto you."[3] The tendency of every person is to seek everything else first and keep the kingdom of God for last. That which should be sought first is left to the last. That is why humanity is not evolving toward perfection. Such occupations as war and preparation for war are not to be called civilized occupations.

2. Matthew 5:48.
3. Matthew 6:33.

From Limitation to Perfection (1)

It is a pity that in this period of civilization people should have wars. And yet we think that we are more civilized than people of ancient times. Ages before Christ, Buddha taught, *Ahimsa paramo dharmaha*, "Harmlessness is the essence of religion." And he taught people to be friendly even to the smallest insect, he taught the kinship of all beings. And we occupy ourselves with wars day after day. Under the conditions existing today we can expect war anywhere in the world. Where does it all come from? It all comes from seeking perfection in the wrong way. Instead of seeking spiritual perfection, earthly perfection is sought. What everybody is seeking is earthly perfection, the earth. But all that the earth holds is limited. And when everyone struggles for earthly perfection, the earth will not be able to answer the demands. Whether we will get it or not, there will always be a struggle.

And now I come to the main point, which is that religion is the way by which perfection is sought, and to explain what religion means. Religion has five different aspects. The first and most principal aspect and the foundation of religion is belief in God. And now one asks, "What is God?" For many say that, "If there is a personal God, I don't care for it. But if you think that there is abstract God, then, yes, it can be." They forget that something abstract cannot be a living being. Abstract is nothing, you cannot call space, God. Space is space. You can neither call space God, nor can you call time God. Besides that, space is our conception. We think of yards and length as dimension. It is our conception. In the same way time is a conception. In reality it does not exist. It is unlimited and it cannot be comprehended. That which cannot be comprehended is without any name. What is intelligible to you, you can give a name to; if it is unintelligible, you cannot give it a name, because you cannot know it. And when we come to those who believe in a personal God, many of them merely have a belief. By that they worship God. They believe in a certain law given in the name of God; they do good works in the name of God. They do good

From Limitation to Perfection (1)

works for the sake of God. But at the same time, they have no knowledge other than a belief that there is a God somewhere. Neither of these types of believer in God have any conception of the real meaning of the God-ideal. They merely have belief in God, and this does not take one much further. In reality, the God-ideal is a stepping stone toward the knowledge of spiritual perfection. It is through the God-ideal that higher knowledge can be gained. And those who wait to see if they will be shown a God before their eyes, or who want a proof of the being of God, are mistaken. That which cannot be compared, which cannot be named, cannot be shown. For instance, you see light. Light is intelligible to you because there is a darkness opposed to it. Things are known by their opposites. Since God has no opposite, God cannot be known in the same way as the things of the earth can be known. Besides, to explain God is to dethrone God. The less said the better. And yet the knowledge of God is necessary for those who seek after perfection. Different religions have different conceptions of God. But not only religion, every person has a conception of God. You cannot think of any being without making a conception in your mind of that being. For instance, if anyone told you a fairy tale, the first thing you would do would be to make a conception of a fairy, what it looks like. If someone talks to you about an angel, you make a conception of it. It is natural tendency to make a conception according to one's own experience, and thus very near to one's own self. A human being does not think of an angel or a fairy as being a bird or an animal, but something like a human. If that is true, then it is not a fault of those who have their own idea about God. But it is a great fault on the part of those who want to take away that idea and wish to give that person another idea. It is not right. No one can give to another one's own conception of God, because each person must make it real for him- or herself. The prophets of all ages have given some ideal to help people to form a conception of God. As a

From Limitation to Perfection (1)

philosopher says, "If you have no God, make one." For that is the proper way, the easiest way of realizing the unlimited truth.

There is the story about Moses who saw a shepherd boy sitting near the river and talking to himself, saying that, "O God, you are so dear. If you once appeared before me, I would be everything for you. I would give you a bath in the river and cover you with my mantle. I would put you to bed in my hut. And I would give you all sweets and delicious things to eat, and take care of you, and protect you from all wild animals, and love you so much and care for you so much, if once I saw you in my life." And the prophet said, "What are you saying, young man? Have you any idea! God, the protector of all beings, you say you will protect. The one who bestows all gifts and who is the sustenance of all beings, even the smallest, the littlest creature is looked after by God, you will cover him? He is unseen, unlimited." And this boy became so frightened. He thought, "What was I doing? What a terrible thing! I have been saying something I ought not to have said. Terrible!" And he was terrified. And when the prophet left him, there arose a voice from within, the same voice that used to come to the prophet in solitude every day, "What have you done, Moses? We sent you to bring our friends together, to bring my friends to me, and you have separated them. Everyone, every lover has their own idea of their beloved. And no other person knows what anyone thinks of their beloved."

In the story about the Eastern Romeo and Juliette, Leila and Majnun, someone said to Majnun, the young lover, "Leila, she is not so beautiful. What is she? Why do you love her so much?" And Majnun said humbly, "In order to see Leila, you must borrow my eyes." Yes, the conception of God in every person is different, distinct, and one person cannot give his or her conception of God to another.

There is another story told about a housewife who was preparing a great feast. When her husband came home, he said, "My good wife, why have you prepared a feast? Is it a holy day?

From Limitation to Perfection (1)

Is it a birthday? What is it?" She said, "It is greater than a birthday, is better than a holy day. It is a great day for me." But he said, "What is it?" She said, "My husband, I never thought that you believed in God." He asked, "And how did you find out?" She said, "While changing sides in sleep you uttered the name of God, and I am so thankful." The man said, "Alas, that which was so sacred and secret in my heart has today been revealed. I can no longer sustain it and live." And he dropped down dead. His conception of God was too sacred for him.

There is outer expression and inner expression, and we don't always know which is which. We may think many are removed from God-ideal and we don't know that they are much nearer to God than we are. It is difficult for anyone to judge who is near to God and who is not. It is difficult to know even in our lives what will please our friend and what will not. It is so difficult. The more conscientious we are of pleasing our friend, the more we find how difficult it is to know what will please and what will not. Not everyone knows it, but then the light of friendship has not been kindled in everyone. Sometimes it remains a word in the dictionary. One who has learned friendship has learned religion. The one who has learned friendship has attained spiritual knowledge. The one who has learned friendship need learn very little else. For in the Persian language, morals are called friendship.

There is another story that explains this idea of the pleasure and displeasure of God. There once was a man who was very pious and who lived a very religious life. One day he said to Moses, "All through my life I have tried to be a good man and I have tried to be religious. And I have always been in a terrible difficulty. But I don't care. I would only like to know what is in store for me. Will you ask God?" Moses said, "Yes." As Moses goes on a little further, there sits a drunken man. The man says, "Come here! Where are you going? Will you ask about me also? I have never done prayers or fastings. I have never done good things, as they say in this world. I know these, my great friends, bottle and glass. Go and ask what is in store for me." And when Moses comes back after his meditation on the top of Sinai, he tells the religious man that, "For you there are great rewards, beautiful things." And when he goes further the drunken man asks, "What is the answer?" And Moses said, "For you there is the worst place possible." And the man stood up and danced and was most joyous. He said, "Oh, I don't care what place is given to me. I am so happy that God thought about me, I, such a humble man, and such a sinner. That I was known by God. I thought nobody knew me." He was most happy. In the end, the two exchanged places. And Moses was surprised, and he asked within. And the answer was that, "This man, in spite of all good, did not deserve our favor. For our grace cannot be bought by good deeds. What are man's good deeds! His whole life's good deeds cannot be compared with one moment's favor of God. How can you buy God's grace with good deeds? And this other man pleased me, for he enjoyed everything given to him. His contentment has won me."

It is the same thing. When we cannot understand the pleasure and displeasure of our own friends in this world, how can we understand the pleasure and displeasure of God? Who on earth can say that God is pleased with this or that? No one could ever have the power to make rules and laws, saying "by this God is pleased," and "by this God is displeased."

And now I come to the other aspect of religion, and that is the aspect of the teacher. For instance, we come to the question of Christ. There are some who see divinity in Christ. They say, "Christ was God, Christ is divine." And there are others who say, "Christ was man, one like us all." And when we come to look at this question, the one who says, "Christ is divine" is not wrong. If there is any divinity shown, it is in the human. The one who says, "Christ was a man" is also not wrong. In the garb of man Christ manifested. Those who do not want Christ to be a man, they drag down the greatness and sacredness of the human being by this argument, by saying that the human is made of sin and by separating Christ from humanity. But there is nothing wrong about calling Christ God or divine. It is in human being that divine perfection is to be seen. It is in the human that divinity is to be manifest. But then there are Christ's own words, that "I am Alpha and Omega."[4] And this is one idea that many close their eyes to. That the one who said, "I am Alpha and Omega," existed also before the coming of Jesus. The one who says, "first and last," must exist also after Jesus. In the words of Christ, there is the idea of perfection. He identified himself with that spirit of which he was conscious. Christ was not conscious of his human part, but of his perfect being when he said, "I am Alpha and Omega." He did not identify himself with his being known as Jesus. He identified himself with that spirit of which he was conscious, that spirit of perfection that lived before Jesus and continues to live to the end of the world, for eternity. If that is so, then what does it matter if some say that "Buddha inspired us," and millions are inspired by Buddha? It is only a difference of name. After all, it is Alpha and Omega. If others say Moses, or Muhammad, or Krishna—what is it? Where did the inspiration come from? Was it not from one and the same spirit? Was it not the Alpha and Omega of which Jesus Christ was conscious? Whoever gives the message to the world and illuminated human beings, raised thousands and millions of people in the world, it cannot be but that same Christ whom one calls by this name and the other by another name. Yet human ignorance always causes wars and disasters on account of different religions, different communities, on account of the importance they give to their own conception, their own corrupted conception differing from the other. Even now on the one hand there is materialism, and on the other there is bigotry. What is necessary today is to come to the first and last religion, to come to the message of Christ, to divine wisdom, so that we may recognize wisdom in all its different forms, in whatever form it has been given to

---

4. Revelation 1:8.

humanity. It does not matter if it is Buddhism, Islam, Judaism, Zoroastrianism, Hinduism. What does it matter? It is one wisdom, that call of the spirit that wakens a human being to rise from limitation, and to reach perfection.

And now we come to the third aspect of religion. The third aspect of religion is the manner of worship. There are many in different ages who have worshipped the sun, but they have believed in God just the same. The sun was only a symbol. They thought, "This is something that does not depend upon oil or anything else, something that remains night and day." And then there were others who worshipped sacred trees and holy places, rocks and mountains of tradition. And others who worshipped heroes of great repute or teachers and masters of humanity. Nevertheless, all had divine ideal. And the form in which they worshipped does not matter. The Arabs in the desert where there was no house, no place, stood in the open air and bowed in the open space at sunset and sunrise. It was all worship of God. It was given in that form. The Hindus made idols of different kinds in order to help people focus their mind on particular objects. These were all different prescriptions given by the doctors of souls. They were not pagans or heathens. They were only taught differently by the wise; different thoughts, different ways were given, just as a doctor would give a different prescription to different people in order to come to the same goal. Therefore, the difference in worship does not make a different religion. Religion is one and the same in spite of a thousand different kinds of worship.

And now we come to the fourth aspect. This is the moral aspect. Different religions have taught different moral principles. But at the same time there is one human moral principle on which all is based, and that is justice. And it is not justice in principles and rules and regulations, but that one law that is the true religious law that is in a person, that is awakened in a human being. As one's soul unfolds itself, so that law becomes more and more clear to one: what is just and what is unjust.

And the most wonderful thing about this law is that a thief or a wicked or unrighteous person may be most unjust to others, but if someone is unjust to them, they will say, "That one is not just to me." That shows they know justice too. When they are dealing with others they forget it, but when it comes to themselves, they know justice just the same. Therefore, we are all responsible to ourselves according to that religious law. If we do not regard it, it naturally results in unhappiness. And everything that goes wrong goes wrong for the reason that we do not listen to ourselves.

And the fifth aspect of religion is self-realization. This is the highest aspect of religion, and everything we do leads to it: prayers, concentration, good actions, good thoughts—everything leads to that one object that is self-realization. And how is it gained? Some say that we realize God by self-realization. But it is not true. For we can only realize self by the realization of God. Whenever a person tries to realize self while omitting God, that person makes a mistake. And it is very difficult for one to realize self because the self one knows is a most limited self. The self to which one is awakened from the time of birth, the self that has made within one a conception of oneself, is most limited. However much one is proud or conceited, however good an idea one has of oneself, yet in one's innermost being, one knows one's limitation, one's small being just the same. One may be a most successful general, one may be a king or queen, yet one knows one's limitation when the time comes that one runs away from one's kingdom. Then one knows that one is not really a king or queen. Earthly greatness does not make one great. If there is anything that makes one great, it is only the effacing of oneself, and the establishing of God instead.

The one who says, "Begin with self-realization," who has many intellectual, philosophical principles, gets quite into a muddle and arrives nowhere. These are wrong methods. And today, there are people who say, "I am God." This is insolence, stupidity; it is foolish to do such things. They spoil the idea of others with this affirmation, with such intellectual studies. They are insolent to the greatest ideal that the prophets and saviors of humanity have always respected. Such people can never reach spiritual perfection. In order to reach spiritual perfection, the first thing is to destroy that false self. First this delusion must be destroyed. And how must it be destroyed? By the ways taught by the great teachers, ways of concentration and meditation, by the power of which one forgets oneself, removes one's consciousness from oneself, in other words, rises from one's limited being. In this way, one effaces oneself from one's own consciousness, and places God in one's consciousness instead of one's limited self. It is by this way that one arrives at that perfection that every soul is seeking.

27

FROM LIMITATION TO PERFECTION (2)

Beloved Ones of God, my subject this evening is from limitation to perfection.[1] Every kind of striving that one has in one's life, whether for a material thing or for a spiritual object, is one's natural inclination to reach from limitation toward perfection. Whatever it may be, wealth or rank or name or comfort or pleasure, it is this limitation that keeps one discontented. When we come to the idea of learning, studying, practicing, acquiring, attaining, there also we see that this striving of a person is to go from limitation to perfection. The saying in scripture that God alone is rich and all others are poor can be seen in one's everyday life. The greater the riches one has, the more one wants. And the most interesting thing is that when one studies the life of a poor person, one finds that the poor person is more content with what he or she has than a rich person with his or her wealth. And sometimes one also sees that a poor person feels more generous in giving than a rich person parting with his or her wealth.

And now we shall look at another aspect of life. People who are learned in a small degree think that they have learned, think that they have read much, and they wish to show it. But more learned people, who have really learned, begin to find that

1. A lecture given at the Sorbonne, Paris, December 14, 1924.

From Limitation to Perfection (2)

they have learned very little and there is still very much to be learned.

Then there is still another picture to be seen and that is the foolish and the wise. The foolish one is ready to teach you without thinking for a moment, ready to correct you, ready to judge you, ready to form an opinion about you. But the wiser someone is, the more diffident that one is to form an opinion about you, to judge you, to correct you. What does this all mean? It means that whatever someone possesses in a small degree, they think they have much of, but when they possesses more, then they begin to feel the need and the want for perfection, for completion.

There is an ancient story of a sovereign that wanted to grant a dervish his desire. And the desire of the dervish was to fill his cup with gold coins. The sovereign thought that it would be the easiest thing to fill the cup of the dervish. And he was looking forward to the pleasure of seeing the cup filled. And the cup was filled, but it was a magic cup, it would not fill. The more money was poured into it, the emptier it became. And the sovereign was very disappointed and disheartened at the thought that this cup could not be filled. The dervish said, "Sovereign, if you cannot fill the cup, you only have to say 'I cannot,' and I shall take my cup back. I am a dervish, and I will go and I will only think that you have not kept your word." The sovereign with every good intention and with all his generosity and with all his treasures could not fill that cup. And he asked, "Dervish, tell me what secret you have in this cup? It does not seem to be a natural cup. There is some magic about it. Tell me what is its secret?" The dervish answered, "Yes, Sovereign, what you have found out is true, it is a magic cup, but it is the cup of every heart. It is the heart of a human, which is never content. Fill it with whatever you may, with wealth, with attention, with love, with knowledge, with all there is. It never will fill, for it is not meant to be filled. Not knowing this secret of life, people go on in pursuit of every object, or of any object they have before them, continually. And the idea is that the more they get the more they want, and the cup of their desire is never filled."

And the meaning of this can be understood by the study of the soul, that a person's appetite is satisfied by food, but behind it there is an appetite that is the appetite of the soul, and that appetite is never satisfied. That appetite is at the back of all the different hungers, all the different thirsts. And since one cannot trace that innermost appetite, one strives all through one's life to satisfy these outer appetites, which are satisfied and yet remain unsatisfied. If one is making a search of objective things, things of the objective world, one may gain a great deal of knowledge of them and yet there is never an end to it. The one who searches the secret of sound, the one who searches the mystery of light, the one who searches the mystery of science, they all search and search and search, and there is never an end to it, there is never any satisfaction. And a thoughtful person wonders if that satisfaction is to be found anywhere, the satisfaction that answers, so to speak, the promise of the soul? And the answer is, yes, there is a possibility for that satisfaction and that possibility is to attain to that perfection that is not dependent upon outside things, a perfection that belongs to one's own being. And this satisfaction is not attained, this satisfaction is discovered. It is in the discovery of this satisfaction that one finds the fulfillment of the purpose of life.

And now the question arises: How does one arrive at this perfection? Religion or philosophy or mysticism, all these things will help one, but it is by the actual attainment of this knowledge that a person will arrive at this satisfaction.

Life can be pictured as a line with two ends: one end of the line is limitation, and the other end of the same line is perfection. And as long as one is looking at the end that is limitation, however good, virtuous, righteous, pious one is, one has not touched what may be called perfection. Are there not many believers in religion, in a God, worshippers of a deity, more among simple people than among those who are intelligent, educated? Do they all arrive at perfection before leaving this earth by their belief in a deity or by their worship?

There are others who learn from books. I have seen myself those who have written perhaps fifty or a hundred books themselves and have read perhaps a whole library, a British Museum. Yet they stand in the same place where they were. As long as one's face is not turned from that end that is the end of limitation, and as long as one does not look toward that ideal of perfection, which is the real Ka'ba or place of pilgrimage, one will not arrive at that perfection.

And what keeps this perfection, which belongs to one's own life, which is one's own being, hidden from one? A screen put before it; and that screen is oneself. The soul, conscious of its limitation, of its possessions with which it identifies itself, forgets its own being and becomes, so to speak, captive in its limitation. Religion or belief in God, worship, philosophy, or mysticism, all these help one to attain this. But if one does not search for perfection through these, even these things will only be an occupation, a pastime and will not bring one to the proper result. One might ask: Is there any definition of this perfection? What sort of perfection is it? Can it be explained in any way? And the answer is that it is only perfection itself that can realize itself. It cannot be put into words, it cannot be explained. If anyone thinks that truth may be given in words, that one is very much mistaken. It is just like putting water from the sea in a bottle and saying, "Here is the sea."

Very often people ask, "But where is the truth? What is the truth? Can you explain it?" But words cannot explain it. Often I thought it would be a good thing to write the word "truth" on a brick and give it into the hands of a person and say, "Hold it fast, here is the truth." There is difference between fact and truth. Fact is a shadow of truth, fact is intelligible. But truth is beyond comprehension because truth is unlimited. Truth knows itself, and nothing else can explain it. What little explanation can be given lies in the idea of expansion.

From Limitation to Perfection (2)

There are those who toil all day in order to make their livelihood, to give themselves a little comfort, a little pleasure, and so their life goes on. And there are those who have a family, who have others to think about, who toil for them, who work for them. Sometimes they forget their own pleasure and comfort for the comfort and pleasures of those who depend upon them. They hardly have time to think about their own comfort, to think about themselves. Their pleasure and comfort is in the pleasure and comfort of those who depend upon them. And there are those who try to be useful in their town, to improve the condition of the town, to help the education of the people of their town. They are engaged in this work, and very often they forget themselves in striving for the happiness of those for whom they are working. There are also those who live for their nation, who work for their nation, who give their whole life to it. They are only conscious of their nation; their consciousness is expanded, and they are larger. There is very little difference between the frames of these people. But there is a great difference between the expansion of each one's consciousness. There are the ones who seem as large as they seem to be, there are others who seem as large as their family, there are others who seem as large as their town, there are others who seem as large as their nation. And there are still others, believe me, who are as large as the world. There is a saying of a Hindustani poet that, "Neither the sea nor the land can be compared with the human heart. If the human heart is large, it is larger than the universe." Therefore, if perfection can be explained in any terms, if perfection can be defined, it is in the expansion of one's consciousness. The one who strives after this perfection need not know or learn what is selfish or unselfish. Unselfishness comes to that one naturally; that one becomes unselfish.

In the last few years humanity has gone through the greatest catastrophe; all nations have suffered and have partaken of it. Every individual, even every living creature on this earth has been affected by it. One might ask, what was lacking? Was education lacking? There are many schools and universities. Was religion lacking? There are many churches still, and many different beliefs still existing in the world. What was lacking was the understanding of the true meaning of religion. What was lacking was the understanding of the real meaning of education.

And now the question arises of how those who have found out that perfection is attained by realizing the self within have attained it. It was not only by what people call external worship. But it was by self-abnegation in the true sense of the word. It is by going into that silence where one can forget the limitedness of the self, that one can get in touch with that part of one's being that is called perfection. And this can best be attained by those who have realized the meaning of life.

28

THE PATH OF ATTAINMENT (1)

Sadhana

The secret of life is the desire to attain something, the absence of which makes life useless.[1] Hope is the sustenance of life; and hope comes from the desire of attaining something. Therefore the wish to attain something is in itself a very great power. The object a person holds to be an object of attainment may be much smaller compared to the power one develops in the process of attainment. Therefore the Hindus call attainment *sadhana*; the power gained through attainment is called in Sanskrit *siddhi,* which is the sign of spiritual mastership.

By learning the mystery of attainment one learns the divine mystery that is suggested in the phrase of the Bible that says: "Thy will be done on earth as it is in Heaven." This phrase is a veil that covers the mystery of attainment. Human beings, who are the instruments of God, on coming to earth, lose, so to speak, a connection with that divine power whose instrument they are; thus depriving not only themselves but even God of helping God's will to be done. Human beings, who are

---

1. In the original *Sufi Message* volume this chapter was composed of three parts. Here they are presented in their original form, including the question-and-answer sessions. This first talk was given in Geneva, October 11, 1923.

born to be the instruments of God, when they do not perform their mission properly they naturally feel dissatisfied. It does not mean that they do not accomplish what they desire; they are unhappy because they do not help God to make God's will be done, by keeping themselves disconnected from God, who is their innermost being. This condition is like a hand coming out of joint: it is not only the hand that suffers, but the person whose hand it is, not being able to use it, suffers also. Therefore in accomplishing the work one undertakes, in attaining to the aim one has in life, one does not only help oneself, but one also serves God.

* * *

Question: *In the* Gayan *we find: "I would have either heaven or hell, but not purgatory." Why do you prefer hell to purgatory?*

Answer: It is a metaphorical expression; but at the same time one can understand by this a philosophical truth: that life means pain or pleasure. The absence of pain or pleasure is death. The heaven as expressed by the scriptures, or hell—both—have either pain or pleasure. What is void of pain and pleasure is not what may be called in our ordinary sense of the word "life." Life is either pain or pleasure. And if one wishes to live, either one must accept pain or pleasure, whatever one can gain. But where these two are absent there is no life, it is death. Now coming to the Bible. From the beginning to the end, what is the teaching of Jesus Christ? To rise above mortality, to find out eternal life, which means: to learn the art of being, the science of being. All scriptures, all religions, every philosophy, or mysticism teaches this. Now there is the question: Why do they teach this? The answer is: there is one thing undesirable, and that is mortality. Death, no sane person will ask for death. Desire for death is unnatural desire. And if mind is craving for death, the soul is longing to live. The soul is living, is life; it does not want to die. Death is something foreign to it; it does not know death. Therefore the smallest insect, whose life is most insignificant, protects itself in every way in order to avoid death. And so it is the longing of every soul. If any soul thinks that it longs to die, it is its mind, not its innermost being.

Question: Is it not true that to express always weakens a thing, and to repress strengthens it?

Answer: There is always a limit to expression and repression. Too much expression might kill a thing, and too much repression might deaden a thing. Too much of everything must be avoided. For instance, sometimes prisoners who are sentenced to life in prison, after being in a prison for a certain length of time, lose their mind. Because the prisoner is alone there, no one to speak to, there is no expression. And by being alone all the time they lose their mind. If these persons are brought among people again, they prove to be insane.

Spiritual Attainment

Beloved Ones of God, I would like to speak today on the subject of spiritual attainment.[2] The way in which spiritual attainment is reached must be seen from quite another point of view. It cannot be attained in the same manner as the material way. And what discourages one is that perhaps after striving for a year, one does not seem to have arrived at anything. The one who strives to attain the things of this world finds the proof of having attained them by holding them. One says, this is mine, because one possesses it. Spiritual attainment, on the contrary, wants to take possessions away. It does not even allow you to possess yourself. This becomes a great disappointment for a person whose only realization of having attained something is in possessing it. Spiritual attainment, however, comes by not attaining.

Then there is the question, what is the difference between the spiritual person and the person who possesses nothing. The

2. A talk given in Geneva, April 2, 1924.

difference is indeed great, for the spiritual person in the absence of any possessions is still rich. What is the reason? The reason is this: those who do not possess anything are conscious of limitation; those who are spiritual persons, in the absence of even possessing themselves, are conscious of perfection. Then one asks: How can those who are limited be conscious of perfection? The answer is: Those who are limited have limited themselves, they are limited because they are conscious of being limited. It is not their true self that is limited. That which is limited is what they hold, not themselves. That is the possibility that made Christ say: "Be ye perfect as your Father is perfect."[3]

Spiritual knowledge is not in learning something, it is in discovering something, so to speak, in breaking the fetters of the false consciousness and allowing the soul to unfold itself with light and power. What does the word *spiritual* really mean? *Spiritual* means spirit-consciousness. When one is conscious of one's body, one cannot be spiritual. It is like a king who does not know his kingdom. The moment he is conscious of being a king, he is a king. Every soul is born a king; it is only afterward that one becomes a slave. Every soul is born with kingly possibility; by this wicked world it is taken away. This is told in symbolical stories, as in the story of Rama, from whom his beloved Sita was taken away. Every soul has to conquer this, to fight for this kingdom. In that fight the spiritual kingdom is attained. No one will fight for you, neither your teacher, nor anybody else. Yes, those who are more evolved than you can help you, but you have to fight your battle, your way to that spiritual goal. An intellectual thinks that by adding to knowledge he or she may attain spiritual knowledge. This is not so. The secret of life is boundless. Knowledge is limited. Eyes see only a very short distance, and the human mind is just as limited—how far can it see? And those who see can see by not seeing, learn by not learning. The way of spiritual attainment is contrary to the way of all material attainment. In material attainment you

---

3. Matthew 5:48.

The Path of Attainment (1)

must take, for spiritual attainment you must give. In material attainment you must learn, in spiritual attainment you must unlearn. Material attainment is one side, spiritual attainment the other side, the opposite direction.

The word *spiritual* simply means spirit-consciousness; if one is conscious of one's body and thinks this is all that can be known of oneself, the spirit is covered. It is not that one has not got a soul, but that one's soul is obscured. In English they say: that person has lost their soul. No, it is only covered. Can anything possessed be lost? If one thinks this, one is limited. Neither objects nor beings are lost. They are covered for a moment, yet they are all there. Nothing made can ever be destroyed. It is only a covering and an uncovering. All relations and connections—nothing is separable. The separation is outward; inwardly they are never separated. They are separated from one's consciousness, but when the consciousness accommodates them, then nothing in the world can separate them. What does one learn by this? That spiritual attainment is to be reached by the raising of the consciousness from limitation to perfection.

There is another side of the question. There is no one, wise or foolish, who is not progressing slowly or quickly toward the spiritual goal. The only difference is that one is attracted to it, facing the goal, making their way toward it, while the other has their back turned to it and is drawn toward the goal without their being conscious of it. Those poor people do not know where they are being taken, but they go just the same. Their punishment is that they do not see the glory they are approaching, and their torture is that they have been drawn toward the opposite pole to the one they desire. Their punishment is not different from that of the infant that goes into the water of the lake and whose mother pulls it back by its shirt, but it is looking all the time at the lake. From a religious point of view it seems very unjust of the perfect Judge that one should be deprived of that perfect bliss that is spiritual attainment. But from the point of view of metaphysics, no soul will be deprived of this knowledge at any time through eternity.

Now coming to the question of what Sufism teaches on this subject. Sufism avoids words, words from which differences and distinctions come. Words can never fully express truth. Words promote argument. All the differences between religions are differences of words; in sense they do not differ, only in words. For in sense they all have come from one source, and to the same source they return. And this very source is a store for them, it is life, light, and power. Then how can differences be made by human limitations? This is the way of the Sufis: if they do not agree with somebody in a particular idea, they take a step higher instead of differing on the lower plane. Therefore for the wise person there is no difficulty. The main thing that Sufism teaches is to dive deep within oneself, and to prepare mind and body by contemplation to make the being a shrine of God, which is the purpose for which it was created.

* * *

Question: *Murshid, may I ask the explanation of three sayings from the* Gayan? *They are: "All longing in the heart deprives it of freedom," "To suppress desire is to suppress divine impulse," "Ideal is the means and its breaking is the goal."*[4]

Answer: "All longing in the heart deprives it of freedom." The truth is, as soon as there is a longing, one is tied by an iron chain, but a stronger chain than an iron chain. Desire is the condition to be bound. It is not a moral, but a statement, a philosophy. If one followed it, . . . [*text missing*] one cannot live without desire. One might just as well be a rock. No doubt one should have the same freedom as the rock, be quite free if one were free from desire. But even the rock is longing for the day

---

4. The precise text of these three sayings from the *Gayan*: "All that produces longing in the heart deprives it of its freedom"; "To repress desire is to suppress a divine impulse"; and "The ideal is the means; but its breaking is the goal."

when desire is coming. The desire of fulfillment will come in the development into human form.

The second question is, "To suppress desire is to suppress divine impulse." Not everybody is able to understand this and to have a proper judgment about this idea. Those who divide "divine" and "not divine" certainly make the greatest error; either all is divine or nothing is divine. The only division is the division of machine and engineer. The mind of God is working and the instrument of God is working. The one is God who is working, the other the machine of God that is working. What comes as a desire has God . . . [text missing] a divine impulse. And the pious one, ignoring this, makes a false conception, making God a captive in heaven.

And the third question is about the "Ideal is the means but its breaking is the goal." The picture of the ideal is like the egg. Its breaking is the fulfillment, when the children come forth. Breaking is like blooming of flowers. Even so it is necessary for the ideal to break. If it is not broken, then the ideal is not used.

Sadhana, the Path of Attainment

In worldly attainment, or spiritual attainment, the first thing to gain is self-discipline.[5] Many experience, though few know why, that things go wrong when one's self is not disciplined. Those who easily give way to anger, passion, or emotions, they may seem for the moment successful, but they cannot continually succeed in life. Very often misfortunes follow, and illness or a failure, and the reason is that one weakness gives way to another, and so the person who goes down, goes down and down and down. It is natural one may sometimes take a step downward, for the path of life is not even. But the wise thing is that if one has gone down one step, the next step is taken upward. It means, no doubt, resisting the force that pulls one downward. But only that resistance secures the safety of a person's life.

5. A talk given in Paris, December 11, 1922.

What generally happens is that one does not mind a little mistake, one does not take notice of a small weakness. One underestimates a little failure, and in this way in the long run one meets with a great failure. The wise thing, therefore, is—to whatever depth one has fallen—to fix one's eyes upward, and try to rise instead of falling. It is very interesting to observe that when God or heaven is meant one always points upward, although in reality God is everywhere, and so is heaven. And what makes one think that God or heaven is upward is a natural impulse in a person, a divine impulse that gives one an inclination to rise above.

And this shows that the attainment of success is the divine pleasure. Failure and its experience are God's displeasure. People who blame destiny for their failure, take the path of least resistance. But there are more difficulties in the path that appears to be of least resistance. Those who struggle with life lessen their difficulties as they go forward. Those who take the easy path, for them the difficulties grow more as they go on. This does not mean that one should choose a path in life with more difficulties. It only means that in the path of attainment difficulties should not be counted. Difficulties rise over the head of one who looks at them with awe, and the same difficulties fall beneath the feet of one who does not take notice of them. The one who fails in the world, also fails to attain to spiritual bliss. Humans are the kings and queens of their domain; their coming on earth takes away their kingdom. During this trial they are tested to see if they use that human virtue that helps them to attain the mastery over their kingdom. Whatever be their life, they will not be satisfied, for their soul's satisfaction is in fulfilling their purpose. The day when they arrive at that mastery, the day when they have regained the kingdom they had lost, they can say, "Thy will is done on earth as it is in Heaven." And in this is the fulfillment of their being born on this earth.

The question may be asked: What is it to be self-disciplined? It is to be able to say "I can" and not "I cannot." Of course, the words "I cannot" are used when a person does not think it would be wise or just to do something. In that case it is different. But when there is something about which a person thinks it is just, it is good, it is right, and that the person then thinks "I cannot," it is there that self-discipline is lacking. When a person says, "I cannot tolerate," "I cannot endure," "I cannot bear," "I cannot forgive," all these are signs of a lack of self-discipline. In order to see this question more clearly, one must picture oneself as two beings: one as the monarch, and the other as the servant. When one of them wishes, it is the monarch who wishes; and the part that says "I cannot"—it is the servant who says "I cannot." If the servant has their way, then the monarch is in the place of the servant, and the more the servant has their way, the more the servant rules, and the monarch is servant. Naturally, therefore, a conflict arises inwardly, and that reflects on the outer life, and one's whole life becomes unlucky. One may be pious or good or religious, it makes no difference. If one does not realize the kingdom of God within and realize one's spirit to be the monarch, then that one does not accomplish the purpose of life.

29

THE PATH OF ATTAINMENT (2)

The secret of the working of the whole universe is in the duality of nature.[1] In all aspects of nature these two forces are working, and it is the working of these two forces that balances life. Therefore in the path of attainment not only power, which manifests as enthusiasm or action, is sufficient, but besides power (enthusiasm), knowledge and the capability of working are necessary.

Very often people fail to attain success, with all their enthusiasm and power of will, and the reason is that either by the power they have they push along their object, like a ball, or with their strength they hammer the rock that they really need to be whole and not in pieces. Power is, no doubt, most necessary in attainment, but in absence of knowledge the power may prove helpless. By power I mean power in all aspects: the power that one possesses in the outward life, and the power of mind and body. It is the power of mind that is called willpower. No doubt, many with knowledge, but lacking in power, will also meet with failure. If an object is pulled from both sides, by power and by knowledge, then also there be no success. It is the cooperation of these two powers that is the secret of all success. Success, be it of material character or of some other na-

1. A talk given in Paris, December 6, 1922.

ture, is always success. Success, however small, is a step forward to something great, and failure, however small, is a failure and will lead to something still worse. Success should not be valued from its outer value, it must be valued from what it prepares in oneself. And failure, however small, makes an undesirable impression in oneself. This shows how very necessary it is to keep the balance between power and knowledge.

It is of great value to try and develop in life power and knowledge in attaining one's object. There are two kinds of people who become tired of the life in the world: those who have risen above the world, and those who have fallen beneath it. The former have attained their object, but the latter, even if they left the world, any other life would not satisfy them. Their renunciation of worldly things means nothing. It only means incapacity. It is the conquerors of the life of the world who have the right to give up the struggle of the world if they wish to. But those from whose hands the life of the world is snatched away from by others and who are incapable of holding it, who cannot progress, who cannot attain in life what they wish to attain, if they left the world, it is not renunciation, it is simply poverty. It is not by any means selfishness or avariciousness to want to succeed in life. For by success one is climbing upward. But when one is intoxicated by one's worldly success, and one closes one's eyes to the further path, one stands still, and that standing still is like death.

When the many successful people whom we see in this world do not progress spiritually, it means that they did not continue in the path of success. In reality all roads lead to the same goal: business, profession, or science, art, religion, or philosophy. When people do not seem to have arrived at their proper destination, it is not because they have preferred one path to another path. It is that they have not continued on the path. Very often, people lacking knowledge, and with more strength than is necessary, destroy their own purpose. While wanting to construct, they cause destruction. The greatest fault of human nature is that people think that they know best, and when they speak to another person, they think that second person knows but half, and when they are speaking about a third person, they think that third person knows only a quarter. And some few who do not rely upon their knowledge, are then dependent upon the advice of others. Therefore their success or failure, and also their thinking, depend upon the advice of others.

It is most difficult in life to have power, to possess knowledge, and together with these to have clear vision. And if there is any possibility of keeping the vision clear, it is by keeping the balance between power and knowledge.

30

STAGES ON THE PATH OF SELF-REALIZATION

Friends, this evening I shall speak on the subject of self-realization.[1] We see in the words of philosophers, mystics, sages, thinkers, and prophets a great importance given to self-realization. But if I were to explain about self-realization, I would say the first step to self-realization is God-realization. The one who realizes God in the end realizes self. But the one who realizes self never realizes God. And that is the difficulty today with those who search after spiritual truth intellectually. They read many books about occultism, and about esotericism, and mysticism, and what they find most emphasized is self-realization. And then they think that what they have to do in the world is to come to that self-realization. And they think they can just as well omit God. But in reality, God is the key to spiritual perfection; God is the stepping stone to self-realization. God is the way that covers the knowledge of the whole of being. And if God is omitted, then nothing can be reached. The wrong method today carried on in many different so-called cults often proves to be a failure when they teach the beginner on the spiritual path to say, "I am God," a phrase of thoughtlessness, a word of insolence, a thought that has no foundation. It leads them nowhere except to ignorance. To the prophets

---

1. A talk given at the Playhouse, Chicago, April 29, 1926.

and thinkers, the sages who taught their followers the ideal of God, it had a meaning, a purpose in it. And people today, not recognizing it, and being anxious to find the shortest cut, they omit the principal thing in order to come to that realization.

Once a man went to a Chinese sage and said to him, "I want to know some occult laws. Will you teach me?" The sage said, "You have come to ask me to teach you something. We have so many missionaries in China who come to teach us." This man said, "We know about God. But I've come to ask about occult laws." The sage said, "If you know about God, you don't need to know anything more. God is all that is to be known. If you know God, you know all."

Friends, in this world of commercialism there is a tendency, an unconscious tendency, even for a person who promotes spiritual truth, to cater to the taste of the people. Maybe owing to commercial instinct, or with the desire to make a success, there is a tendency to cater to what people want. If people seem to be tired of the God-ideal, those with that tendency want to give them occultism, want to call it mysticism, want to make it a mystification of anything, because the God-ideal seems so simple. And there is even a fashion—today one, tomorrow another—in belief. One thinks that the ideal of God is an old-fashioned thing, something of the past. In order to make a new fashion that one mars that method that was the royal road made by all the wise and thoughtful of all ages, the method that will surely take the person to perfection. Safety and success on that path are sure.

And now I want to discuss a most vital point on the subject of God. There is a person of devotion and of simple faith, of religious belief, who believes in a God, who calls God the judge, the creator, the sustainer, the protector, the master of the last day, the lord, the forgiver, and so on. And there is second person who is perhaps intellectual, who has studied philosophy, who says that, "God is all, and all is God. God is abstract, and it is the abstract that is God." Now, in point of fact the first one has a God, even if that God is only in the imagination, and the second has none, just the abstract. The second calls it God because others say God, but in that one's mind there is only the abstract. For instance, when you say space, there is no personality attached to it, no intelligence recognized in it, no form, no distinct individuality or personality in it. The same thing with time. When you speak about time, you do not imagine time to be a person or sovereign. You say it is time, which means a conception that you have made for your convenience. A person who says that the abstract is God, has no God, just has the abstract. What is it then? The same as space or time. In this I do not mean to say that the one or the other is right. What I am explaining is that from a mental point of view one has a God, even if God is in one's imagination; the other has not, whether that one admits it or not. As soon as one identifies God with the abstract, one has the abstract.

And now we come to the question of who is right. My answer is both are right, and both are wrong. One is in the beginning, and the other is at the end, because the one who begins with the end, will end at the beginning. And the one who begins from the beginning will end at the end. But one might think, "In this short life, why must we make ourselves a kind of illusion, why should we arrive at the truth in the end? Why not begin with truth?"—since everyone is so anxious to get the absolute truth just now. But, friends, if truth were such a thing that could be said in words, I would have been the first person to have given it to you just now. But truth is a thing that must be discovered; one has to prepare oneself to realize it. And it is that preparation that is called religion, or occultism, or mysticism. Whatever you may call it, it is that preparation. You prepare yourself by one way or the other in order to realize truth in the end. And the best way that all the thinkers and sages have adopted is the way of God.

And now I come to the question of belief in God. There are four stages of belief in God. Each stage is as essential and important as the other. And if one does not go stage by stage, gradually evolving toward the realization of God, one does not come to anything. It must be remembered that belief is a step on the ladder. Belief is the means and not the end. It leads to realization, and it is not that we come to a belief. And if one's foot is nailed on the ladder, that is not the object. The object is that one must step on the ladder and climb upward. If one stands on the ladder one defeats the object with which one journeys on the spiritual path. Those, therefore, who believe in a particular creed, in a religion, in God, in the hereafter, in the soul, in a certain dogma, they are no doubt blessed by their belief and think they have something. But if they remain there, there will be no progress. If it were only necessary to have a religious belief, then thousands and millions of people in the world today who have a certain religious belief could have been most advanced people. But they are not. They go on year after year believing something that they have believed perhaps for many generations, and still continue with it and remain there just like the one standing on the step of a staircase, a place not made for one to stand but to go on. When one stays there, one comes to nothing.

If I were to describe the first belief, it is the masses' belief. If one says, "There is a God," then everyone says, "Yes, there is a God," because the others say it. If one is religious, then everyone says, "Yes, we also go with him." And you might think that today, at this stage of civilization, people are too advanced to have a mass belief, but that would be a great mistake. People are the same today as they were a thousand years before, or perhaps worse, if it comes to a spiritual question. Someone who is called "the person of the day" in a nation, is looked upon favorably for a time by the whole nation; thousands and millions lift the person up, hold the person high. But for how long? As long as one more powerful person has not said, "No, it is not so." And then the whole country throws that person down.

Just before the war I was visiting Russia. And would you believe, in every shop there was a picture of the czar and czarina, held in high esteem. It was a sacred thing for them. There was the religious ideal attached to the emperor as he was the head of the church. And they used to be filled with joy when they saw the czar and czarina passing in the street. It was a religious upliftment for them. And it was not long after that that they had processions in the street where at each step they took, they hammered the crown in the street. It did not take them one moment to change their belief. Why? Because it was mass belief. It is a very powerful belief. It changes nations. It throws them down and raises them up; it brings wars. But what is it, after all? A mad belief. And yet no one will admit it. If you ask someone, they say, "I am not one of them." At the same time all move together when an impulse comes for good or bad.

Then there is a second step toward belief, and that is belief in an authority, such as is happening today with the people of Italy. They believe in a leader. They say, "I will not believe in the ordinary person, in my neighbor, in my colleague, I believe in that man whom I trust." This belief is one step higher, because it is a belief in somebody in whom one has trust. When a person says, "I am a Christian," it means a belief in Jesus Christ and his teaching. It is a belief in someone, not in everyone, just the one in whom you believe. That is the second step in belief, the belief in authority. One might say, "We don't even care for belief in authority today," but it is not true. For instance, everyone accepts a discovery made by a scientist before having made investigations about it. Investigations come afterward. When a person comes forward and says, "I have discovered this," everyone accepts it. Maybe another scientist will produce something else one may believe. But the one who says something with authority is believed by the multitude.

And then there is a third stage in belief, a stage still further, and this belief makes one still greater. That belief is the belief of reason, that one does not believe in any authority, nor in anything that everybody else believes, but one has reasoned it out; that one sees its reason. This belief is stronger still, for of the beliefs I have explained before one cannot give the proof of those beliefs. It only shows that if a scientist says "so and so," many people say "so and so." But in this case one can stand up and say, "Yes, I have reasoned it out." But this has its limitation just the same. Since reason is the slave of mind, reason is as changeable as the weather. This reason obeys your impressions. If you have an impulse to insult a person, or to box with that person, you can produce many reasons for it. It may be that afterward there will be contrary reasons. But at the same time, while one has this impulse to the right or wrong, there is always a reason with it. Do you think the criminals in jail have committed crimes without a reason? No. They have a reason too. It does not fit in with the law perhaps, it does not satisfy society, but if you ask them, they have a reason. And at the same time, the reason you have today, may perhaps change next week. Nevertheless, this third belief we have just now explained makes one stand on one's feet for that moment, if not forever, and gives one a greater power to defend one's belief.

And then again there is a fourth belief. That belief is a belief of conviction, which stands above reason. There is a sense of conviction in a person that is not discovered for some time in life, but there comes a time when it is discovered, and that is a blessed time. Then there arises an idea, an idea that no reason can break, an idea, a feeling that is not a passing feeling, but that is a conviction. However high the idea may be, you seem to be an eyewitness of that idea; you are as strong, as powerful, as a person who has seen with their own eyes. Something says, "Yes, I have seen it." You can be convinced of ideas so fine, which cannot even be expressed in words. You are more convinced of them than even if you had seen them with your own eyes. It is that belief that is called by Sufis and Persian mystics *iman*, which means conviction.

I remember the blessing my spiritual teacher, my murshid, used to give me every time I parted from him. And that blessing was, "May your iman be strengthened." At that time I had not thought about the word *iman*, which in the East means belief, or faith. But on the contrary, I thought as a young man, "Is my faith so weak that my teacher wants it to be strong?" I should have preferred if he had said, "May you become illuminated," or "May your powers be great," or "May your influence spread," or "May you elevate higher and higher," or "May you become perfect." This simple thing, "May your faith be strengthened," what did it mean? I did not criticize it, but I pondered and pondered upon the subject. And in the end I came to realize that no blessing is more valuable and important than this. For every blessing is attached to a conviction. When there is no conviction, there is nothing. The secret of healing, the mystery of evolving, the power of all attainments, and the way to spiritual realization, all these come from the strengthening of that belief that is a conviction, that nothing can change it forever.

And now we come again to the question of God, because this is the first important question we must make clear in our mind before we take a step further in spiritual progress. Although, I must first say that, "To analyze God means to dethrone God"; so the less said on the subject, the better. But at the same time, the seekers after truth who want to tread the spiritual path with open eyes and whose intellect is hungering for knowledge, should know something about it.

There is a Hebrew story that once Moses was walking near the bank of a river. And he saw a shepherd boy speaking to himself. Moses was interested and halted there to listen to what he was saying. The shepherd boy was saying, "O God, I have heard so much of you. You are so beautiful, you are so lovely, you are such a dear, that if you ever came to me I would clad you with my mantle, and I would guard you night and day. I would protect you from the cruel animals of this forest, and bathe you in this river, and bring to you all good things, milk and buttermilk. I would bring you a special bread, and love you so much. I would not let anyone cast his glance upon you. I would be all the time near you. I love you so much! If only I could see you once, God, I would give all I have." Moses said, "Hello, what are you saying?" The boy looked at Moses and trembled and was afraid. "Did I say anything wrong?" he asked. Moses said, "God, the protector of all beings, you think of protecting him, giving him bread? He gives bread to the whole universe. You say you would bathe him in the river. He is the purest of all pure things. And how can you say that you will guard him who guards all beings?" And the boy trembled. He thought, "What a terrible thing I did, such wrong things." He seemed to be lost. But as Moses went a few steps further there came a voice, "Moses, what did you do? We sent you to bring our friends to us, and now you have separated one. No matter how he thought of us, he thought of us just the same. You should have let him think the way he was thinking about us. You should not have interfered with him. Everyone has their own imagination about God. It is best if everyone is left with their own imagination."

Dear friends, in our daily life we may hate someone, yet the same one is loved by another; we may criticize someone, yet the same one is praised by another. If that is so, then the conception of everyone about everyone is different. The same person is considered saint by one and satan by another.[2] If that is true, then the God that we know or can know is nothing but our conception, a picture that we have made of God for our own self, our own convenience. It is the greatest mistake for anyone to interfere with the conception of God of another, or to think another one should have the same conception of God as oneself. It is impossible. So many different artists have painted the picture of Christ yet each one is different. And since we allow every artist to have their own conception of Christ,

---

2. Used here, as in Islam and in the Hebrew Bible, the word *satan* or *shaitan* is not a proper name but indicates any evil being.

so we should allow every person to have their own conception of God. Therefore, we need not blame the old Chinese and Greeks and Indians who believed in many gods. Many gods is too small a number. In reality, each one has his or her own God. Besides, all the different conceptions are nothing but covers over one God. Let them call that God by any name, think of God by whatever imagination they have. It is, after all, the highest ideal, and the ideal of each one is as high as that one's imagination can make it. And urging upon someone that God is abstract, and formless, and pure, and that God is nameless, all these things do not help that person to evolve because the first step on the path of God is to make a conception of God. It is simply to help the seekers after God that the wise in all ages sometimes made a little statue and called it god or goddess and said, "Here is God." They said, "Here is God. There is a shrine. Go there." And to the one who was not satisfied with this, to that one they said, "Walk two hundred times around the shrine before you enter the temple, then you will be blessed." When the worshipper got tired, they naturally felt exaltation because they walked in the path of God.

And now coming to the idea of self-realization. In relation to the belief in God, you might ask me that, "If we leave everyone with their particular imagination or ideal of God, will they then progress and one day come to the realization of the self, which is the highest attainment taught by all the great teachers of humanity?" I say, "Yes."

There are three stages on the way to spiritual perfection. Those who are unaware of the possibility of spiritual perfection, they are greatly mistaken when they say that, "A human is imperfect, a human cannot be perfect." They are mistaken for the reason, that they have seen only the human in the human. They have not seen God in the human. Christ has said, "Be ye perfect even as your Father in heaven is perfect."[3] This shows that there is the possibility of perfection. It is true also that a

---

3. Matthew 5:48.

human cannot be perfect, but a human is not human alone, in a human there is also God. Therefore, the human remains imperfect, but the God part in the human seeks for perfection. That is what the world was created for. Humans are here on earth for this one purpose, that they may bring forth that spirit of God in them to discover their own perfection.

And now I will explain the three stages toward this perfection. The first stage is to make God as great and as perfect as your imagination can. It is in order to help one to perfect God in oneself. That is why the teachers gave different prayers, the prayers of God, calling God the judge, the forgiver, most compassionate, most faithful, most beautiful, most loving. All these attributes are our limited conceptions. God is greater than what we can say about God. But when we make all these conceptions, and make God by our imaginations as great as we make him, it must be understood that by making God great, God cannot be made greater than God is. We cannot give God pleasure by making God great; however, it is by making God great that we arrive at a certain greatness, that our vision widens, our spirit deepens, our ideal reaches high, that before us we create a greater vision, a wider horizon, for our own expansion. We should, therefore, by way of prayer, by praise, contemplation, try to make God as great in our idea as possible. Now, the truth behind this is that those who see good points in others and want to add what is lacking in others, those persons become nobler every day. Imagine, by making others noble, by thinking good of others, they themselves become nobler and better than those of whom they think good. And the one who thinks evil of others becomes in time wicked, because that one covers the good within and produces thus the vision of evil. Therefore the first stage and the first duty of all seekers after truth is to make God as great as possible for their own good, because they are making an ideal within themselves, they are building within themselves that which will make them great.

Stages on the Path of Self-Realization

And now there is a second stage. That second stage is the work of the heart. The first is of the head. To make God great intellectually, with thought and imagination, is the painter's work. Now the work of the heart. Our love forms that ideal. In our everyday life we see the phenomenon of love. The first lesson that love teaches us is, "I am not, thou art." The first thing to think of is to erase yourself from your mind and think of the one whom you love. As long as you do not arrive at this idea, so long the word love remains only in the dictionary. Many speak about love, but very few know it. Is love a pastime, an amusement, a drama, is it a performance? The first lesson of love is sacrifice, service, self-effacement.

There is a little story of a peasant girl who was passing through a field where a Muslim was offering his prayers. And the law is that no one should pass by a place where a person is offering his prayers. After a time this girl returned the same way, and the man said, "O girl, what a terrible thing you have done today." She was shocked. She asked, "What did I do?" He said, "You passed by this way! It is a great sin. I was praying." She said, "I want to know, what were you doing?" He said, "I was praying, thinking of God." She said, "Were you thinking of God? I was going off to see my young man. I did not see you. How did you see me when you were thinking of God?"

To close the eyes for prayer is one thing, and to produce the love of God is another thing. That is the second stage in spiritual realization, where in the thought of God you begin to lose yourself in the same way as the lover loses the thought of self in the thought of the beloved.

And the third stage is different again. In the third stage the beloved becomes the self, and the self is there no more, because the self as we think it to be no longer remains. But the self becomes what it really is. It is that realization that is called self-realization.

31

HUMAN BEINGS, MASTERS OF THEIR DESTINY (1)

Beloved Ones of God, this evening I am speaking on the subject of human beings, the masters of their destiny.[1] I would like to quote a saying from the *Gayan*, "The present is the reflection of the past, and the future is the re-echo of the present." Destiny is not what is already made. Destiny is that which we are making. Very often fatalists think that we are in the hands of destiny, driven in life in whatever direction destiny drives us. But in point of fact we are the masters of our destiny, especially from the moment we begin to realize this fact. Among Hindus there is a well-known saying that the creation is Brahma's dream, in other words, that all manifestation is the dream of the creator. I would add that destiny means the materialization of a person's own thought. For success and failure, for rise and fall, the person is responsible, and it is the person who brings it about, either knowingly or unknowingly. There is a hint of this in the Bible; the principal prayer that is taught by Christ has these words at the end that, "Thy will be done on earth as in heaven."[2] It is a psychological suggestion to humankind to make it possible that the will of God, which is easily done in

---

1. A talk given at the Waldorf Astoria, New York City, December 13, 1925.
2. Matthew 6:10.

heaven, also be done on earth. And that English saying that "Man proposes and God disposes" supports this also; it suggests the other side of the same idea. These seem two contrary things, yet explain the same theory, that what is meant by destiny is changed by a person, and destiny changes a person's plans.

The question of destiny can be better explained by giving you a picture of the artist meditating on a certain design that she has in mind. To create the design in her mind, that is one stage. Now she wishes to bring it on the canvas. When she draws this picture on the canvas, it may suggest to her something that she had not thought of when she made the design in her mind. And when the artist has finished the picture that she had first designed in her mind, she sees that it is quite different from what she had originally thought.

This shows that our life stands before us as a picture, and when all that has been designed before, when that is brought about, this picture suggests something else to our soul. It suggests a certain improvement to be made, something that is lacking in it, that might be put in it. And it is in this way that the picture is improved. Because there are two artists, one who designs the plan that has been made in her mind on the canvas, and the other who takes suggestions from the picture itself as she goes on designing the picture. There is a difference; one is merely an artist, the other is a master. The latter is not bound to the plan; the former has designed something and is bound to what she has designed; she is limited.

One can say the same thing with a composer of music. The composer thinks a certain melody in his mind; he contemplates upon it and wishes to put it on paper. But when he plays his composition on the piano, the music suggests an improvement to him. He plays the same idea he first had thought of, but he is able to perfect and finish it when he has heard it with his own ears.

That is the picture of our life. There are those who are driven by the hand of destiny, who do not know where they come from, do not know where they are going. They are put in a certain condition in life. They are busy with something, occupied with something, and they see there is no other way of getting on; they may desire something quite different, they may have difficulty putting their mind to what they are doing, but they still think, "So I must go on." Those are the ones who have not yet understood the meaning of this secret. But there are others who even after a hundred failures are still determined that they will succeed at the next attempt. These ones are the masters of their success.

And now we shall come to the idea of what a human being is. In the *Gayan* it says, "When a glimpse of our image is caught in a human, when heaven and earth are sought in a human, then what is there in the world that is not in a human? If one only explores him or her, there is a lot in a human." When a person says, "But I cannot help it, this is my habit," when a person says, "I cannot help it, I am like this," when a person says that, "I have always done so, I cannot do differently," when a person is fixed in a situation and cannot alter it, that person does not know the meaning of the quotation I read. Everything is there in the human. If only one could explore within oneself and find out what treasure there is within oneself. Those who have explored the human being have found out, they have discovered that a human has two aspects: one aspect is living and the other is dead. One is the engineer, the other is a machine. When the engineer part of one is buried, the part of one that is called a mechanism is there. Then one is a mechanism, one is a machine, one works like a machine from morning till evening. When the engineer part sleeps, what is one? A machine that is running with the oil and steam given to it. This machine part of the human is subject to conditions, whether favorable or unfavorable, to climatic conditions, and personal influences that come from all sides.

And then there is the side of a person that may be called the engineer. This side of the human is living. And it is a side of the person that may be called the free will or the self-expression, where there is intelligence, where there is power. And the greater this part of one's being is, so great is the person, because so much more of the person is living, is conscious of that part in oneself that is the engineer. In religious terminology this may be called the divine spark, and as humans have inherited their physical being from the dense earth that has made them a mortal being, there is one part of their being that is immortal. It is that part of their being that is called the divine spark, it is that part of their being that is the heritage of God.

In ancient religious terminology, in the Bible, for instance, one often reads: the father in heaven. That means that the human being is considered as the child of God. What does it mean? As humans have inherited a part of their being from the earth, so have they inherited the essential part of their being from God. In other words, the human is an expression of God. In the human there is the being of God, and that being can especially be distinguished and defined as the creator. God is the creator and the human is the creator at the same time. Humans give proof of God being the perfect creator by their own creative faculty.

And now coming to the question, how does one attain to this path that is called the path of mastery? In all periods of world history, in all the world's traditions, one sees that there have been wise ones, there have been those who have searched after truth. And the outcome of their search after truth, what they gained, was mastery. The prophets of all times—Buddha, Jesus Christ, Muhammad, Moses—in one way or another, what their lives have shown was mastery.

But in a small way one can also see it in those who came first to America, a country where there was nothing, and all this was made and created as a great wonder in the world. Many came from faraway distances and settled here, many who had nothing in the beginning and now have everything. One can also see in this an example of mastery. But mastery does not end there. If we have gained the earth, that is not the only object; there is something further still. There is a larger scope in life, and as soon as one begins to see that larger scope, one sees that there is much space to be filled, much to be done besides all that one does materially.

There is a story of Timur, the Mughul emperor, a man whom destiny had made to be great. And yet he was not awakened to that greatness. One day, tired of the strife of daily life and despairing over his worldly duties, he was lying on the ground in a forest waiting for death to come and take him. And a dervish happened to come by who saw him asleep and who recognized in this man that destiny had made him to be a great personality. And here he was, unaware of it. The dervish struck him with his stick, and Timur woke up and asked the dervish, "Why have you come to trouble me here? I have left the world and have come to the forest. Why do you come to trouble me?" The dervish said, "What gain is there in the forest? You have the world before you; it is there that you will find what you have to accomplish, if only you realize your power to accomplish." He said, "No, I am too disappointed, too pessimistic, that any good will ever come to me. The world has wounded me. I am sore. My heart is broken. I will no longer stay in this world." The dervish said, "What is the use of having come to this earth if you have not accomplished something, if you have not experienced something? If you are not happy, you do not know how to live." Timur said to the dervish, "Do you think that I shall ever accomplish anything?" The dervish answered, "That is why I have come to awaken you. Awake and pursue your course with courage. You will be successful; there is no doubt about it." This impression awakened in Timur the spirit with which he had come into the world. And with every step he took forward, he saw that conditions changed and all the influences and forces that were needed for success became open before him as if life, which before had closed its doors, now opened before him. And he reached that stage where he became the famous Timur of history.

And another example of the same kind in the history of India is Shivaji, who began as a robber. One day he came to be blessed by a sage whose name was Ram Das. He asked the sage, "Will you bless me?" The sage asked, "Why, what do you want?" He answered, "I am a robber, I am going to rob the travelers." The sage, who was compassionate and who was merciful, saw who it was, and what would come out of this man, did not break his heart, and said, "I will bless you, go, but become a great robber." And what did he become, this great robber? A king. And his attempt then was to be a still greater robber, to be an emperor.

However, in all walks of life, it will prove to the seeker after truth that there is a key to success, a key to happiness, a key to advancement and evolution in life, and this key is the attainment of mastery.

And now the question is: How to attain mastery? There are three stages. The first stage of attaining mastery is to get self-control. And when once self-control is gained, then the second stage is to control all influences that pull one away from one's path, that push one aside from the way one wishes to take. And if one has been victorious in this second stage, then there is a third stage, which is the control of conditions, of situations. The one who is responsible, the one who has control over conditions and situations, is greater than a thousand people who are qualified and work. The controller may sit in a chair and do nothing and that controller will accomplish more than the one who is doing something all day long yet has accomplished very little. Very few can imagine to what extent one can gain power. And especially as life today is a life of continual strife for nothing, a busy life without much accomplishment, we cannot imagine to what extent the power of the master mind can accomplish things. Only it is behind the scene. Those who do little, they come forward and say, "I can do so much," and those who really do something, they say little.

All that is on the earth, gold and silver, gems and jewels, they are all for humankind. And all that is happiness: power, intelligence, harmony, peace, inspiration, ecstasy, joy, these also belong to humankind. One can just as readily make a heavenly thing one's treasure as a thing of the earth. It is not necessary for one to leave all the things of the world and go away from here. One can attend to one's business, to one's profession, to one's duties in life, and at the same time develop this spirit in oneself that is the spirit of mastery. The spirit of mastery is likened to a spark: by blowing continually upon it it will grow into a blaze and out of it a flame will rise.

Those who will continually keep before them the idea that, "All that is lacking outside must not trouble me, for it is all within myself, and if I shall blow on the spark of mastery by continual contemplation, then one day that flame will rise and life will become clear," their power will indeed be great.

32

HUMAN BEINGS, MASTERS OF THEIR DESTINY (2)

Friends, it is my pleasure and privilege to address for the first time the Students and Teachers Association of Wichita. My subject this evening is human beings, the masters of their destiny.[1] In the first place, I would like to say that the word *man* comes from the Sanskrit word *mana* or *manu*, which means the mind. It is symbolical and expressive. It shows that one is not one's body, but one's mind. There are two opposite opinions existing in the world. One belongs to those who are called fatalists. They believe in fate. And the other is the opinion of those who believe in the free will. And if we look at life from the point of view of both, we shall find some reasons for and against each. When we look at life from the point of view of the one who believes in free will, there are many instances where there is a qualification, a condition for progress, an inclination for it, and every possibility. And at the same time, there is some unknown hindrance and one cannot find out what it is. A person may work for years and years and not succeed. And against the fatalist there is also an argument, that there are many who hope and believe that all good things will come of themselves. But just by hoping and believing good things do not come. It takes an effort and persistence; it needs patience

1. A talk given at the High School, Wichita, Kansas, April 20, 1926.

to accomplish things. And this shows that both possibilities are true. And at the same time, the middle way is the best, the way of understanding how far free will works and also where free will is hindered.

And what is it that hinders free will in being successful in life? Life can be divided, according to the mystic's point of view, into two aspects. One aspect is the preparatory aspect, and the other aspect is the aspect of action. The preparatory aspect is before a person was born, and the other after a person's birth. A person is born into a certain condition, which condition becomes the foundation of the course of the person's life. A person is born into an addicted surrounding, or in a rich family. What does it show? It shows that the person is born in a condition that already gives the foundation to build a life. The credit for what the person does with that condition belongs to that person. But that condition is something the person has not made; from this the person has to develop and evolve through life. And the question is how this condition is brought about.

There are many different ideas among Eastern philosophers on this question. The way that the wise and the mystics look at this question is that the human being is a ray of the spirit, which is likened to the sun, and each soul is a ray shooting forth from that sun. Therefore, the origin of all souls is one and the same just as the origin of the various rays is one and the same sun. But as these rays shoot forth they pass through three different phases, in other words, penetrate through three different spheres. The metaphysics of the East recognizes the three spheres this way. When the ray shoots forth, the first sphere it passes through is called the angelic sphere, the next is called the sphere of the genius or jinn, and the third is called the physical sphere. Now, the nature of each sphere is such that the ray or soul, when it penetrates through a certain sphere, must clothe itself in the garb of that particular sphere, just as a person from a tropical country going to a cold climate must adopt the clothes of that climate. Thus the soul, which by origin is intelligence and which is a ray of that sun that is the source and goal of all beings, adopts or dons a certain garb with which it is able to enter, to stay, and to pass through that particular sphere. Therefore, according to the metaphysics of the East, a human is an angel, a jinn, and a human. In these three conditions the soul is the same, but the garb it has taken makes it seem different. Passing through the angelic sphere the soul is angel, passing through the sphere of genius, the soul is jinn, passing through the physical sphere the soul is human. Therefore, if there is an angel, it is human; if there is a jinn, it is human. It is the soul's condition in the preparatory stages of angel and jinn that in the end makes it human.

But then one might ask: What about the animals and about other beings and other objects that show some part of life in them, such as trees and plants and rocks? And the answer is that all these are preparatory coverings that make the clothes, the garb, for the soul to take.

There is a saying of a great sage of Persia who lived five hundred years before Darwin gave his idea of biology, and you can find it in thousands of Persian manuscripts where it says that, "God slept in the rock, God dreamed in the plant, God awoke in the animal, and God realized himself in the human." It tells that this process from mineral to vegetable, from animal to man is really the progress of the garb. For instance, in a country where they did not know how to make clothes, the first clothes were made of the bark of a tree. Then as people went on making clothes, they found better material, and finally came to the finest material. The human is the finest material, its garb, not its soul. Its soul is the same as that of the human of a thousand years ago. The material has changed and has progressed with the evolution of the soul that has adorned itself with it. And in this way the variety of creatures have been made manifest.

There is also another outlook on this subject: that although the soul as a ray goes forward to the physical sphere, yet its nature is to go backward, because of the law of gravitation. Just as the body, which is made of clay, is drawn to the earth, so the soul, which belongs to the spirit, is drawn to the spirit. "But," one may say, "we can see the body drawn to the earth, we can see all things of earth drawn to the earth, but we do not see the law of gravitation working in the soul." We see it but we deny it, because we do not look at it in that way. For there is a dissatisfaction, a discontentment in every soul. People may be in a palace or in a cottage, but no matter what condition they live in, there is an innate yearning and longing that even they themselves do not know. One thinks today, "I long for money," tomorrow "for position," another day again "for a friend," "for fame" or "a name," and one goes from one thing to another. It just goes on. And when in the end one has reached one's object one wants something else. It is the law of gravitation, that something that is the spirit, the sun, that is at the back of it. That is why in ancient times people worshipped the sun god as a symbol of the sun within us, the sun that cannot be seen by our eyes, which is the source and goal of all beings, from which we have come and to which we are drawn. As it is said in the Qur'an, "From God we all come and to God we have to return."[2] That means there is a spirit, the spirit of all things, the essence of life from which we come and toward which we are drawn.

And now there is another side of it to be thought about. That there is an action of the souls coming from their source toward manifestation, and an action of souls withdrawing from the physical sphere going backward. The souls who are coming forward are coming with that life and light, with that electricity, intelligence, freedom, and freshness that they can impart to those they meet. And souls coming from manifestation have also to give something on their way: their thought of the wickedness of the world, of the goodness of the world, their desire of accomplishing things, their experience of life, all these things they are taking back. All the good they have done, the evil they

2. Sura 2:156.

have done, the good and bad actions they have done to others, all these things they are taking back. And there is an exchange as naturally as between people coming and going from the Far East to America and America to the Far East, both meeting in Europe. They give each other whatever they have. In this exchange, one says, "Let me give you this introduction. I know a good friend for you." And when that person travels here they have a condition with which to begin their life already made for them. Still another finds that the wrong person has sent them to the wrong place, and they are lost.

In the Western countries there is much made of what they call reincarnation in Hindu philosophy. In the East people speak very little about these things, and sometimes these conceptions have been exaggerated so much that they confuse their real spirit. And the real meaning of the idea is the impression of the soul who has come from the source. That impression has made that soul the same person who has given the impression. For instance, the soul of Shakespeare going backward to the source met many souls coming toward the earth, and they became impregnated with all the expressions and thoughts that Shakespeare had developed. When that soul comes with those thoughts, it is born with that inspiration from Shakespeare. And in the same way debts need to be paid, that one has to pay the debts of the other. Because one has the benefit of the other, that one has the debts as well. In the East one says that, "You have to look after your children or to pay for your family is the debt you have to pay." The more we think about this subject the more we shall find that preparation is made for a person before the person is born on earth. And it is that preparation that made the person able to live life on earth.

And now coming to the question of life on earth. Is this a life that is fixed and designed or is there free will? Very often people do not understand the meaning of the words *free will*, and those especially who claim to have much free will have the least of it. They are so conscious of their free will, and yet they do not know where it comes from. When they have an inclination to laugh or cry, to sit or move, they think that, "Because I thought like doing it, I did it," but they do not know where the thought came from. It may have come from a friend, perhaps from someone unknown. Do we not feel every day at some time an oppression, seemingly without reason, or a humor or a feeling of despair, or a desire for action and at other times a feeling of lethargy? Some think whatever comes into their mind is free will. But free will is quite different from that. People have two aspects of their being. One aspect is merely a machine, a mechanism that is fixed to work, and subject to influences and conditions as well as climatic and planetary influences. That is the case of the average person. If there is one part of the engineer in a person, there are ninety-nine parts of the machine in that person. And sometimes when they think of free will, it is that one part of the hundred they have. But most often what they have is the machine's ninety-nine. When a person gets an impulse that person thinks, "That is my impulse." But it was suggested by another person. And the desire that springs in a person's mind is perhaps the influence of conditions, their wish perhaps a planetary influence. And there are thousands of influences unknown to us. But as people do not know the influences working behind their vision, they think, "It is my free will."

Now, the machine part in a person's life comes from the garb that person has taken on. It is the body that is a machine, and another, finer machine, inside, is the mind. But both of these are apart from that spirit of free will that is the soul. The more conscious one is of that spirit of free will, the more one wakens the mastership in oneself. In the East they call it the master mind, the person who awakens to that spirit of free will. Very often we muddle these two instruments. We are made of two aspects, a physical and a mental aspect, the body and the mind. And those who make it work to their free will begin to experience mastership in life.

Friends, the great heroes whom we read about in books, whatever they have accomplished in life—whether inventors, composers, generals, statesmen, stateswomen—all show that spirit of free will that is the pure essence of the spirit or of the soul. That spirit was developed in them, and that brought about the great accomplishments they achieved in their lives. You have a great example in America, a country, a land where there was nothing except forests and deserts and a few races living there. And what has been made of this country by those who came and who had patience and strength of will and lived here and made it all as it is! It gives a great and wonderful example to all. But if we think about life, this is not all there is to accomplish. There is much more to accomplish in life than new inventions, great accumulation of wealth, and different aspects of civilization. There is something more to be accomplished. And when we put that out and become contented with all we have, we do not progress any further. There is a need of the soul that needs to be accomplished, and that is the higher destiny.

There are two purposes of life. One is the individual purpose of life and the other is the collective purpose of life. The purpose of an individual's life is different. For instance, in the orchestra the clarinet has one purpose, the violin another, and the cello yet another. Each instrument has to take its own place in the orchestra. And so there is a purpose of each individual's life, a separate purpose. And then there is a collective purpose, and that is the purpose of all lives, of every life. That purpose is to come to the realization of that spirit that is within, which is the source and goal of all things, a spirit that was capable and is capable of all this manifestation. It is therefore that religious people have called it "Lord," the "architect of all," the "composer of all" so as to express their feeling that it has all the power of creation. It is the power of the one and only spirit. But one might think, "How to realize it? Is it possible to realize this power intellectually?"

It seems that the war[3] has brought a wave upon the world of realizing spiritual truth. No doubt, it seems that people are awakening to the spiritual truth, but to my mind many are going backward instead of going forward. Do you think that there is greater peace than before? People thought the war would bring about peace. But first came the outward war, and now there is an inward war. Now in people's mind there is a war.

We talk so much about freedom. But where is it? When we move about, we cannot do it without showing a passport. And it is becoming more strict than it has ever been. There are a thousand things today that show that there is less freedom than there was fifty years ago. The conventionality of today, the commercialism, and the extreme materialism of today have removed people far from the spiritual ideal that was the central theme of civilization. There is no doubt that a majority today is awakened to or at least seeking for the higher truth. But the reason is that people have become so material and life has become so material that now every soul consciously or unconsciously feels for something different from what they get. Naturally a person has a desire to look for something else.

The politicians are working for better conditions and yet they have not come to see things more clearly. So it is with the scientists today. They are inventing many things. Yet they think there is something to be discovered and that is not yet discovered. The other day I had an interview with a very great scientist in New York. And at the end of the conversation, I found how greatly scientists today desire to find some evidence of inspiration, of power, of light, that is not yet explored. But very often people take wrong ways. For instance, there are different seekers after truth today in the States. During my visit in the States I have seen some who think that by reading books, occult books, they will come to realization. It is like looking for the moon on earth. One must look in the sky. It is the same thing. They want intellectually to find truth. They can never

3. World War I.

get it. In order to get to the secret of life, one has to take quite a different way. I do not say that intellectual study is not of great importance in interpreting the truth to others. But in order to find truth, there is something greater than the study of books that is needed. A man came to me who had read perhaps a hundred books on occult science and he himself had written fifty books. And he came to me and said, "Truth I have not yet found." I said, "You will never find it." It is not learning, it is unlearning. It is not to be learned and taught, it is to be discovered. It is not something you can get from outside. It is there already. It is not something new you will learn. It is what your soul has known.

Then there are others who think, "Well, I do not care what truth it is, it is to see some wonders, some spirits, some wonders that others cannot do; that is worthwhile." It is like children with toys. They are for curiosity. They will go to jugglers who will give them illusions, and after that they will come to some understanding. And again there are others who want to seek in this book, in that book, in this school, in that school. They are restless people; they are amusing themselves. They do not want truth. The seeker after truth has a different rhythm, a different inclination. The wobbling and moving boat will not reach its destination. It is the ship that is heavy that will reach its destination. One must first make oneself that boat, earnest and serious. How can an insincere person who has no self-confidence, a person who doubts, a person with a weak will reach that stage?

There are many things one has to overcome before one sets forth upon the journey to higher realization. But at each step one takes toward the realization of truth, one will feel more self-confident. And the more one overcomes all doubts and the more self-confidence one has, the greater will be one's will; and the closer to truth one reaches, the more light one will see. And what is that light? It is the light of self-realization.

33

THE LAW OF ACTION

Beloved Ones of God, I ask your indulgence with my subject for this evening on the law of action.[1] To say that results are similar to deeds sounds simple, for mostly everyone knows it. But it is not always the case that everyone follows it. And the reason is that knowing a law does not enable one to observe the law. Besides, the nature of life is so intoxicating that, absorbed in the activity of life, one mostly forgets this rule. It is natural, however, that this most simple thing is very difficult to practice. And the very reason that it is simple, is because one neglects to think seriously about it.

In order to prove this theory that the results of a deed are similar to the deed, one need not go far. One can see numberless examples in one's own life and in the lives of others. For it is like an echo: what one does has an echo, and in that echo is the result.

And now we come to the saying of Zarathustra that says that actions may be divided into three kinds: deed, speech, and thought. One may not do wrong, but one may speak wrongly; one may not speak wrongly, but one may think wrongly, and the wrong is done just the same. And how many make an excuse by saying, "I said it, but I did not do it." People can even

---

1. A talk given at the Sorbonne, Paris, March 23, 1925.

excuse themselves by saying, "I did not say it, I only thought it." According to the idea of the mystic, the world in which we make our life is an *akasha*, and *akasha* means capacity. It is pictured by them as a dome, and whatever is spoken in it has its re-echo, and therefore no one can do, say, or think anything for one moment that will become nonexistent. It is recorded, and that record is creative. It is not only that what one does, what one says, or what one thinks that is recorded in the memory or in the sphere, but that record also creates at every moment, so that every line and letter of this record becomes the seed or the germ that produces a similar effect.

I once heard a sculptor say—and how truly he spoke—that every person is the sculptor of his or her own image. But I would add that not only is this true, but every person is the creator of his or her own conditions, favorable or unfavorable. The difficulty is that people never have patience to wait till they see the result, for the result takes some time to appear, and before that there may be contrary effects. For instance, a person who had just robbed another person and, when coming home, met with more luck, and found a purse full of gold coins in the street. Naturally the robber would think, "What a good result after good work! Now that it is shown that I have done good work, I must continue it. It is only the simple ones who say things against it. But what they say is just words; I have seen the good results in my own experience." And life is so intoxicating that it gives a person no time to think that the result of one's deed is perhaps waiting; that what happens today may be the result of something else.

When we consider the law of action, it can be divided into five different aspects. One aspect of the law of action is the law of the community. A law that suits one community may not suit another community, for it depends upon the particular development of that community. This law is made for the comfort and convenience of the members of that community. And another aspect can be called the law of the state; it is a law by which different classes of people and different communities are governed as one whole. No doubt, these aspects of law are as limited as the human mind is limited. Naturally, therefore, many laws are rejected, and many new laws are made and brought into practice. And as time goes on, so people will see that the members of the community or the state will always wish for changes to be made in the law. This has always been and will always be.

And now we come to the third aspect of the law, and that is the law of a church, a law that perhaps comes from tradition, and a law that people accept not only because it is a law by which they are governed, but because it is a law that is concerned with their faith, with their belief, which is sacred to them. It is this law that makes a conscience, more than any other aspect of the law.

But then there is another aspect of the law, and that is the law brought by the prophets from time to time. And what is this law? This law comes as an interpretation of the hidden law that the prophet could see. But at the same time, a law that is given by a prophet is related to the period in which the prophet lived, to the people of that period and to their particular evolution. And when we study the different religions given by different prophets to different people in this world in different periods of the world's history, we shall find that the truth that is behind the religions is the same. And if the teaching differs, it differs only in the particular law they have given. People have always disputed in vain about this difference in the laws that the different teachers have given to their people, not realizing how much that law had to do with the people to whom it was given and with the time when it was given.

But these four laws that I have mentioned: the law of the community, of the state, of the church, of the prophet, all have their limitations. There is, however, one law that leads one toward the unlimited, and this is a law that can never be taught and that can never be explained. At the same time, this law is rooted in the nature of the human being. And there is no person, however unjust and wicked that person may seem, who has not this faculty in their innermost being. It may be called a faculty, for it is the faculty of knowing proper from improper, of discerning right from wrong.

But now we come to this question: What determines something to be right or wrong? It is four things: the motive behind action, the result of the action, the time, and the place. Wrong action with the right motive may be right. And a right action with a wrong motive may be wrong. We are always ready to judge an action, and we hardly think of the motive. That is why we readily accuse a person for their wrong, and readily excuse ourselves for our wrong because we know our motive best. We would perhaps excuse another person as we excuse ourselves if we tried to know the motive behind their action too. A thought, a word, or an action in the wrong place turns into a wrong one even if it was right in itself. A thought, word, or action at a wrong time may be wrong even if it may seem right. And when we analyze this more, we shall say as a Hindu poet has said, "There is no use feeling bad about a wrong deed of another person. We should content ourselves knowing that that person could not do better."

And now there is another side to look at. Things seem to us according to how we look at them. To a wrong person everything looks wrong, and to a right person everything looks right; for a right person turns wrong into right, and a wrong person turns right into wrong. The sin of the virtuous is a virtue, and the virtue of a sinner is a sin. Things depend very much upon our interpretation, as there is no seal on any action, word, or thought that determines it to be wrong or right.

And there is still another side to look at: how much our favor and disfavor play their role in discerning right from wrong. In someone whom we love and like and admire, we wish to see everything wrong in a right light. Our reason readily comes to the rescue of the loved one. It always brings an argument as to what is right and an excuse for what is wrong. And how readily do we see the faults and errors of the person whom we disfavor. And how difficult it is for us to find a fault, even if we wanted to, in someone whom we love. Therefore, if in the life of Christ we read how he forgave those who were accused of great faults or great sins, we can now see that it was natural that the one who was the lover of humankind could not see a fault, and the only thing he could see was forgiveness. We see that a stupid or simple person is always ready to see the wrong in another person and ready to form an opinion and to judge. But you will find a wise person always diffident in expressing an opinion of others, always trying to tolerate and always trying still more to forgive.

The Sufis of Persia have classed the evolution of personality into five different grades. The first category is those who err at every step in their life and who find fault with others at every moment of their life. One can picture this kind of person as someone who is always likely to fall, or who is on the point of tumbling down; and while they are falling they at once catch another and pull that one down with them. And this is not a rare case to be found if we study human psychology. Those who find fault with another are very often the ones who have the most faults themselves. The thing is that the right persons find fault with themselves first, and wrong persons find fault with themselves last; only after having found fault with the whole world, do they find fault with themselves. And then everything is wrong; then the whole world is wrong.

The next grade of personality is that of those who begin to see the wrong in themselves and the right in the other. Naturally, they have the opportunity in life to correct themselves, because they find time to find all their own faults. Those who find fault with others have no time to find fault with themselves. Besides, they cannot be just; the faculty of justice cannot be awakened unless one begins to practice that justice by finding fault with oneself.

And the third type is those who say, "What does it matter if you did wrong, or if I did wrong. What is needed is to right the wrong." They naturally develop themselves and help others also to develop.

And then there is the fourth group, who can never see what they call good without the possibility of its becoming bad, and who can never see what is called bad without the possibility of that bad turning into good. The best person in the world cannot hide his or her fault before them, and the worst person in the world will show his or her merit to their eyes.

But when one has risen to the fifth category of people, then these opposite ideas of right or wrong, good or bad, seem to be like the two ends of one line. When that time has come they can say little about it, for people will not believe them. They are the ones who can judge rightly, yet they will be the last to judge.

There are three different ways that people adopt in order to progress toward human perfection. But those who are not evolved enough to adopt the third way or the second way, should not be forced to adopt them. If they were forced at this stage, it would mean that they were only taught a manner. For these three ways are like three steps toward human perfection.

The first degree is the law of reciprocity. It is in this degree that one learns the meaning of justice. The law of reciprocity is to give and to take sympathy, and all that sympathy can give and take. It is according to this law that religion is made, the law of the state is made, the law of the community is made. The idea of this law is that you may not take from me more than you could give me. I will not give you more than I could take from you. It is a fair business: you love me, I can love you; you hate me, I can hate you. And if people have not learned the just measure of give-and-take, they have not practiced justice. They may be innocent, they may be loving, but they have no common sense, they are not practical. And the danger in this law is that people may value more what they themselves do, and may diminish the value of what is done by another. But those who give more than they take are progressing toward the next grade.

It is easy for us to say that this is a very hard-and-fast law. But at the same time, it is the most difficult thing to live in this world and to avoid it. One must ask a practical person, a person with common sense, if it is possible to live in this world and to be regardless of this law of give-and-take. And if the people of this world did no better than keep this law properly, there would be much less trouble in this world. There is no use thinking that people will become saints or sages or great beings. If they became just, it would already be something.

And now we come to a further step. This is the law of beneficence. And this law means to be unconcerned with how another person responds to us in answer to what we do to the person in love and sympathy. What concerns one is what one can do for the other person. It does not matter if a favor is not appreciated. Even if the favor were absolutely ignored, still the satisfaction that the beneficent person gets is out of what he or she has done, not out of what the other who has received it has expressed. When this sense is born in one, from that day one begins to live in the world. For one's pleasure does not depend upon what one receives from others, but one's pleasure depends upon what one does for others. And, therefore, one's happiness is not dependent on anything, one's happiness is independent, one becomes the creator of one's happiness. One's happiness is in giving, not in taking.

But now what do I mean by giving? We give and take every moment of the day. Every word we speak, every action we do, every thought and feeling we have for one another, this is all giving, this is all taking. But it is this person who will forget his or her sorrow. It is this person who will forget his or her miseries. It is this person who will rise above the pains and miseries of this world.

And a step further brings us to the third law, and that law is the law of renunciation. To those who observe this law, giving means nothing. For they are not even conscious that they give; they give automatically. They never think "I give"; they think that it is "being given." This person may be pictured as someone walking on the water. For it is this person who will rise absolutely above the disappointments, distresses, and pains of life that are so numberless. Besides, renunciation means independence and indifference: indifference to all things, and yet not by the absence of sympathy, and independence in regard to all things, and yet not independent in the crude sense of the word.

Renunciation, therefore, may be called the final victory. Only one in a million can attain to this ideal, and the one who has attained this ideal is the one who may be called elevated, liberated.

34

PURITY OF LIFE

Purity of life is the central thing of all the religions that have been taught to humanity in all ages.[1] They only differ in the way of looking at the purity of life; but that has been the central idea. It thus seems that it has not only sprung from religion, but it is the outcome of the nature of life that one sees in all living creatures in some form or other, this feeling of purity so to speak working out its destiny. One sees this tendency in the animals who look for a clean place to sit and among birds who go to the lake or river to bathe and clean their feathers. And in humanity the same tendency is even more pronounced. Even a person who has not risen above the material life shows this faculty of cleanliness, but behind this there is something else hidden, something that is the secret of the whole creation and the purpose for which the whole world was made.

Purity is a process through which the life rhythm of the spirit manifests, that spirit that has worked for ages through the mineral and vegetable kingdoms, through the animal and the human kingdoms to pass through with all this experience of the way and to arrive at that realization where the life of the spirit finds itself pure, pure in its essence, in its pure condition, in its original condition. The whole process of creation and

1. A talk given in Southampton, England, May 8, 1922.

spiritual unfoldment shows that the spirit that represents life, and in life the divine, has wrapped itself in numberless folds and in that way has, so to speak, descended from heaven to earth. And the next process is to unwrap itself, and it is that unwrapping that may be called purity. In the Arabic language the word for purity is *saf*, from which root the word *Sufi* comes, which means the unfoldment of the spirit toward its original condition. What does *pure* mean? For instance, when a person says "pure water," it means it is not admixed with sugar or salt; it is pure, it is original. Therefore, the search for one's original self, the desire to reach this original self and the means of getting to it is, in reality, the purity of life.

But the term can be applied with the same meaning to every form found in the world. When it is used pertaining to the body it means that what is foreign to the body should not be there, and that is cleanliness. That is the first stage of purity. And so it is with mind: when a person is called "pure-minded," what does that mean? It means that what is foreign to the mind does not belong but what is natural to the mind remains. And what is natural to the mind? We need look no further than the mind of a child. What one sees and admires in the little child is its tendency to friendliness, its being always ready to see or admire something beautiful instead of criticizing it, its willingness to smile in answer to anybody's love or smile, to learn to believe without questioning "What is it?" or saying "I believe this" or "I don't believe this," its being a natural believer, a natural friend, who by nature is responding and yielding, who is a natural admirer of beauty without criticism who overlooks all that does not attract it, who knows love but not hate—all of that shows what the original and natural state of the human mind is.

When the human mind comes into this world what is added to it is in addition. It may seem good for the moment, it may seem useful for the moment, but still it is not pure. A person may be called clever, a person may be considered learned, a person may be called witty, but with all these attributes the mind is not pure. When you say that a person is pure-minded, it means being beyond all that. Yes, but then there is a question: Is it then desirable that a child should never learn anything that is worldly, and remain always a child? This is just like saying: Is it then desirable that the spirit never come to earth and always remain a spirit? No. The exaltation of the spirit is to have come to earth and from the earth to have risen to the spirit state, and from that realized its perfection. And therefore all that the world gives in the way of knowledge, in the way of experience, in the way of reason, all that one's own experience and the experience of others teaches us, all that we learn from life, from the sorrows, disappointments—all that helps us to become loving, to become kind. Through all these contradictory experiences, one after the other, if one held one's spirit high, went through all these things and yet did not allow his or her spirit to be stained, it is that person who is pure-minded.

The person who is considered pure-minded but who has no experience of the world, does not know joy or evil, has no credit. That person is a simpleton. A rock does not know what evil is. That person is no better than a rock. The greatness is in having gone through all that which takes away that purity of mind that a person is born with and having risen through it all without being pushed under, but holding to that original purity, rising above all that pulls one down and keeps one down on the earth. It is a kind of fight through life. The one who does not have cause to fight, has not known life. One is perhaps an angelic person, perhaps a pious person, and that we can call someone that out of respect, but, speaking plainly, that person is a simpleton.

There are so many phases one has to go through in the process of knowing the purity of life that the phases through which one has passed seem of no importance. But the phase that one is passing through is of importance. Outward purity matters little when a person goes to the inward purity of life. The first purity is the purity of the physical world where one keeps to the laws of cleanliness, to the laws of health and hygiene, and from the psychic, physical, and hygienic point of view one takes one step forward toward spirituality. Then the next is what is generally called purity of life. That purity of life is the purity of one's conduct in dealing with others, and very often a person takes one direction in the purity of life and in another direction forgets it. The churches, religions, and national and social laws very often make rigid principles concerning the purity of life, and a person begins to know the human-made purity that is necessary to go through to reach the higher plane. However, one can learn the principal rule of purity of conduct from anything; the principal rule is this: that all speech or action that brings fear, that produces confusion, that gives a tendency to deception, that takes away that little twinkling spark in one's heart that is the spark of trueness, all that one would feel embarrassed, ashamed, uncomfortable, or full of anxieties about—all these things—keep a person away from what is called purity of life.

One cannot always tell that a particular action is a wrong action or a right one, but one can always remember this psychological principle, and one can judge for oneself, whether any action that has these effects takes away that natural purity and strength and peace and comfort of mind that is one's natural life. When a religious authority says, "Oh, this person is guilty of a fault," that one is often wrong. We do not know the condition of another person. No one can judge another person; it is one's self that must be one's judge. Therefore, it is no use teaching the purity of life. Religion teaches it, schools teach it, others make laws about the purity of life, yet with all these human-made laws the prisons are full of criminals and the newspapers are every day more and more full of telling about the faults and crimes of the world. That cannot stop crime. It is people who should understand for themselves what is good for them and what is not good for them, and they should be able to discriminate what is poison and what is nectar. They should know it, weigh it, and measure it, and judge it, and that they can only do by understanding the psychology of what is natural to them and what is not natural to their nature. The unnatural action, thought, or speech, is that which makes one uncomfortable before, during, or after it has taken place, but that means that all such things that give discomfort are not from the seeking of the soul. The soul is seeking for something that will open it up and make it free and give comfort in this life, something that will give it freedom. Therefore, it seems as if the whole life is tending toward freedom, toward the unfoldment of something that is choked up by coming on earth; and this freedom can be gained by true purity of life.

Of course it is not for everybody to understand what action, what thought brings remorse or causes discomfort. And another thing, the life of the individual is not in his or her control. Every rising wave of passion, of emotion, of anger, or wrath, or of affection, these waves carry away one's reason, blind one for the moment, and one can give in easily to a mistake, and in a moment's impulse give way to an unworthy thought or action. And then comes remorse. But still, those who wish to learn, who wish to improve themselves, those who wish to progress further, at the thought of their faults and mistakes will go on because every fault will be a lesson, and a better lesson. Then they will not need to read in a book or learn from a teacher because their life becomes their teacher.

This does not mean that one must wait for one's personal experience to learn the lesson. If one were wise one could learn the lesson from others, but at the same time one's fault must not be taken as one's nature. It is no one's nature. A fault means what is against one's nature. If it was in one's nature it could not be a fault. The very reason that makes it a fault is because it is against one's nature. How can nature be a fault? When someone says, "I cannot help that I am angry and I cannot help saying what I wish to say when I feel bitter," they do not know—they could if they wished to. It means they do not wish to when they say, "I cannot help it." It is lack of strength in one when one says "can't." There is nothing that one can't. The human soul is the expression of the Almighty, and therefore the human mind has the power of the Almighty in its will if only one can use that power against all things that stand in one's way as hindrances to one's journey to the goal. And by regarding some few things in life as faults one covers up little faults that sometimes are worse than faults that are pointed out by the world. For instance, when a younger person is insulting to an elderly person, people do not call it a very great fault. Sometimes such a little fault can rise and have a worse effect upon one's soul than the faults that are recognized as faults. A person with a sharp tongue, with an inquisitive nature, with satiric remarks, with thoughtless words can commit a fault that can be worse than so-called great sins. You do not know what is in an action. You cannot always judge a thing from the action. The judge has to see what is behind the action, and when a person has arrived at this stage of judgment, then he or she never dares to form an opinion, to judge. It is the ordinary one who makes a thousand mistakes every day and overlooks them who is always ready to judge others.

And when one passes through this sphere of the purity of life there comes another sphere of purity, and this sphere is to make one's heart pure, free from all impressions that come from outside and that are foreign to one's nature. And how does one do it? By overlooking the faults of others, by overlooking the shortcomings of others, by forgiving the faults of one's friends. By an increase of love one gives way to the desirable impressions that come upon one's heart and collect there, and in that way one keeps one's heart pure. If during the day an ill feeling comes over a person, a feeling of hatred for a friend or relative, a feeling of annoyance, a feeling of criticism, a feeling of bitterness, then one who wishes to cover one's heart from that impression, who does not wish to think about it, who does not wish to let it enter, should think it is poison. It is just like taking a poison in one's blood, introducing a disease. For many diseases come from a bad impression being kept in one's heart. And the bitterness that a person takes from others, that others have perhaps done something that one does not like, or that one feels bitter about, if one keeps those in one's heart it is just like injecting a poison in one's heart, and in time that poison breaks out as a disease in one's physical being. And it is such diseases that cannot be cured, that cannot be healed, that are difficult to heal because they are not from a physical source but are from the inner source. The external purity or cleanliness does not make much difference to the inner purity, but inner unclean feelings, bitterness, spite against anybody—these cause disease both inwardly and outwardly.

But when one has gone through this process and has tried to keep one's body and mind and one's life and character pure, then there comes a stage of still greater and higher purity, and that is attained by high ideals, by a righteous path, by good actions, by good thoughts. One has to attune oneself to be free from all foreign impressions in that sphere of one's journey in order to keep away from one's mind all else but God: all that one thinks about, all that one feels, all that one sees and admires, all that one touches or perceives is God. It is still greater purity when one does not allow any thought or feeling to enter one's mind except God. In the artist's picture the artist sees God, in his or her merit the artist sees God, in the color and brush of the artist, in the eyes of the artist, which observe nature, in that faculty of the artist that produces the picture, the artist sees the perfection of God. And therefore to the artist God becomes all and all becomes God.

And when one has arrived at this purity, there are many things that come in one's life to test one: one's enemy who annoyed one, those whom one cannot bear, those whom one cannot like, those who are intolerant to one. One comes in contact with situations that are difficult. Every possibility appears for one to give up that purity for a moment, but every moment that purity becomes poisoned, it is that moment in the life of a sage that is called a sin. I remember the words of my Murshid, who said, "Every moment that God is absent from one's consciousness is a moment of sin," and when God is in one's consciousness, every moment of that consciousness is continual virtue. Therefore, when a person has arrived at that pitch he or she lives in virtue. Virtue is not a thing that one experiences from time to time, but one's life is virtue, what one says and does and what is done to one is all virtue; and that shows that virtue is not one little experience. Virtue is purity of life. Really I would not consider virtue a worthwhile thing if it came and went away. It is only worthwhile when it lives with us, when we can depend upon it and when we can live and move and have our being in it. That is worthwhile. If it only came for a moment, and if it visited us for one minute, it is not a virtue, and we would rather not have it. We would rather prefer poverty to the wealth that came for a moment and went away. Therefore, that is the stage when one begins to understand what virtue means. One begins to understand the glimpse of that virtue that came. One thought it was virtue but now it is the whole life and the whole life becomes virtue and one lives in it and life means virtue. It is lack of life that is sin.

But then there is a further purity and that is purity or freedom from the thought of oneself, from one's own thought. And by thought of self I do not mean the thought of one's real self. Thought of one's limitation covers what is true in one's being, one's true self. It is this limitation that makes one feel at times that "I am good" or "I am bad." One then realizes that "I am neither good nor bad, I am what I am; neither good makes me perfect nor bad makes me imperfect." Good and bad do not exist when one is above them. It is purity from all shapes and colors, purity from all the forms of life. It is like rising above heaven and hell, and it is like touching the throne of God. It is just like bathing in the truth of God. That is exaltation when one has risen above one's limitation and has become conscious of that perfection whom we call God, whom we worship and whom we love, and who is the goal of that endeavor.

35

THE IDEAL

Beloved Ones of God, I would like to speak to you this afternoon on the subject of the ideal.[1] If anyone asked me what is the life of life and what is the light of life, I would answer them in one word, and that is the ideal. If anyone asked me what throws light on the path of life; if anyone asked me what gives one interest in life I would answer in one word, and that is the ideal. A person with wealth, with qualification, with learning, with comfort, but without ideal to me is a corpse. And a person without learning, without qualification, without wealth or rank, but with an ideal is a living person. If one does not live for an ideal, what does one live for? One lives for oneself, which is nothing. The one who lives and does not know an ideal is powerless and lightless. The greater the ideal, the greater the person. The wider the ideal, the broader the person. The deeper the ideal, the deeper the person. The higher the ideal, the higher the person. Without an ideal, whatever may be the life, that life is worthless.

What do I mean by an ideal? However small an object may be that you love, that you look up to, for which you are ready to sacrifice yourself and all you possess—that is an ideal. I pre-

---

1. A talk given at the home of Baroness D'Eichthal, Paris, December 19, 1924.

fer that fanatic who says, "On this idol of rock I will give my life, I have worshipped it as a god," to the person who says, "I do not know, I just live on from day to day." A sincere ideal, however small, is an ideal.

There are those who will go through any sacrifice to serve their nation; they have their ideal. There are those who, in order to keep the dignity of their family, of their ancestors, will endure troubles and difficulties and yet will keep their honor; they have some ideal. However narrow they may seem to be, however conservative they may seem to be, yet they have a virtue; it should be recognized.

The records of the world's history show that those who have been able to maintain their virtue have very often been able to maintain it because their parents maintained it, because their ancestors had dignity; therefore they could not have done otherwise. There is something in it, it is not altogether to be discarded. A person who does not consider these things will go on living and may even have a profitable life; but it will be an ordinary life, a life that has no depth, a life that has no value. There is nothing in life that can make it worthwhile except an ideal.

There are others who have a racial ideal, saying "These are the qualities of my race that I value, I maintain them, and in order to maintain them I shall go through any sacrifice; that is my ideal." There are others who have the honor of their word. Once they have given their word, it is forever. There are other idealists who have the honor of their affection, the honor of their love, the honor of their friendship. Once they have given it, it is given; to go back on it is the greatest disgrace to them. Both in giving their heart and in accepting a heart there is stability, there is character, there is honor. The breach of that stability is worse to them than death. All these things, however small they may seem, however childish they may appear, have great value, they are the only things worthwhile in life. I shall tell you a story of an extreme ideal.

The Ideal

A few little girls were playing together when Maharaja Singh of Jaipur was taking a walk in that street disguised as an ordinary man. One little girl said, "I am going to marry a millionaire." Another little girl said, "I am going to marry a commander." And there was another girl who said, "I am going to marry the king of this place, the maharaja." The maharaja, who was old enough to be her grandfather, overheard this. He was amused and told the parents of that girl, "When the time of her wedding comes, you should apply to me, and a dowry will be given from the state, so that she will be happy all her life."

Years passed, and the king passed away. And the time came for the parents to think about arranging their girl's wedding. And when the question came before the girl, she said, "How can it be? I was married already. Did I not give my word? Is it not enough?" They said, "It was a word given in your childhood. It meant nothing at all. It was play, and the maharaja is now dead; it is nothing." She said, "No, I will not hear another word about it. I am a daughter of a Rajput. I have given my word, and I will not go back on it." It is an extreme ideal. It has a fanatic aspect. Nevertheless, it is an ideal. There are others. There is an ideal of a general, whose name I have just now forgotten. When the time of defeat came, he still raised the flag of his nation and said, "The nation is not defeated."

There are a thousand ideals like that. One could say that they lack wisdom, that they lack balance, reason, and logic, and yet they stand above logic and reason, they stand above what one calls practicality and common sense. Many practical people with common sense have come and gone. But if we remember the names of any who have made an everlasting impression upon the world they are the idealists. No doubt, that ideal in which we all feel that we come from the same source and return to the same source is the greatest, because in that ideal we unite with one another and serve one another and feel responsible for being sincere to one another. I think that even if a person has learned some virtues, that person cannot very well practice those virtues if they have no ideal. Ideal naturally teaches virtues, which rise from the human heart.

There is a story of a king who judged four persons for the same fault. The wise king said to one that he must be exiled, to the other that he would be put in prison for his whole life, to the third that he should be sentenced to be executed, and to the fourth he said, "I am surprised, I never expected such a fault to be done by you." And what was the result? The one who was sent to prison, he was quite happy with his comrades there. The one who was exiled, he built up his business outside the country. The one who was sentenced, was sentenced. But the fourth went home and committed suicide.

What prompts someone to sacrifice is only one thing, the ideal. And one can only sacrifice one thing, and that is one's own life. A person without ideal has no depth, is shallow. However pleased in one's everyday life one may be, one can never enjoy that happiness that is independent of outward life. The pleasure that is experienced through pain is the pleasure experienced by the idealist. But what of the pleasure that has not come out of pain? It is tasteless. Yes, life's gain, people think so much of it. What is it after all? A loss caused by an ideal is a greater gain than any other gain in this world.

* * *

Question: *Can one conquer the ideal? Can one get to have an ideal if one has not got it from one's birth?*

Answer: Yes, it is difficult, but at the same time it is better to pursue an ideal through life and always follow an ideal.

Question: *But those who have no ideal?*

Answer: There is someone's writing, whom I have forgotten, "If you do not have a God, make one."

The Ideal

Question: *I think everyone has an ideal, even if it is ever so small.*

Answer: Even to start with a narrow ideal is better than to have none.

Question: *Can one lose the ideal?*

Answer: Then to have another ideal, for there are two ways of losing it. One way is that one has lost the ideal by becoming pessimistic, or by being disappointed in the ideal. But I should think that one must make one's ideal so independent that nothing outside oneself may have the power of breaking it. I think that a person who can see the faults of their beloved friend, has not yet loved that friend, because their love must be able to add to the friend's shortcomings all that is necessary in order to complete it. It is not that the beloved is complete, but that the lover completes it. Many say, "I have loved, but I have been disappointed," but I tell them, "You have dug, but you have not dug deep; you have reached the mud, but not the water."

Question: *Is idealism catching?*

Answer: There is nothing more catching than idealism.

Question: *What is the test you would put to an ideal that is true, that it may lead one on?*

Answer: I think that an ideal is an ideal. If it leads you so far and no further, then another ideal will come to lead you further, but the ideal is the way to take.

Question: *If it is a true ideal, it will lead one on and on. It will not have to be dropped and risen above to . . . ?*

Answer: Yes, but it is very difficult to distinguish between a false and true ideal. It is not only difficult, it is impossible. For if something is false, then it is as false as it is real. And if it is real, it as real as it is false. The best way is just to take as true that which at the time appears true to one. But we should not discuss it with others, or try to defend it. We do not know. We do not know that what we find true today, we may not consider true tomorrow. But never say, "Tomorrow I shall not say the same thing is false." For all these terms, good or bad, right or wrong, virtue or sin, and false or true, are relative; and change according to differences of time and space, which means that it depends from what height we look at it, from what position we see it. In other words, in order to simplify it, I should say, that what seems right in the morning, may seem wrong in the evening. What may seem wrong in the day, may seem right at night. Another example is if we are standing on a step in a staircase when looking at things, the right things will seem wrong by looking at them from another step, and the wrong things will seem right by looking at them from another step. It is how you look at them. Therefore, the best thing is that whatever for the time being we consider to be right, just, good, and a virtue, that is the thing we ought to do. But we should not impose or urge what we consider right or good or true upon others who do not consider it in the same way as we do.

Question: *In education how should we do?*

Answer: Of course, for children the question is different. In order to gain freedom we do not begin with freedom. In order to arrive at freedom we begin with discipline. This is always the mistake of the time, that in order to come to freedom they give freedom, and therefore they spoil things. For if you begin with liberty then you will end in discipline. If you begin with discipline you will arrive at liberty. Freedom is the ideal to gain, and the result of our work, and not the thing to begin with it.

Question: Those more advanced have the responsibility? Among the grown up there are some who are like children before the wise ones.

Answer: No one is responsible for anyone else. We are all responsible for ourselves. And many times you may make a great mistake by thinking another person not so advanced as yourself. But at the same time, if one wants to know how to deal with them, I should say, in a modified form in the same way as one deals with children.

Question: But how may we find that we are on the way that is true? Our upbringing may have its influence upon our ideas.

Answer: Truth is the part of our own being and the most essential, and the most important part. And therefore all that we consider true at the moment is true for that moment. It is only our discerning sincerely that is required. For as we fool ourselves then shall we be fooled. Those who go far away from truth, it is because they fool themselves, for they are not careful, they are not attentive to keep to that truth that their own soul says is true. What for the moment you consider as true, that is true for you.

Question: One might be limited by the principles one thinks are wrong that have been put in us by our upbringing. One wishes to get rid of those.

Answer: But I say, then the principle that one thinks to be wrong, one must not hold to be true. If the whole world says that it is true and you think that it is false, then it is false. For it is false at least for you and that counts most in your life.

Question: Sometimes it is very hard to know whether it is true or false. One's upbringing is such a strong force that one reasons with oneself and thinks, this is impossible, this is useless; one is handicapped.

Answer: Yes, if one knows that what one has learned is all false, then one must unlearn.

Question: *By what test? Can we not take that in the silence and find out the truth? Is there not a place where one can find the truth?*

Answer: As long as one is pursuing the truth, one is going in the truth already.

Question: *Truth does not change, it is only our point of view that changes. In that silence we can find that light?*

Answer: Ultimate truth is the absolute truth, which cannot be compared with anything else, there must be a distinction made between fact and truth. Facts are the two things between which you choose the one as real and the other as false. But when you come to the ultimate truth, it is just like light. In the presence of light there is no darkness. Therefore, that truth that is ultimate truth has no comparison; it is not relative. That truth is something that makes all truth.

Question: *Can you get it by the silence?*

Answer: Of course, silence is the chief thing.

36

THE JOURNEY TO THE GOAL (I)

Beloved Ones of God, this evening I wish to speak on the subject of the journey to the goal.[1] When we picture life as a journey, there are a thousand things that will prove this fact to us. We see when taking a journey that we are with a great many people looking at life and going forward. Those who have arrived at their station have got out of the train, and the little friendship or sympathy or antipathy that we had with them only lasted till then. Those who have left, what they have left with us is that impression that we carry of them. That impression makes us either happy or unhappy; either it makes us love them even in their absence, or it makes us hate them, wishing that we shall never see them again. When we think of yesterday, when we think of last week, when we think of last month, and when we think of the years that have passed in our lives, it only shows that they have passed and we have gone on. It is like the sensation that one has in the train, as though the train were standing still and the trees were running by. In life we have that same sensation, that life is passing and we are standing still.

And then we also see in this traveling that some are prepared, with all that is necessary in this world, while there are others who are not prepared. Both have to journey just the same, those

---

1. A public lecture given in Bern, Switzerland, January 22, 1925.

who are prepared and those who are not. The only difference is that for those who are prepared, this journey is easy. There is a fable about the monkey and the sparrows. When autumn seemed to be coming closer the sparrows said, "We must have a nest, we must build it, it must be ready because the autumn is coming nearer." A little monkey overheard this and was very frightened because it was the first time for this young monkey to face the autumn. It went with great anxiety to its parents and said, "We must build a home, we must build a nest where we can be protected. I did not know the autumn was coming, but someone told me it was coming." While they were discussing this the sparrows made their nest ready. But the monkeys put it off from one tomorrow to another tomorrow. And so it is in this world we find two kinds of personalities. There are those who say, "What does it matter? We shall see what will come," and when they are faced by a difficulty, by a need, by a want, then they begin to realize that it would have been better if they had prepared beforehand.

And it is the same with education. When young persons are learning there is always an attraction for them to play, to enjoy life; and when that golden age of childhood that gives facility for learning and for acquiring knowledge is passed, then it is too late. And the same thing with the youths; the days when they should be careful of what they spend, and the time when they have spent all they have, and not earned anything, then they begin to feel the loss. The greatest wealth is health and energy and intelligence and life itself. If this health is not preserved and looked after from youth, then even though one may not feel it at that time there will come a time when one knows that one did not prepare for it. I once asked a person who was old and strong and healthy, "Sir, will you tell me what blessing you have, what is it that keeps you at this age so strong and healthy?" He said, "This is the conserved energy of youth which is now maintaining my life." Very few young people think about this. Youth is an intoxication. When they are in that intoxication, when they are full of energy, they do not think about it, of what they have to spend in order to go far in the journey of life.

And then we come to the idea of humanity. Today what we consider learning or education consists mostly of grammar and history and geography and mathematics and calculations. But that kind education that we should have as current coin—a good manner, a strong will, a right attitude of mind—that kind of education seems to be overlooked. We find it nowhere. And if a person has the education, qualification, rank or position, yet lacks manner; that person lacks a great part of life. If a person has all these things such as rank and position and qualifications yet does not have that strength of mind that is necessary to carry one through the whole of life's path, that one is lacking a great deal. A person who lacks money misses little, but the person who lacks power of mind misses everything in life. Weakness develops, and develops, and develops without one's knowing it. When one sees a little spark of weakness in oneself, one thinks, "What is it, it is nothing," but one does not know that the spark will one day turn into a glow, and the glow will turn into a flame. For those who lack manner, those who lack strength of mind, those who lack a right attitude, it is then too late, they cannot be corrected. And the nature of life is such that the thoughtless life will pull one into thoughtlessness, and then thoughtlessness will also draw the thoughtful person toward itself, and therefore there is more chance of falling than of rising in life. And besides, friends, among thousands of persons there is hardly one who is taking this journey with open eyes, for nearly all journey with their eyes closed. People so much depend upon their friends, upon their relations, upon those who love them, upon those who admire them, but do not know that those who love them will demand from them any quality missing in them.

Therefore what is necessary in life, is that one must possess oneself, and not think, "Oh, what does it matter, my father was a king and my grandfather was an emperor; it does not matter." What relations you have, how great and good they may be, is not of any use to you. We each have our journey to make, and we have to answer the demands of this journey. How wonderful it is to watch others in the little journeys we make. One person comes along in a little group of travelers and gives pleasure to all, puts before them all the good he or she has, shares with them and gives a good impression to all, wins their hearts. When that person has gone, what he or she has left with the friends is joy, that beautiful impression that they will always keep. And there is another one who has hurt or harmed or produced some disturbance among those traveling with him or her. And when that one has gone, they pray that they will never meet that one again. One day a maid said to her mistress that there was a funeral passing through the street. She was much impressed and said, "Certainly the person who died went to heaven." Her mistress laughed at the idea of this maid's authoritative exclamation that this dead person went to heaven. She said, "Did you see this dead person going to heaven?" "It is simple, Madam," she said, "for everyone who was going with the funeral was weeping. Certainly this person made a good impression on those among whom that person lived."

People lose all when absorbed in their daily life, not knowing that life passes and the call comes before they think of it. People make great mistakes, but among all mistakes there is one principal mistake, and that mistake is that they go on through life thinking that they will stay here forever. And since they are without preparation, the call naturally comes to them as a blow instead of as an invitation. And when we think, friends, of the journey beyond, we begin to see how many there are in this world who even do not know that there is a hereafter. And if one knows of the hereafter, then one has one's preconceived ideas as to the coming of the hereafter: there is either a religious or philosophical belief, but neither that can suffice for our purpose. What can suffice for our purpose is to become acquainted with the road along which we have to pass, and by becoming acquainted with that road one also begins to see that that was the road whereby the soul descended to earth. This road is that bridge that stands between the physical and the spiritual part of one's being, and therefore the nature of this journey is different. The journey in the world we make outside ourselves. But this journey that we are making is within ourselves, and it is by being acquainted with that road that leads us to that destination where we are meant to go; it is this that is acquired as divine knowledge by the help of meditation. There are many in this world curious to know what we shall find beyond this life. And it is this curiosity that gives way to those who wish to attract humankind by falsehood; it gives them the chance to make up stories and to satisfy people's curiosity. For who can know of this way but we ourselves; we are the traveler and our own spirit is the way. It is we ourselves who must see our way, and it is with our own eyes that we must see what we will find on this way. Therefore, the teachers of life's secret do not say that we will see this or that on the way. They say one will find whatever one will find, and your duty is to open your eyes that you may travel on the way and see for yourself. Once a murid asked his teacher; "How I should like to see what it is like in heaven and what hell looks like." "Close your eyes," said the teacher "and you will see it." "Shall I see heaven first?" The teacher said, "Yes." He closed his eyes and he went to his meditation. "And now," said the teacher, "see hell also in meditation." And when he opened his eyes, the teacher said, "What did you see?" He said, "Neither did I see in heaven that paradise of which people speak, or those beautiful plants and flowers and all the beautiful things of comfort and luxury, I saw nothing." "And what did you see in hell?" said the teacher. "I saw nothing. I had expected to see fire and people being tortured, but I saw nothing. What is the reason, did I see or did I not see it?" "Certainly you have seen heaven and hell, but the brimstone and fire, or the beautiful gems and jewels of paradise, you have to bring them yourself. You do not get them there." And this gives us the secret to Omar Khayyam's saying. "Heaven is the vision of a fulfilled desire. Hell is the shadow of the soul on fire."[2] What is most necessary for us to learn and understand is that from a perfect source we come and to a perfect goal we go. But many seek that source unconsciously, and most of us seek that source wrongly. But few seek that source consciously, and fewer still seek that source rightly.

And now coming to the question of the right way to seek that source. The way to seek it is first to learn the psychology of one's own life. What makes one fall, what makes one rise, what makes one fail, what makes one succeed, what gives one happiness, what brings one sorrow. Then one should study the nature of pleasure and pain, whether it is lasting pleasure, whether it is lasting pain, or whether it is momentary pleasure, or whether it is momentary pain. And then find out the deceitful and false nature of one's own impressions, how under a cover of pain there was pleasure, how under a cover of pleasure there was pain, and how in the worst person there is some good to be found, and how in the best person there is something bad to be traced. This widens one's point of view, and this prepares the ground of one's heart to realize the secret of enjoyment. And the next thing that one has to do is to control one's activities, physical and mental, that one must know that the nature of life is to go on, and therefore this suspension of life gives that traveling attitude of life a scope within, instead of only giving it a scope without. However much a person reads about and studies these things, that does not bring a person satisfaction; satisfaction comes out of experience, and experience is gained from meditation.

Besides, in this journey no one asks you what family or people you come from, what nation or what race you come from, with what faith you were raised. What is asked is that are you prepared for this journey. It is your preparation that is your

---

2. Stanza LXVII of FitzGerald's 4th edition.

passport, it is your readiness that is your ticket to show on this path of life. There are no personalities considered here; what is considered is the evolution on the spiritual path. In the East the schools of the Sufis have existed for thousands of years, a school that had its beginning even before the time of Abraham. It is the message of that wisdom that is now being given here in the Western world. And at this time when the need is felt everywhere in the world, the doors of this school are being opened in many different nations of the world, and also in Switzerland. It is to the serious seekers, who do not seek for phenomena or wonder working, or go after this information for the sake of curiosity, but who have a serious mind and a steady intention of going on this path—it is to these that this school opens the doors of its heart to welcome them.

37

THE JOURNEY TO THE GOAL (2)

Beloved Ones of God, my subject this evening is the road to the goal.[1] Before proceeding on my subject, I should like to say that there are two different stages in human evolution, and these two different stages may very well be called the minor and the major stage. In Hindu Puranic symbology, these two characters are called the younger and the elder brother or sister.

There is a stage of childhood when the child only knows what it wants and is only happy when it gets it, no matter what may be the consequences. That minor stage of soul is when one in reality desires only what one can see, hear, perceive, touch; beyond that one does not care. One wants only what is desirable, one does not wish anything else. And the major state is when someone has experienced life more or less, has known pleasure and pain, enthusiasm and disappointment, and knows the variability of life; only then has one reached the stage of majority. The minor and major do not depend upon a certain age, nor do they depend upon a particular education; no, they depend upon inner life. When one has gone into life as far as one could go, and when one has passed the limit of the minor state, then one arrives at the major state. In the East there is a custom that has become a kind of religious etiquette: not to

---

1. A lecture given in the Netherlands, September 6, 1921.

wake someone who is asleep but to let that person sleep well. If this is not done it is considered a crime. In other words, you must treat the world according to nature and not go against nature. Do not force someone in the minor state into the major; one must first sleep well before one can awaken.

Now, about progress for the spiritual path, there are two different characters on the spiritual path. The first are those who say, "Yes, I would like to go on this path, but where shall I arrive?" They want to know all about it before traveling this path, and if their friends are going with them. And if not, they are not ready to go either, because they are not sure of the way, will not go alone, and want to know when and where they will arrive, and if it is safe to journey on that particular path. When they travel on the path, they look back and try to look forward, asking: "Shall I reach the goal? Is it really the right path?" A thousand times doubt comes, fear comes; they look back, forward, around. If others could only tell them how far they have journeyed. They are restless, wanting to know how far they are from the goal. They, therefore, are children still, although they have a desire to journey. For these people there are toys: the mystical hints for mental research keep them busy. They may look on the map of the journey to see where they go.

Now we are coming to the conditions of the major path. About this character the Bible says: "Unless the soul be born again, it will not enter the kingdom of God."[2] In the first place, if I were to say what the journey is and its object, the answer would be that the whole creation was purposed for this journey, and, if it were not for this purpose, there would be no creation at all. And before any take the journey, they practice in some form or other, in play, how they will make this; but they have not yet started in reality. For instance, some desire to be rich and devote all their time, their energy, their life, their thoughts to that object; and, so to speak, they journey to that goal. If some people desire power, they work for that and get

2. John 3:3.

it. If they want position, they use all their strength to reach this goal naturally, in a playing way. The proof of this is that every activity of which they are in pursuit to attain the thing desired brings them to desire something else. If they are rich, they want to be famous; if they are famous, they want something else; if they have one thing, they strive for another and are never satisfied. It shows that humankind, externally busy in the pursuit of worldly things, is not satisfied in its soul but has a constant yearning in the soul for something more, which keeps people uneasy. A very good explanation is that which Rumi, a great Sufi teacher of Persia, gives us in his book, the *Masnavi*. There he says, "What is it, in the flute made of reed, that appeals to your soul, that goes through you, pierces your heart?" And the answer is that it is the crying of the flute, and the reason for its crying is that it once belonged to the plant of the earth, from which it was cut apart. Holes were made in its heart. It longs to be back and united with its source, its origin. And so the soul feels a longing for its origin. In another place in his book, Rumi says so it is with all who have left their original country for a long time. They may roam about and feel very pleased with all they see, but there will come a moment when a strong yearning is in their hearts for the place where they were born.[3]

One sees that those in the world who have really suffered, who have been disappointed, are brokenhearted and do not wish to tell anybody of their experiences, don't want any company but wish to be alone. And it is then as if there was someone waiting with open arms, awaiting that soul as a child comes to its mother. This shows that there is, somewhere, a consoler greater than any in the world, a friend dearer than anyone in the world, a protector stronger than any earthly one. Knowing that the world is not to be depended upon, they look for that great one in themselves.

A friend who is a friend in life and after death, in pleasure and pain, in richness and poverty, one on whom you can always

---

3. *Masnavi*, book 1.

depend, who always guides aright, who gives the best advice—that friend is hidden in your own heart. You cannot find a better one. Who is this friend? Humanity's own being, the true inner being. That friend is the origin, source, and goal, the final goal of all. But the question arises: What if that friend is one's own being? Why then call it a friend? Why not call it oneself? The answer is that no doubt, in point of fact, this friend is really one's own being; but when compared with the present realization of the greater self, one finds oneself smaller than a drop in the ocean. One cannot very well call that friend oneself until one has forgotten one's own self, until one is no more oneself. Until and unless one has arrived at the state of perfection, one had better be quiet rather than insolent in talking about that which one has not yet become.

All occult schools, all over the world, prescribe, as the first lesson, quietude: no discussion, no dispute, no argument. The conditions for those on the path are altogether different from those of the outer world. The true knowers of life have kept their lips closed about that subject, and no method has been more successful and profitable than the method of the prophets of all lands who give humankind the first lesson of love for God. Of course, religious authorities of different times have kept humanity ignorant of the knowledge of God and have only given it the belief in God.

Absence of knowledge has made people of reason rebel against that which they could not understand. There remained no link between knowledge and understanding, and that is how the reign of materialism came to the world, a reign that is still spreading around. In such times of materialism chaos comes into the world; all is confusion and unrest. All wish to do good but do not know how. Such times Sri Krishna has called the decay of dharma, when spirit has gone and form only remains.[4] No doubt warning comes in time as an intuition to the soul; but in the intoxication of the time, the mist is so great

---

4. Bhagavad Gita, 4:7.

that the message is not heard, not understood, not received until the messenger has disappeared.

Now, coming to the journey, what is the manner and the method of it? We see that when a person rises above all things of the world—such as power, wealth, possession, all that gives pride and vanity—there comes a desire in the heart, a remembrance of the origin of the perfection of love and peace. No one in the world can pretend to have arrived at this stage, because every moment of one's life speaks louder of what one really is than of what one says.

A person's first tendency toward humanity is a loving attitude, a charitable attitude to such an extent that forgiveness leads every action in life. A person shows patience in actions, tolerance to humanity, and considers that each is at a stage of evolution and cannot be expected to act better than that point of evolution permits. One does not make one's own law and want others to follow it; one follows the law for all. When a person's attitude is a loving attitude, a tendency to serve, to forgive, to tolerate, a reverence for all—good and bad, young and old—then that person begins the journey. To explain what path this is, there is no better symbol for it than the path of the cross. No one without courage, without strength of will, and without patience can go on this path. When one has to live among people of all natures, one must make one's own character soft as a rose and make it finer, so that no one can be hurt by the thorns. Two thorns cannot harm each other. The thorns can hurt the rose, but the rose cannot tear the thorns. Think what the life must be of the rose between two thorns. The journey begins with a path of thorns, and one must go barefoot. It is not easy to be tolerant, always to be patient, to refrain from judging others, and to love one's enemy. It is a dead individual who walks on this path, one who has drunk the bowl of poison. The beginning of each path is always difficult and uninteresting, hard for everybody. Ask the violinists about the first days when they practice the scales and cannot even form the tones;

often they have not patience enough to go on till they can play so well that they are satisfied.

The first part of the path is permanent strife, a struggle with life; but as one approaches the goal, the path gets easier. The distance seems larger, but the path is easier, the difficulties less. The journey is achieved first by realizing in oneself: What am I? Am I body, mind, or what else am I? Do I originate from earth or from somewhere else?

As soon as one has started on the journey, one's lower nature rises up. All the follies and weaknesses want to drag one down to earth, and the struggle of breaking these chains requires the strength of a Samson. Then comes the struggle between beauty in matter and spiritual beauty. Beauty in form is more realistic; spiritual beauty is hidden in mist until one comes to a stage where spiritual beauty becomes the beauty that is shining with light. Another struggle is that when people have acquired knowledge, power, and magnetism, they are conscious of having a greater power than others, of knowing more than others, that they can do more than others. To use those faculties rightly is another struggle. One must not pride oneself on these accomplishments. There is an enemy who starts with travelers on the journey and never leaves them: pride and spiritual egotism. It stays as long as an individual is on the path.

Think of the temptation, on having received inspiration and power, when one can think, "I can do and know and understand more than you." That is a constant struggle till the end, and every moment one falls and tumbles down. Only the steady travelers will persist in rising up every time, as without patience they may lose the path. Those who journey on this path will get help, as Christ said, "First seek the kingdom of God, and all things will be given to you."[5]

The goal is the important thing, and the right attitude of the soul toward it, and not the things you meet on the path. The inner circle of the Sufi school, which is now presented to the

---

5. Matthew 6:33.

Western world, is meant as a guidance on this path. Nobody in the world can carry a person on this path. The only thing is that a little advice can be given by those who have journeyed on the path to those who really wish to travel it.

Thank you for your kind sympathy and response. God bless you.

38

ACKNOWLEDGMENT

Beloved Ones of God, I should like to speak this afternoon on a subject concerning psychology, especially what we may acknowledge and what we may not acknowledge in life.[1] What generally happens in life is this: people acknowledge what they should not acknowledge, and do not acknowledge what they should acknowledge. As a rule, it is best never to acknowledge a fact that one does not wish to give life to. For instance, when one begins to see that one's friend is not as kind, is not as affectionate, is not as pleased as someone ought to be as a friend, as soon as one acknowledges it, one at once gives strength to something that so far has been only a shadow. A person who feels, "Everyone in my family, in my surroundings, dislikes me, they disapprove of me; I have a tiring effect upon them," certainly gives life to that fact.

A friend came to me and said, "I do not know what kind of bad planet has its influence upon me, but for the last three years, everything I touch goes wrong; nothing that I touch brings success or pleasure." I asked, "How long?" and she said, "Three years now." I said, "I am very sorry, you have come too late. And yet it is not too late. But for three years you have given fuel to this fire." The friend asked, "How did I give fuel to

1. A talk given at the home of Baroness d'Eichthal, Paris, January 10, 1925.

Acknowledgment

this fire?" I answered, "By your acknowledging it." What happens is that every little fact that has a bad effect upon one's life, if we acknowledge it, we give life from our own to that fact and thus make it a living thing. And so it is also with many illnesses. Very often people get into the habit of saying, "Oh, I am so tired." For them it is not necessary that they should cut stones or cut wood or carry stones or carry wood. They will be tired before doing it. They need not wait for an action, for a thing to make them tired. No sooner do they think of tiredness, than it is there. There are many cases where there is no need to be tired, and the person becomes tired by the fact of having acknowledged it. It is the same thing with sleeplessness. Once you acknowledge to yourself, "I cannot sleep," that is enough of a cause to keep you awake all night. There are many illnesses of this kind, especially the acknowledging of depression. To acknowledge I am depressed, I am sad, certainly there may be no other reason for being depressed, for being sad; the very fact of acknowledging I am sad will make a person sad.

To the one who acknowledges this life to be one's friend, life will prove to be one's friend. To the one who acknowledges this life to be one's enemy, life will prove in every way to be one's enemy. There are many who take notice of those who are working against them, and by taking special notice of it, they make them do it even more, because they make an impression upon them. But you might ask, "Does there not exist any animosity in persons, without thinking about it?" Yes, it may exist, but by taking notice of it, by acknowledging it, you give life to it. If you do not acknowledge it, it will die in time. For animosity is a fire, but not a perpetual fire. It is the acknowledging that gives fuel to the fire. If you do not acknowledge it, the fire will be extinguished.

Many might say that it is hypocrisy not to acknowledge a fact, but that hypocrisy is better than the truth. But in fact that is not to be called a hypocrisy when you know its meaning, its worth, its understanding. That doctor is not a hypocrite who says to the patient, even seeing that the patient has a high fever, "It is all right, it is nothing." By saying that there is a high fever, the doctor will certainly increase the fever of the patient, and many doctors do so. Everything a physician or a religious person does to make a person who is on their deathbed think of death, only encourages the person toward death, is pushing the person toward death. One could prove a greater friend to someone on their deathbed by not acknowledging their trouble, their difficulty, their coming death. I have heard of many cases where as soon as the doctor has given up hope, the whole family begins to talk about it to the patient, and the patient's departure is hastened by six months.

What should we acknowledge? That which we always escape from acknowledging, and that is our faults. By acknowledging our faults, we shall kill them. When we acknowledge them as our enemies, we shall destroy them. But that is the one thing that we want to hide, and that is the one thing that we want to keep hidden, even from our own sight. To look one's own fault in the face is the best thing to do: to analyze it, to weigh it, to measure it, and to understand it better. By this one either destroys it or understands it, or one turns the same fault into a merit. Very often people think it is wise to tell a person that, "No, you are not my friend; no, you have not been very attentive or kind to me." When a person tells another these things, even if they were not existing before, the first person inspires the second person with them. Besides, all misfortunes, all dangers that threaten and frighten one, very often they are not so great as one thinks; they can be avoided if one did not acknowledge them. For how a person feels about the danger depends upon the particular pitch to which the heart is tuned. For instance, take ten people standing before the same danger: if one can weigh their fear, one will find that the degree of fear that they have is very different in each of them.

There is an interesting story of the Prophet Muhammad, when he and a disciple were exiled and their enemies were pursuing them in the desert. They were standing behind a rock, and the running of many horses was heard. "Oh, Prophet," said the disciple, "they are pursuing us, they are many, they are many—there is an army behind us." "Oh, they are going somewhere else," said the Prophet. "They are coming here; I hear it." "They will go to some other direction," said the Prophet. "But what shall we do if they come here? They are so many and we are only two." "Are we two?" said the Prophet, "no, three—you, I, and God."

For everyone does not look at danger from the same point of view. To one, the smallest thing is too great; for the other, the greatest thing is nothing. It is as one views it. Once you see the danger as being great, you will make it greater. And by not acknowledging the greatness of the danger, you will diminish its greatness.

There is another thing that one must acknowledge: one must acknowledge in one's friend, in one's companion, in those one wishes to help, the good part in their character. By acknowledging it, by noticing it, you will fortify it; it will become greater. And do not think that it is against humility to acknowledge even your own merits, because if you are unconscious of your own merits, the plant is suffering there without water. It does not mean that by acknowledging one's merit, one's virtue, one becomes proud or conceited. If one wants to, one can keep oneself free from pride or conceit. But by recognizing one's merit, one certainly waters that plant that is worth rearing.

It is the same method you can carry from psychology to esotericism. In esotericism you have a problem before you. There is a truth that you have to discover, which is covered by a fact. And if you are accustomed to deny a fact in order to discover a truth, you will be ready then in the esoteric work to deny the fact that hides the truth and discover thereby that truth that is worth discovering. The one who understands this will understand the meaning of all the concentrations and meditations that are studied and practiced by the Sufis; they are all one means for one purpose; they are all in order to deny fact in order to establish truth.

* * *

Question: *What kind of fact is it that obscures the truth, which we remove by meditation?*

Answer: By explaining the meaning of the word "fact," I should like to say that the fact is a shadow which for the moment represents something that has a certain meaning to it, which we can witness and which at the same time will not continue its reality forever. For instance, a person says, "Sandow, in fact, is a strong man."[2] Yes, it is a fact that he is a strong man, but because he will not be eternally strong, that is a fact; it is not a truth. And, therefore, the knowledge of our own existence and the knowledge of the existence of the others, all this knowledge that we have is a changeable knowledge, and since it is changeable, it is a fact. Truth is behind it. But when we discover within our own self, and when we discover in the others that something that is everlasting and will never change, that is the truth.

Question: *In great trouble, how is one to dominate one's thoughts?*

Answer: Of course, when conditions have gone so far that it is most difficult to dominate the trouble, then one has to control them. But at the same time, by making a great excitement over it, we shall not make the trouble any less; on the contrary, it will be greater. I will tell you an amusing story that explains this. There was a prime minister of Hyderabad not long ago. He was one of the ancient royal families who carried with them a certain kind of ideal, manner, and culture. And once, sitting at the table, entertaining some foreign friends, it happened that a part of his palace had caught fire. Of course, as was the custom of the palace not to come hurriedly when bringing news,

---

2. Eugene Sandow (1867–1925), a famous Prussian bodybuilder known as the "father of modern bodybuilding."

the aide-de-camp came very gently between the courses and whispered in his ear what was happening. To the great surprise of the aide-de-camp, the prime minister only said, "Yes," and went with the next course that had arrived. And then when the next course was coming, he begged pardon of his friends and said, "I will come back in a moment." Quietly he went, as if nothing had happened, giving orders what to do to extinguish the fire, and then came back quietly. A great part of the palace had already burned; but the guests left from dinner without knowing it. Next day they read in the paper that a great part of the palace had burned. They were very surprised to see such a thing, such patience, such self-control, such a mastery over oneself. It does not mean that the minister did not feel the loss; he felt it perhaps more than anyone could have felt it. But he did not show it. It was not his manner to jump about. It was not his manner to run and rush; it was not his manner to make a fuss for nothing. Suppose he had done as everyone does, what would he have done? He would have excited the others also and made things worse. It is better that the palace was on fire than the spirit being on fire; that is better.

39

RESPONSIBILITY

Beloved Ones of God, I wish to speak this evening on the subject of responsibility.[1] I will quote first from the Arabic scripture: that God sent his trust on the mountains, and they refused to bear it. And God sent his trust on the trees, and they were unable to bear it. And then God sent his trust to humankind, who readily accepted it.[2] Trust, in this case, is responsibility. One's value is as great as one's responsibility. For what mountains cannot bear and trees cannot lift up, that humankind has carried through life. That is why a responsible person naturally shows a spiritual quality in all connections, in all relations. Be it your friend or master or servant or relative, if the person is responsible for the trust you give him or her, it is that which makes the value of the person. Be someone a minister or a king or a president of the state, their greatness, their value is according to their responsibility and according to the power with which they carry it out through life.

But there is another point of view from which to look at it, that people may become great by their responsibility, and at the same time they may fall, for there is a stumbling block. For the more conscious people become of their responsibility, the

---

1. A public lecture given in Suresnes, France, June 28, 1925.
2. Qur'an 33:72.

less they recognize the power of wisdom that is working beside them. It is, therefore, that at this time of materialism there are great personalities who accomplish great things, and yet in the end they show a limitation, and that limitation is from being drowned in the responsibility they have taken and of having forgotten God, the other power that is working beside them. However great someone may be in wisdom, in power, yet they are limited. And if their wisdom and power be compared with divine wisdom and power, it is not even as much as a drop compared with the sea. Saʻdi, the Persian poet, has made a remark in his *Rose Garden* in simple words. He says: "The constructor of this whole universe is active in constructing even my affairs, but my anxiety about my affairs is my illness." By this he means "it is something I cannot help, but at the same time I recognize that all that I wish to accomplish is already being done by someone else who is far greater, more powerful and wise than I." Jalal ad-Din Rumi points out in a verse from his *Masnavi* that the smallest insect receives its proper nourishment. Either it is attracted to its nourishment or the nourishment is sent to it. Humans, who are responsible for themselves and who take responsibility upon themselves for other living creatures, would never even think of the small insects living at the bottom of the wall of the house, under the earth, hidden under leaves, covered by the grass. But they receive their nourishment, what is needed to keep them alive. And so birds and animals all receive their nourishment and all that they need to build their nest without the help of humans.

The unfortunate task falls upon human beings to toil and make their living, but it is the price that they pay for self-reliance, for self-dependence, for the responsibility that they take upon themselves. And in so far they take responsibility upon themselves, they no doubt do a great work for humanity. But if they become absorbed in that responsibility so that they only rely upon their limited resources, and they forget that source from where their help comes, and if they are unaware of that

Responsibility

power and wisdom that is beside them, then no doubt, with their great responsibility and with all the power and might they may have, they will fail in the end.

And now coming to a question that a person asks today: Is there not an energy working, a force, that is devoid of wisdom? And the answer is that there cannot exist a quality, an attribute, without the possessor of that quality, of that attribute. Energy cannot exist without the energetic one to whom the energy belongs. Might cannot exist without the mighty one whose attribute it is. Intelligence cannot exist without the intelligent one to whom that intelligence belongs. And when a person asks: Well, is it not an energy, a force, a power from which all this comes? But one does not call oneself energy, or force, or power. One says: "I am I, an ego, a being." If this being is produced from an object, it cannot be a being too. It should not claim itself to be a being. This shows that a being comes from a being, that there is a being behind it all, and that being is perfect in its power and wisdom. But then a person is inclined to say that that being is a being larger than me, because one's ego compares that being with oneself. One wants to see the other being, how it stands in comparison with oneself. And the answer to this is that it is a being who includes you, and I, and all. And, therefore, there is nothing else that you can compare this being with. Nor can this being be explained, for neither is the wisdom of this being like our wisdom, nor is the power of this being like our limited power.

Those who have tried to learn the life of dependence upon that being have been saints and sages. No doubt, they have practiced the recognition of the divine power and of divine wisdom by becoming passive to it, by becoming responsive to it. And by this practice their load of responsibility was taken away from them, and their lives were made easier for them, and they experienced a great ease and peace in their lives. Very often a thoughtful person envies a little child who is so happy, without cares, without anxieties. The child represents the divine kingdom. It is as if all that is there belongs to it, all that is good and beautiful is its.

But now there is a question: How far must one depend upon divine wisdom and power, and how far must one feel responsible for oneself and for those who depend upon one? What sometimes happens is this: a person takes a principle and practices it. But in order to practice that principle, one must prepare oneself. If one is not prepared for that principle, one must not practice it. If someone who toils every day for their livelihood sits down and says that God must supply it, the supply will not come so soon, they will be disappointed. In order to practice it one must first of all prepare oneself to come to that faith. It is that confidence and faith that will bring the supply, but the confidence and faith should first be cultivated gradually, and the principle should not be practiced at once. If one has a business affair somewhere and one says, "Well, it will all be done by itself, I shall not go there," that will be wrong, because that one has started by being responsible for it. One cannot at once take oneself away like this. But one must practice every day that principle of recognizing that wisdom and power that is beside oneself.

I would never advise anyone to give away one's responsibility in recognition of the might and wisdom of God; but one should be full of courage and confidence in the face of difficulty and seeming trouble, by recognizing that there is a mighty power, that there is a perfect wisdom behind one, and that all will be well. By that one will rise above one's limitation of power and wisdom and will be able to draw power and wisdom from that unlimited source that in the end will lead one to success. Then even in the case of failure, this recognition of a perfect power and wisdom working beside oneself will give one the strength to bear it and to be resigned to the will of God.

40

THE CONTINUITY OF LIFE

Beloved Ones of God, I would like to speak a few words on the question of the certitude of the life in the hereafter.[1] This is a question that occupies every mind. Sooner or later in life a person begins to wonder if there is such a thing as continuity of life. There are many who, by their pessimism, think that there seems to be nothing afterward. And there are others who, owing to their optimism, think whether there is something or whether there is not something, it is just as well to think that there is something. Nevertheless, this thought is most painful when a person thinks that there will be nothing after death. And however many reasons one may have in support of this belief, that belief itself is worse than death. There are some who through different phenomena wish to get proof of the life in the hereafter. But they meet with ninety-nine disappointments and perhaps one reality. And when we come to the idea of the Sufis, their idea is that life lives and death dies. In other words, to life there is no death, and to death there is no life. But this way of attaining to the certitude of life is not only an intellectual one. For by studying all the philosophies and metaphysics all through life one may in every way prove to oneself by reasoning that there is continuity of life. Yet this realization gained

---

1. A talk given at the home of Baroness d'Eichthal, Paris, March 28, 1925.

by the effort of mind will not give one that feeling of certitude that one would wish to have. Sufis, therefore, practice that process through which they are able to touch that part of life in themselves that is not subject to death. And by finding that part of life, they naturally begin to feel the certitude of life. It makes them more certain of life than of anything in the world because they see changeability and limitation in all things. For everything that is constructed is subject to being destroyed. Everything that is composed is subject to be being decomposed. Everything born is subject to death. But in finding that life, they find their own self, and, as that is the real life, all else that they know about life begins to lose its importance.

And now you will ask: In what way does one discover that life in one that was never born and will never die? By self-analysis, but a self-analysis according to what mystics know of it, which means the understanding of what this vehicle that we call the body is to us, and in what relation we stand to it, and by understanding what this mind that we call mind consists of. And then by asking: "What am I then: am I this body, am I this mind?" There comes a time when one begins to see that one is oneself the knower of the body and of the mind. But one only arrives at this realization when one can hold the body and mind in one's hands, as objects that one uses for one's purpose in life. Once one has done this, then the body and mind, these two things, become like the two floats a person puts on in order to swim in the water without danger of drowning. The same body and mind that cause one's mortality, at least in one's thought, the very body and mind then become the means of one's safety from being drowned in the water of mortality.

In reality, mortality is our conception; immortality is reality. We make a conception of mortality because we do not know the real life. By the realization of the real life, the comparison between real life and mortality makes one know that mortality is nonexistent. Therefore, it would not be an exaggeration if I said that the work of Sufis is an unlearning. What they are accustomed to call or recognize as life, they then begin to recognize as death. And what they are accustomed to call death they then begin to recognize as life. And, therefore, for them both life and death are not conditions to which they are subject, but are conditions that they themselves bring about. A great Persian Sufi, Bedil, says, "By myself I become captive, and by myself I become free." If I were to interpret this in simple language, I would say that, "By myself I die, and by myself I live." But why do Sufis say this? Why does not everyone say it? Because for Sufis, it is a condition that they bring about. For another person, it is a condition in which that person is helpless.

And now you will ask me in what way this realization is to be brought about. The first thing is that one must learn in every little thing in life the way of unlearning. In my own work I find it difficult when a person comes to me and says, "Now I have learned so far, will you add more to my knowledge?" And in my heart I say, "The more you have learned, the worse it is for me; and if I wanted to add to it, it would not be adding, it would be taking away from what you have in order that I may unburden you from all you have learned, that you may be able to unlearn first and that through this unlearning what will come will be the true learning." But one might say, "Then is it all useless for us to learn what we learn in life?" And the answer is, "No, it is all useful, but for what? For the object for which one has learned it; for it is not all learned on account of that object you are searching after." When you wish to search after the secret of life, the learning that one calls learning, that is the first thing to unlearn. No doubt, this is something that is difficult for everyone to understand. And yet when we read the lives of Rumi, a great teacher, and his teacher, Shams-i Tabriz, the first lesson the latter gave to Rumi was, "Unlearn all that you have learned." And now you may ask me, "Is this unlearning forgetting all that one learns?" Not at all. It is not necessary. This unlearning means to be able to say with reason, with logic, the contrary to what one knows. When you are accustomed to saying, "This is wrong, that is right; this is good and that is bad; this is great and that is small; this is higher and that is lower; this is spiritual and that is material; this is up and that is down; and this is before and that is after," if you can use the opposite words for each with reason and with logic, you have unlearned naturally what you once had learned. It is after this that the realization of truth begins. Because then the mind is not fixed anymore. And it is then that one becomes alive, for then one's soul has been born. It is then that one will become tolerant, and it is then that one will forgive, for one will understand both one's friend and one's foe. Then one never has only one point of view; one has all points of view. You might ask, "Is it not dangerous to have all points of view, then I wouldn't have my own point of view?" Not necessarily. You may have one room in the house or you may have ten rooms. You may use each as you like. As many points of view as one can see, so large is one's point of view.

But all this is attained by the meditative process: by tuning oneself, by bringing oneself to a proper rhythm, by concentration, contemplation, meditation, and realization, by both dying and living at the same time. In order to rise above death, one must first die. In order to get above mortality, one must know what it is. But this is certain, the greatest and most important thing that one can wish to accomplish in life, is one and only one thing: to rise above the conception of death.

* * *

Question: *How can you rise above the conception of death?*

Answer: As I have already said, the most necessary thing is to play death and try to know what death is. And it is a great learning, how to play death. For what we do is a very false thing, and that is we play life when we are subject to death. If we played death, it would be a real thing; it would not be a hypocrisy. And it is out of that that we shall discover life. For we experience death by playing life, and we experience life by playing death.

What we call death is the death of this body. But if we attach ourselves to this body as ourselves, then it is death. A simple man asked a person, "How can I know that I am dead?" "Well," the person said, "it is very easy. When your coat has become rotten and torn and worn out, then it is death." Of course, when the coat was worn out and torn, then this man began to think that he was dead, and he was weeping bitterly. Then some thoughtful person came along and told him, "It is only your coat that is torn. How can you cry? You are still alive." This story shows exactly the mystical idea. For the mystic, the body is a garment. But it is no use realizing it intellectually. Because if one says intellectually, "My body is my garment, but then what am I, and where am I?" And as I have said, it is by the meditative process that one finds where one is, and what one is. And, therefore, this does not remain as a belief; it becomes faith, and even greater than faith: it becomes conviction.

Question: *In what way can we play death? How can we do it?*

Answer: There was a king who thought that he would give up his kingdom and he would become a murid. That is to say, he would become a disciple of a teacher, and give up all worldly things and just go in the spiritual thought. And when he went to Bokhara, under the guidance of a teacher, the teacher gave him a probationer's work. And that work was to sweep and clean the whole house where all the pupils lived, and to collect the garbage and take it out of the village. Of course, the pupils were very much in sympathy with this man, and they were shocked that this man, who used to sit on the throne and be a king, had to do this, a thing that he was never accustomed to do, that it must be a terrible thing for him! No doubt, the teacher, knowing the object that he had before him, could not do otherwise. He said, "He must do it, for he is not yet ready." Once all the disciples went, and they said, "Teacher, we are all in sympathy with this man, and we think he is so fine and so nice and so cultured, and we would so much like if you would relieve him of this duty." And then they said to the teacher, "It has been a long time, now he must be relieved of it." The teacher said, "We shall have a test." One day when he was taking his garbage pail outside the town, somebody knocked against him, and all was spilled on the ground. He looked back and said, "Well, it is not the days of the past, what can I tell you?" And when the report was brought to the teacher, he said, "Did I not say that the time has not yet come?" And after some time, a test was made again. And when the same thing happened, this man looked at the one who pushed him and said nothing. The teacher said, "Did I not say that the time has not yet arrived?" But the third time when he was tested, he did not even look at the man who spilled his pail; he gathered up all that was spilled and carried it along. The teacher said, "Now is the time, now he can play death." All the teachings that Christ has taught, that if one should strike you on one side of the face, give the other side; if one should ask you to go one mile, go still further; if one asks you for your overcoat, give your cape also[2]—when we think of it, what does it all mean? Is it not all teaching to play death? Therefore, if at any time the teachers of truth have prescribed to their pupils any process of behavior with their fellowmen, that process can be called nothing else but playing death. But one might think that this is very hard, that this is very cruel on the part of the teacher. But the instructor had to go through the same cruelty once at a certain period of his or her life. But sometimes the greatest cruelty is the greatest kindness. It is hard, but the hardest path can be conquered by this. And if I were to speak about it in simple words, it is like this: How many times do we take to heart unnecessary things? How many times do we cause, or take interest in, disharmony that could just as well have been avoided? How often do we resist evil that we could have just as well not resisted? This is all playing life.

2. Matthew 5:39–41

And what I have said before is playing death. When we play death, we arrive at life. When we play life, we arrive at death.

Question: *Is it not sometimes to become insensible at the pain of others to just look at them and not share with them?*

Answer: What I have said, is that playing with death is rising above the sensible and insensible, because sensible and insensible belong to a certain stage. One can rise above that stage; then all is sensible. Besides one can always find among those who play death or who have played death that they are the ones who are most sympathetic and the most open to the pain of others. Because when they are playing death automatically they are playing life too. And therefore, although they are dead to all the wrong things that come to them, they are alive to everything that can help them to help others.

Question: *May I ask in what consists that state, where at certain days and at certain hours, one no longer feels one's body and all the thought is alive and awake?*

Answer: It is a condition. As I say, any condition that automatically comes is not a normal thing, even if it be a high condition. But if it automatically comes, it is not normal. The normal thing is to be able to experience any condition one wishes to. To be able to experience death, to be able to experience life, that is the right thing. The one who always experiences death and does not experience life, that is abnormal too.

Question: *How to have a balance?*

Answer: To have a balance one must do everything from morning to evening that is balanced.

GLOSSARY

Ahimsa paramo dharmaha (Sanskrit): "Harmlessness is the essence of religion."

ajnana (Sanskrit): Lack of realization or "ignorance" (imperfect knowledge).

akasha (Sanskrit): Capacity. In Hinduism, it is used to mean the essence of everything that exists in the material world.

ananda (Sanskrit): Happiness or bliss or divine joy.

asana (Sanskrit): A certain way of sitting, a certain way of walking, and a certain way of standing. It is practiced for achieving control over muscles and nerves.

atman (Sanskrit): Soul. The eternal core of the personality that transmigrates or attains release in Hinduism.

Bedil: Persian Sufi. He is considered one of the prominent poets of Indian School of Poetry in Persian literature and is regarded as having his own unique style.

bhavasagara (Sanskrit): Life of the world. Hindus believe life is floating in this ocean of the activity of the world, not knowing what one is doing, not knowing where one is going.

Birbal: Prime minister of Emperor Akbar with charismatic wit.

Brahma: Hindu creator god.

Brahmins: People from highest ranking in four varnas of Hindu society with developed intuition and had insight into the law of harmony, the law of attraction and repulsion.

deva (Sanskrit): God or angelic person.

dharma (Sanskrit): Religion or duty. According to the Hindus the observers of duty are considered religious.

gayan (Sanskrit): Song. The title of a work by Hazrat Inayat Khan, *Gayan: Notes from the Unstruck Music.*

iman (Arabic): Conviction. To accept truthfully, to be convinced, and to verify something, to rely upon or have confidence in something.

jnana (Sanskrit): Realization or "spiritual knowledge" or "wisdom." It denotes a knowledge of the Self that is inseparable from the Divine.

mana (Sanskrit): Mind.

manusha (Sanskrit): Human person.

murid (Arabic): "Seeker," a Sufi initiate, a spiritual student.

murshid(a) (Arabic): "Guide," a Sufi spiritual teacher.

rakshasa: Monstrous person. In Hindu mythology a malignant demon.

Rama (Vedic Sanskrit): A major deity in Hinduism. He is the seventh and one of the most popular avatars of Vishnu.

Ram Das: Samarth Ramdas or Ramdas Swami, was an Indian Hindu saint, philosopher, poet, writer, and spiritual master. He was the great guru of Shivaji Maharaj.

Rumi: Jalal ad-Din Muhammad Rumi (1207–1273): Persian Sufi poet and founder of the Mawlawi (Mevlevi) order.

Saʿdi: Musharrif al-Dīn ibn Muslih al-Dīn, Saadi (1213-1291): Persian poet, one of the greatest figures in classical Persian literature.

Shivaji: Shivaji Maharaj (1630–1680) was a seventeenth-century king who founded the Maratha Empire in India, a Hindu kingdom that challenged the Mughal and Adilshahi rule.

siddhi (Sanskrit): Sign of spiritual mastership. Spiritual or magical power or capability that arises from perfect spiritual practices.

sophia (Greek): Wisdom; the message of wisdom.

SOURCES

Note: All but three of the original sources of the texts in this volume can be found in the *Complete Works of Pir-o-Murshid Hazrat Inayat Khan, Source Edition* (New Lebanon, NY, and Richmond, VA: Omega/Sulūk Press; London and The Hague: East-West Publications; Katwijk, the Netherlands: Panta Rhei Publishers, 1982–). The *Complete Works* volumes are also available online at www.nekbakhtfoundation.org. Chapters 22 and 37 appeared in *Social Gathekas: Sufi Wisdom on Social Harmony and Service* (Richmond, VA: Sulūk Press, 2020). The original text of chapter 19 remains unpublished; it will appear in a future volume of the *Complete Works*.

1. The Alchemy of Happiness — 1922, vol. II, 130
2. The Aim of Life — 1924, vol. I, 244
3. The Purpose of Life (1) — 1926, vol. I, 55
4. The Purpose of Life (2) — 1926, vol. II, 380
5. The Art of Personality — 1926, vol. II, 430
6. Reconciliation — 1923, vol. II, 118
7. Attitude — 1926, vol. III, 255
8. The Secret of Life — 1923, vol. II, 856
9. What Is Wanted in Life — 1925, vol. II, 828
10. Life, a Continual Battle (1) — 1923, vol. I, 73
11. Life, a Continual Battle (2) — 1923, vol. I, 78
12. The Struggle of Life (1) — 1922, vol. II, 251
13. The Struggle of Life (2) — 1924, vol. I, 207
14. Reaction — 1924, vol. II, 741
15. The Deeper Side of Life — 1926, vol. I, 23
16. Life, an Opportunity — 1926, vol. II, 454
17. Our Life — 1925, vol. II, 763

18. Communicating with Life	1926, vol. II, 225
19. The Intoxication of Life (1)	1921
20. The Intoxication of Life (2)	1923. vol. II, 864
21. The Meaning of Life	1923, vol. II, 831
22. The Inner Life	1922
23. The Inner Life and Self-Realization	1926, vol. II, 360
24. The Interdependence of Life Within and Without	1925, vol. II, 507
25. Interest and Indifference	1926, vol. III, 74
26. From Limitation to Perfection (1)	1926, vol. II, 486
27. From Limitation to Perfection (2)	1924, vol. II, 759
28. The Path of Attainment (1)	
Sadhana	1923, vol. II, 775
Spiritual Attainment	1924, vol. I, 181
Sadhana, the Path of Attainment	1922, vol. II, 240
29. The Path of Attainment (2)	1922, vol. II, 223
30. Stages on the Path of Self-Realization	1926, vol. II, 301
31. Human Beings, Masters of Their Destiny (1)	1926, vol. I, 36
32. Human Beings, Masters of Their Destiny (2)	1926, vol. II, 252
33. The Law of Action	1925, vol. I, 139
34. Purity of Life	1922, vol. I, 145
35. The Ideal	1924, vol. II, 773
36. The Journey to the Goal (1)	1925, vol. 1, 73
37. The Journey to the Goal (2)	1921
38. Acknowledgment	1925, vol. I, 29
39. Responsibility	1925, vol. II 93
40. The Continuity of Life	1925, vol. I, 164

BIOGRAPHICAL NOTE

Hazrat Inayat Khan was born in Baroda, India, in 1882. Trained in Hindustani classical music from childhood, he became a professor of music at an early age. In the course of extensive travels in the Indian subcontinent, he won high acclaim at the courts of the maharajas and received the title of Tansen-uz-Zaman from the Nizam of Hyderabad.

In Hyderabad Hazrat Inayat Khan became the disciple of Sayyid Abu Hashim Madani, who trained him in the traditions of the Chishti, Suhrawardi, Qadiri, and Naqshbandi lineages of Sufism, and at last blessed him to "Fare forth into the world."

In 1910, accompanied by his brother Maheboob Khan and cousin Mohammed Ali Khan, Hazrat Inayat Khan sailed for the United States. Over the next sixteen years he traveled and taught widely throughout the United States and Europe, building up the first Sufi order ever established in the West.

In London Hazrat Inayat Khan married Ora Ray Baker. They raised their four children in London during the First World War and afterward in Suresnes, France, where a little Sufi village sprang up around their home, Fazal Manzil.

The doors of Hazrat Inayat Khan's Sufi Order[1] were open to people of all faiths. Appealing to experience rather than belief, Hazrat Inayat Khan's discourses and spiritual instructions illuminated the twin themes of the presence of God in the depths of the human soul and the interconnectedness of all people. Numerous books were compiled from Hazrat Inayat Khan's teachings during his lifetime and posthumously. In September 1926 Hazrat Inayat Khan bade farewell to his family and disciples and returned to India. On February 5, 1927, he died and was buried in New Delhi.

1. Known today as the Inayatiyya.

INDEX

A

acknowledgment, 288–93
advanced age, 120–21
affection, 136–37
  honor of, 267
agreement, 46
Ahimsa paramo dharmaha, 196
aim of life, 7–13
ajnana (lack of realization), 19
akasha (capacity), 251
Akbar, Emperor, 190
alchemy, defined, 2
ananda (happiness), 20
angelic essence, 114
angelic person, 44, 260
angelic sphere, 242–43
anger impulse, utilizing, 98
animosity, 289
another, interest in, 187
art of personality, 35
asana (way of sitting), 97
aspect of action of free will, 242
atman (soul), 1
attachment, 136–37, 143, 146
attainment. *See* path of attainment; spiritual attainment
attitude, 56
  of body, 45
  for direct communication with God, 34, 62–63
  of mind, 45, 276
  steadiness of, 59–60
  towards oneself, 56–58
automatic working of life, 182

B

balance in life, 166–67, 304
Bedil (Persian Sufi), 300
being in accordance with life, 68
being in tune with the infinite, 67–68
belief(s)
  in God, 6, 196–97, 225–28, 231, 284
  understanding and tolerance between those of different, 106
Beni Israel, 110
bhavasagara (life of the world), 136
Bible, 22, 99, 140, 153, 184, 195, 211, 212, 234, 237, 282
Birbal, 190
birth of the soul, 184
blame, 86, 105
body, state of not feeling the, 304
Brahma, 22, 234
Brahmins, 44–45, 178
breath/breathing
  and concentration, 96
  as essence of life, 5
  exercises, 5
  teaching, 100, 108
Buddha/Buddhism, 19, 57, 104–5, 196, 237
  and Christianity, 107, 110–11

C

celestial chamber in the human heart, 163–64

certitude of life, 298–99
chamber of divine light, 162
child of God, 237
children, concentration in, 115–16
Christ, Jesus, 110, 111, 140, 141, 237
   conception of, 200–201, 230–31
   on forgiveness, 254
   friendship with the fishermen (lower evolution), 179
   message of truth by, 139, 141
   on perfection, 195–97
   on purpose in life, 27, 30
   teaching of, 212, 214, 227, 234–35, 286, 303
Christianity and Buddhism, 107, 110–11
chukar, 160
collective purpose of life, 247
common sense, 117, 255, 256, 268
communicating with life, 127–34
concentration, 115, 119, 180. *See also* meditation
   and breathing, 96
   in children, 115
   faculty of, 5
   habit of, 96
   for self-realization, 177–78
conception
   of death, rising above, 301–2
   of God, 24, 197–99, 230–32
conscientiousness, 60, 90, 169
consciousness, 184. *See also* soul
   expansion, 209
   of the inner life, 158
   presence of God in, 264–65
   and self effacement, 92
   and sense of duty, 29
   spiritual, 32, 33, 39, 92
conscious of human feeling, 92
contemplation, 180
contentment, 35, 89, 90, 200, 244
continual guidance, 61
continuity of life, 298–304
control
   on influences, 239
   of the reaction, 97–98
   of situations, 239
Creator's interest, 188
criticism, 60, 259, 263

D

date-like personality, 37–38
death, 9, 11, 290
   desire for, 212–13
   playing, 302–4
   rising above conception of, 301–2
debts of life, 170–72
decay of dharma, 284
deed, 94
deeper side of life, 102–11
d'Eichthal, Baroness, 70
dependence on others, 69
dervishes, 20, 52, 146–47, 206, 238
desire, 216
   for death, 212–13
   of fulfillment, 217
   for perfection, 193–95
   suppressing, 217
   unfulfilled, 206–7
destiny, 184, 234–36
   human beings as masters of their, 234–49
   and meaning of life, 151–52
deva (angelic person), 44
dharma (duty/religion), 29
dignity, 41, 95, 267
direct communication with God, 62–63
disagreement, 12–13, 41, 46, 47, 53, 109

discipline, 217, 218–19, 271–72
discontentment, 90, 244
dishonesty, 58–59
dissatisfaction, 24, 244
distrust, 58, 112, 173–74
divine ideal, 202
divine impulse, 218
   suppressing, 217
divine kingdom, 296–97
divine mind, 130
divine perfection, 201
divine plan, 184
divine pleasure, 218
divine power, 59
divine power, recognition of, 296
divine spark, 237
divine spirit, 164
divine wisdom, recognition of, 296
duty, 28–29

E

earning money, 27–28
earthly perfection, 196
Eastern philosophers, 242
education, 275–76
   and ideal, 271
ego, 74, 89, 143, 144, 296
endurance, 25
esotericism, 108, 291
exaltation, 118
experiences of life, 118
expression, limit to, 213
external purity or cleanliness, 264
external worship, 210

F

faculty, 253
   of concentration, 5
   of inner life, 163
   instinct, 127

   intuitive, 128, 129
   of mind, 74, 76–77
   of perceiving impressions, 128
   of retaining thought, 74
false ideal, 270–71
false self, 90, 178, 204
fatalists, 241
fear of the condition, 66–67
feeling of kinship, 141
finding one's object/purpose, 8
Firdausi, 131
forgiveness, 41, 254, 285
freedom for looking inside, 161
free will, 81, 183–84, 237, 241–42,
   245–46
friendship, 199, 267

G

gaining power, 19–20
garb, 243
Gayan, 14, 18, 212, 216, 234, 236
genius/jinn, 242–43
gentleness, 40–41
God
   belief in, 6, 196, 197, 225–26,
      231
   the Beloved, 22–23
   communication, 34, 62–63
   conception of, 24, 197–99,
      230–32
   displeasure of, 199–200, 218
   the judge, 224–25
   knowledge of, 6, 284
   owning, 191
   parenthood of, 142
   perfection of, 264
   pleasure of, 199–200
   presence in consciousness,
      264–65
   union with, 45
   will of, 297

God-ideal, 197, 199, 224
God-realization, 223
God-spirit, 131–32
grape-like personality, 37–38
guidance from spiritual teacher, 174–76
Gulistan, 15

H

happiness
  alchemy of, 1–6
  yearning for, 10
harmonizing with rhythm of life, 64–70
healing power, 42–43
heart
  divine essence in, 5–6
  of a human, 206–7, 209
  quality, 117–18
Hejaz, 53
higher consciousness, 29, 32
Hindi language, 190
Hindu idea of self, 167
Hindu philosophy, 245
Hindu Puranic symbology, 281
Hindus, 22, 71, 136, 178, 202, 211, 234
  ideal of duty in, 29
Hindustani, 49–50, 59, 70, 155, 209
honesty, 58
honor of word, 267–68
horoscope, 44, 178
human beings, as masters of their destiny, 234–49
human ignorance, 201
human perfection, 255
humbleness, 39, 50, 79
hypocrisy, 289–90

I

the ideal, 266–73
idealism, 24, 39, 174, 175, 270
ideal life for the average person, 109–10
ignorance, 19, 57, 104
iman (conviction), 228–29
impression, 153–55
imprudence, 57
impulse(s)
  feeling, 99
  having only good, 100–101
  rising above, 100
  in saints, 100
In an Eastern Rose Garden, 179
inclinations of people, 16
India, 32, 44, 97, 106, 110, 120, 122, 146–47
indifference, 187
  and interest, 187–90
  learning, 192
  of sages, 190–92
individuality, 36, 225
individual purpose of life, 247
influence on a person, 181
  to attract, 51, 52–53
  to make difficult situations easy, 51, 53–54
  outer, 183
  to progress, 51–52
innate desire of unfoldment, 194
innate yearning, 244
inner guidance, 61
inner learning, 11–12
inner life, 157–67
  and self-realization, 168–80
inner self, exploring, 33–34
inspiration, 129–30
  and faculty of inner life, 163–64
  and knowledge of life, 155
instinct, 72, 127, 224

instrument of God, 217
intellect, 53, 92, 117–18, 229
intellectual knowledge, 11, 19
intellectual magnetism, 38
interdependence of life within and
    without, 181–85
interest, 186–92
intoxication of life, 135–42
  and activity of life, 138
  battle, 77–78
  environment and condition in
    life creating, 138–39
  intoxication of childhood,
    144–45
  intoxication of youth, 145
  kinds of intoxication, 143–44
  love for, 139
  message of God to overcome,
    140–42
  moments of emotion causing,
    135–37
  principle of intoxication, 146–48
  soberness from, 148–49
  spiritual or religious truth,
    139–40
intoxication of the time, 284–85
intuition, 44, 117, 127–29
  and inspiration, 129–30, 131–32
  and revelation, 132–34
  and science, 131–32
  and self-confidence, 127–29
  of a true dream, 154–55
  and vision, 132
  and willpower, 130–31
intuitive faculty, 128, 129

J

jinn, 162, 242, 243
jnana (realization), 19
journey to the goal, 274–80, 281–87
judging others, 261–63

K

Kabir, 122
karma, 111
  influence on every soul, 81
Khayyam, Omar, 29, 279
knowledge
  of battle, 71–72, 73
  of God, 6, 284
  of life, perceiving, 153–56
  of peace, 71–72
  of warfare, 82
  yearning for, 10, 118–19

L

language
  of the heart, 161
  of life, 133
law of a church, 252–53
law of action, 250–57
law of attraction and repulsion, 44
law of beneficence, 256
law of harmony, 43–44
law of personality, 45
law of reciprocity, 255–56
law of renunciation, 256–57
law of the community, 251–52
law of the prophets, 252–53
law of the state, 251–53
life. *See also specific* entries
  aim of, 7–13
  communicating with, 127–34
  as a continual battle, 71–75
  continuity of, 298–304
  deeper side of, 102–11
  of dependence, 296
  of a hermit, 62
  interdependence of life within
    and without, 181–85
  opportunity of, 112–22
  as pain or pleasure, 212–13

playing, 303–4
purity of, 258–65
yearning for, 9
limitation
   to perfection, 193–210
   and responsibility, 295
longing, 244
losing ideal, 270
love, 136–37
   of God, 6
   honor of, 267
   of knowledge, 16–18
   for life, 18
   between persons of lower and higher evolution, 179

M

magnetism, 38, 43
mahatmas, 119
making best of the present, 29–30
making wealth, 27–28
mana, 152
manifestation, 244
   secret of, 188–89
manner of worship, 202
manusha (human person), 44
Masnavi (Rumi), 283, 295
mastery, 237–38
   attaining, 239–40
   over oneself, in troubled situations, 292–93
materialism, 27, 214–15, 284, 295
material person, reaction of, 93, 94–95
meaning of life
   destiny, 151–52
   knowledge of life, perceiving, 153–56
   searching for, 150–51
Mecca, 52

meditation, 61, 69, 180, 278, 301
   to find truth, 292
   habit of, 96
message of God, 140–42
message of wisdom, 141
metaphysics
   of the East, 242–43
   point of view of, 189, 216
middle age, 120
mind, nature of, 4–5
mind of God, 54–55
moral principles, 202–3
mortality, 18–19, 299–300
   from spiritual point of view, 10–11
Moses, 198, 199, 229–30, 237
motive, 189
   behind action, 253
Muhammad, Prophet, 24–25, 52–53, 171, 237, 290–91
murid, 302
murshid, 47–48, 58, 89, 91–92, 229, 264–65
music, 133
   inspiration from, 129–30
mysticism, 4, 14, 63, 107, 207, 212, 223, 224, 225
mystics, 96

N

narrowness of outlook, 46
natural rhythm, 33
nervous power, 73–74
nervous system, conditioning of, 96

O

object of God, 155
occultism, 223–25
occult schools, 284
oneness, 45

opportunity of life, 112–22
optimism, 76
Order of the Sufis, 142
outer experiences of life, 183
outer life, 157, 160
outward purity, 260
owning, 191

P

pain of others, insensible at, 304
parenthood of God, 142
path of attainment, 220–22
    sadhana, 211–13, 217–19
    spiritual attainment, 213–17
path of mastery, 237
patience, 25, 241–42
    in troubled situations, 292–93
peace, 119
    knowledge of, 71–72
    seeking, 21
    yearning for, 10
perception, 38–39, 45, 128, 167
    of life, 30
perfection of God, 264
Persian mystics, 228
personality
    art of, 35–45
    grades of, 254–55
personal magnetism, 38
philosophical belief, 277
phrenology, 154
physical magnetism, 38
physical sphere, 242
physiognomy, 154
pleasure, 1, 118, 138
    and displeasure of God, 199–200
    and happiness, 10
    and seeking happiness, 20–21
pomegranate personality, 37–38
power, 11
    of feeling, 122

    of indifference, 189
    of interest, 189
    of mind, 37
    of self, 177–78
    of the soul, 189
    of trust, 58
    of wealth, 69
    of will, 78–80
    of wisdom, 295
    yearning for, 9
praise, 86, 105
prayers, 108
    concentrating through, 5
preparatory aspect of free will, 242–43
preparing for future, 30–31
principle of democracy, 39
Providence, 25
psychology, 159
pure intelligence, 158
pure-minded, 259
purity of life, 258–65
purposes of life, 247
    preliminary, 26–31
    spiritual journey, 32–35
    understanding, 23–26
purposes of life, preliminary
    making best of the present, 29–30
    making wealth, 27–28
    and natural rhythm, 33
    preparing for future, 30–31
    sense of duty, 28–29

Q

Qur'an, 55, 56–57, 73, 244

R

racial ideal, 267
rakshasa (animal person), 44–45

Rama, 214
Ram Das, 239
reaction, 93–101
reading, concentrating through, 5
real self, 90
reconciliation, 46–48
reincarnation, 110, 111, 245
religion, 108
   aspects of, 196, 200, 202–3
   meaning of, 3–4
   and truth, 12
religious belief, 277
religious ideal, 227
religious truth, 139–40
renunciation, 90, 256–57
   of worldly things, 221
repression, limit to, 213
responsibility, 55, 294–97
restlessness, 90
revelation, 155–56
   and intuition, 132–34
rhythm of life, 64–70
right attitude to God, 61
Rose Garden (Sa'di), 295
Rubaiyat (Khayyam), 29
Rumi, Jalal ad-Din, 22, 283, 295, 300

S

sacred power, 59
sacrifice, 162–63, 233
Sa'di, 15, 57, 106, 120, 133, 295
sages, 163
   Chinese, 224
   in the East, 43
   in India, 168–69, 190, 239
   indifference of, 190–92
   of Persia, 243
Satan, 90
satisfaction, 35, 47, 63, 135, 144, 182, 207, 218, 256

science/art, interest in, 187
secret of enjoyment, 279
secret of life, ignorance towards, 206–7
secret of magnetism, 58
seeking happiness, 20–21
seeking peace, 21
seer, 161
self, 167
self-abnegation, 210
self-analysis, 299
self-confidence, 25, 129
self-control, 73, 239
   and age of life, 96
   educating children about, 97
   and spontaneity, 99
   in troubled situations, 292–93
self-denial, 96, 163, 184
self-dependence, 295
self-discipline, 217, 218–19
self-effacement, 233
self-expression, 237
self-interest, 186–87
selfishness/avariciousness, 221
self-pity, 90
self-realization, path of, 203–4, 249
   and inner life, 168–80
   stages in, 223–33
self-reliance, 295
self will, 183–84
sensation, 118
sense of duty, 28–29
sensitiveness, 79–80, 82
   and willpower, 82
service, 2, 5, 63, 121, 165, 172, 233
Shah Nameh (Firdausi), 131
Shivaji, 239
siddhi, 211
silence, 40–43, 96, 273
sin, 264–65
Sita, 214

sitting postures, 45
slave of mind, 228
sleeplessness, 289
solitude, 167
sophia (message of wisdom), 141
soul. *See also* consciousness
   appetite of the, 207
   birth of the, 184
   karma's influence on every, 81
   power of the, 189
   as a ray, 243–44
   spirit-consciousness, 214–15
speech, meaningful, 40–41
spirit of mastery, 95, 240
spiritual attainment, 9, 12, 24–25, 31–32, 40, 134
   inner journey for, 169–73
   of self-sufficient person, 180
spiritual awakening, 164–65
spiritual beauty, 286
spiritual bliss, 218
spiritual consciousness, 32, 33, 39, 92
spiritual goal, 214
spiritual happiness, 122
spiritual ideal, 248
spiritual influence, 51–52
spirituality, 27
   and religion, 169
spiritual journey, 32
spiritual knowledge, 12, 199, 214
   teachers of, 27
spiritual life, 158–59
spiritual magnetism, 38–39
spiritual mastership, 211
spiritual outlook towards democracy, 40
spiritual path, 63, 89, 172, 282
spiritual perfection, 196–97, 204, 223, 231
   awakening to, 27
spiritual person, reaction of, 93

spiritual progress, 229
spiritual purpose, 33
spiritual quality, 294
spiritual realization, 184
spiritual teacher, 32, 60–61
   guidance from, 174–76
spiritual things, interest in, 187
spiritual truth, 139–40, 141, 247–48
spiritual unfoldment, 259
spiritual work, 88
Sri Krishna, 284
staying happy, 29–30
steadiness of attitude, 59–60
struggle of life, 83, 86–87
   with circumstances, 84, 85
   with oneself, 84–85
   with others, 84, 85
study of life, 108
success, 221
Sufi Movement, 60, 70, 141
Sufi Order, 60, 61
Sufis, 108, 228, 280, 298–300
   outlook on struggle, 85–87
   principle of intoxication, 146–48
Sufi school, 286–87
Sufism, 47–48, 216
Sufis of Persia, 254
sun, worshipping, 202
superstitions, 152–53
sympathetic magnetism, 38
sympathy, 45

T

Tabriz, Shams-i (Rumi's teacher), 300–301
teacher, 200–201. *See also* murshid
thinking, concentrating through, 5
thoughtlessness, 223, 276
Timur (Mughul emperor), 238–39
tranquility, 21, 152, 166

true happiness, discovery of, 12
true ideal, 270–71
true profit, 86–87
trust, 25
   power of, 58
   as responsibility, 294
   in spiritual teacher, 32–33
   while treading spiritual path, 172–73
truth, 208, 249, 273
   attaining, 12–13
   realization of, 301
truth-seeking people, 17
tuning oneself to the infinite, 69–70

U

union with God, 45
unlearning, 299–300
unselfishness, 209
upbringing and ideas, 272–73

V

Vedantists, 20
virtue, 6, 20–21, 253, 265, 268–69
vision and intuition, 132

W

wakeful condition, intoxication in, 139
wakening of the ideal, 109–10
walnut-like personality, 37–38
weakness, 25
what is wanted in life, 64–70
will, 181–82, 276
   of God, 297
   and luck, 185
willpower, 78–80, 130–31, 220
   cultivation of, 80–81
   and sensitiveness, 82
wisdom, 105, 117
   and lack of courage, difference between, 82
wise, being, 78, 80–81
women, intuition in, 128
words for expression, 216
worship, manner of, 202

Y

yogis, 96, 108
youth, 116–17, 275–76

Z

Zarathustra, 250–51

Inayatiyya
A Sufi Path of Spiritual Liberty

Sulūk Press is an independent publisher dedicated to issuing works of spirituality and cultural moment, with a focus on Sufism, in particular, the works of Hazrat Inayat Khan and his successors. To learn more about Inayatiyya Sufism, please visit **inayatiyya.org**.